THE REMEDY

A *True Story*

by
Andrew Malcolm

AKME

ISBN 1-874222-90-8

A CIP catalogue record for this book
is availiable from the British Library

First 'published' in the form of an updatable
computer-printout in July 1997
First produced as a laser-printed paperback
December 1999

To Mum and Dad, co-bearers

AKME Publications, Brighton, England

Contents

THIS, as went the original prologue to *Bandit Queen, is a true story, and whatever writs may fly, this avowal will stand. No event or person in what follows is fictionalised.*

1

Life before Oxford

IT IS A TRUE STORY — that is the point — but from no side, I fear, is it a pretty or an agreeable one. However, it may interest people in the world of books and academe, be they authors, publishers, educators or lawyers, and will perhaps also provide material for moralists, psychologists, and even philosophers, I don't know. My only certainty is that now feels the time to set it down, a task for which I have long had no stomach, and to let those who will, read. A full blow-by-blow account, including all of the tale's legal and psychological detail, would soon become a tedious slog through the myriad back streets that comprise the vast city of English Law, and through the yet dingier warren of pathways beneath in which run the human emotions that drive it, so I will here attempt little more than a sketch-map of both domains, whose further intricacies I must leave to the reader's imagination.

Most people in publishing have probably by now heard of *Malcolm v. Oxford*, my marathon lawsuit over the University Press's breach of contract to publish a philosophy text I offered them entitled *Making Names*, but few seem to know the extraordinary facts or properly to understand the legal and other implications of the case, which is certainly the most important in its field since the 1920s, and arguably ever. Despite meriting respectively three and six references in the standard contract-law textbooks *Chitty* and *Treitel* (Sweet & Maxwell, 1994 & 1995) there has been an almost complete silence on the affair in the newspapers, meagre coverage of it in the law journals (one article in the *Entertainment Law Review*), no law report, not a single line of analysis in *The Author* magazine, and only a strange mis-statement of it in Charles Clark's *Publishing Agreements* (Butterworth, 1993), formerly an authority on the subject. Eeriest of all, it has even been omitted from *The Times Index*. This general oversight was partially rectified by the appearance in 1996 of Hugh Jones' *Publishing Law* (Routledge), in which a section is devoted to the extraction of some of the case's key points. Necessarily though, Jones glosses certain aspects which his readers may wish to have explained, and begs many questions, not the least of which is: why on earth did I spend six years and Oxford an estimated half a million pounds fighting over such an apparently simple matter? Since, for reasons that will soon become obvious, no established publisher will want to have this account broadcast, I am thinking of calling it *Pariah*, and letting it loose, like a message in a bottle, upon the high seas of the Internet. Already this seems to present a fine publishing paradox — the first of several — to which this new, uncorporatised electronic medium perhaps offers a fine solution. My presentation will be broadly chronological, although from time to time I shall digress when there arises a topic that merits further examination.

Hugh Jones' book begins, very properly, with a chapter entitled *Authors and Ideas,* whose first section is in turn headed *Original Ideas.* As Plato himself might have insisted, in the beginning is the Idea. A brief glance around a popular bookshop may make one wonder just how many modern books do in fact begin with authors' ideas, let alone original ones, but be that as it may, in a very literal sense mine, I believe, did. At school I studied science (maths, physics and chemistry to 'S' and university scholarship levels), before switching at Cambridge to 'moral sciences', as philosophy was then known there. Already, at school, I had become dissatisfied with certain of the assumptions and dogmas of science and had found greater insight in the writings of the philosophers, to which I had been introduced in a sixth-form option. After school, I spent two years travelling and working in Europe, Iran, Afghanistan, India, the Far East and the U.S.S.R. before taking up my university place, where, in between editing a scurrilous magazine and getting into the usual kinds of trouble, I studied under the tutelage of such authorities as Renford Bambrough, Bernard Williams, Casimir Lewy and Elizabeth Anscombe, Wittgenstein's executrix-translator. On gaining a degree and moving to Brighton, I was invited to give introductory philosophy courses at several adult education centres around Sussex, and after a few years of this work developed one or two novel twists of argument or presentation which began to cohere, it seemed to me, into an interesting and unexpected new pattern. Eventually I stumbled upon what I believed, and still sometimes believe, to be an unusually fruitful condensation of their nub. In short, I had an idea.

Are not ideas, even in the commonplace, non-philosophical sense, the most precious, most truly marvellous of all things? Some might even claim that it is their endowment, above all, which sets *homo sapiens* apart from, and above, every other species. Who has not experienced the delight, after weeks of being troubled by some thorny problem, of waking up one day to the discovery, as if by unconscious magic, of its solution: perhaps a safe, diplomatic path revealed through a dangerous social minefield, or an elegant configuration of some awkward architectural layout, or a neat simplifying of a complex computer programme. So it was with me: my lectures had led me through to certain positions shared by many other philosophical writers about the peculiar sort of fictionality that attaches to the objects of science's accepted explanatory world, and my puzzle had for some while become one of finding a fully adequate, non-abstract way in which their conclusion might be expressed. Then, quite out of the blue one day in early 1973 as I was sitting on Brighton beach staring out to sea, an idea for such an expression came to me which seemed at once both sound, profound and lucid. It came as a piece of imagery, essentially alinguistic, yet also based on a pun, a pun which works in all languages, making it perfectly universal and international. I believed that I had found something literally fabulous, and perhaps even beautiful.

And here, of course, the trouble soon started. An idea, especially if it has pretensions of this grand, philosophical kind, can quickly become as much a curse as a joy. Not only in trying to voice it, which is probably foolish anyway, does one run the obvious risk of being branded a crank (especially in philosophy, where unwilling listeners usually have first to be persuaded that they suffer from the supposed problem), but if the perceived elucidation seems to any degree novel and important, it will be likely to render all of one's *other* ambitions at best secondary and at worst trivial. An idea that can appear to open certain abstract, imaginary doorways may imperceptibly close at least as many real-life ones. In my case, out of the swim as I was of intellectual society, it was an especially isolating experience too. Not the least grim fact of the affair is that despite all of the time and argument that has passed since my fateful seafront moment, I have to this day sustained no more than a couple of decent conversation with anyone about the idea which inspired all that here follows.

Now, to digress briefly, I don't know what, apart from the need to keep a roof over their heads, motivates the people who do so to go into publishing, or in particular into philosophy publishing, or indeed into 'professional' philosophy, but I do know what motivated me to start writing my book: it was the feeling that I had had an idea *worth writing*. I hadn't been wanting to write something but wondering what it should be, or been trying to get published for the sake of prestige or fame, or simply been trying to earn my living by the pen; rather, an idea I judged worth writing *had come to me*. Now, a belief in the value of an idea is usually accompanied by a belief that it may be enlightening, that is to other people. This relationship can seem almost a logical one; as is casually remarked somewhere in the book itself, "let's just say, if you think you've seen a truth, you have to try to tell it." Of course, some authors may write to satisfy their personal passions, for literature or science or philosophy or whatever it may be, and who will judge such enthusiasts perverse if they claim not to care what other people think of their work, or even whether the world sees it at all? I, however, was not at that time of such a reclusive disposition, and believed that what I had found should be offered up to the test of others' opinions, if only so that its reasonings and presentations could be set to flames as so much intellectual bric-a-brac.

With hindsight, I suppose I should dismiss such uncynical bravado as a kind of youthful delusion, about myself, philosophy, publishing, and many other aspects of the world, but back in the 1970s, infatuated as I was by my idea, hindsight was not a faculty I much enjoyed, or would have been likely to heed if I had. I did realise, however, that there lay ahead a great deal of work to do it justice in any expression, for the scale of its ambition was daunting, and perhaps beyond my literary capabilities. On the other hand, if the idea were true, half-true, or even one whit truer than our current generally-received notions, nothing else would much matter; and besides, my education had always stressed the importance of nurturing such sparks. I decided to stop lecturing, which by then had anyway become deadeningly routine, and to devote all of my time to the project. Although the subject-matter of the original book is far removed from that of this present setting-down, many readers will doubtless already be asking for more clues about the content of the text that was eventually to become the cause of so much trouble; some may even leap straight to the conclusion that therein lies the proof of the whole pudding. Events will, I think, prove such a leap to be wide of the mark, but nevertheless I will here hazard an outline, which later can be coloured in as opportunities arise.

If I were pressed to give an instant summary of the book's central concerns and questions, I think it would be: the relationship between man and what we call 'nature', the limits and conditions of human knowledge, and (forgive the puns) in particular the matter of how literally we should and should not take certain now commonplace scientific explanations like the atomic and quantum theories. Is it, for simplistic example, scientifically coherent, or even technically useful, for conscious, sentient creatures like ourselves to be conceiving of all substance, including our own, as consisting entirely of inanimate particles and forces? My starting-point was my collection of adult-education lecture notes, from which over the next couple of years I assembled roughly a dozen more or less conventional philosophical and scientific essays. Most of these were in 'plain text', but as a relieving gimmick, I cast my analysis of cause-and-effect as a dialogue between two eponymous characters whose names therefore alternated relentlessly down the left-hand margin of each page. The final chapter took the form of a playscript, an attempt to present in dramatic verse the book's founding imagery. With the simple optimism of a novice, I took this odd bundle (working title then *The Children of Electra*) quite unannounced to Penguin's office near Victoria Station, and offered it to their philosophy editor, a youngish, friendly man by the name of Mike Dover. He, rather to my surprise, at once took the bundle seriously and commissioned a nuclear physicist to referee it. After some months of consideration their verdict was that it was too long, contained too much science ("there are at least two books here..."), but that the verse-play was interesting and the dialogue chapter the most successful; they added that if I could extend this dialogue form throughout a science-pruned version of the bundle, they might well publish it. There were other hopeful beginnings too, now largely lost in the mists of time; I remember a promising approach to Routledge being embarrassed by the discovery of an old-school acquaintanceship, and an editor at George Allen & Unwin, Russell's publisher, also taking an interest. He invited me to lunch, but then insisted over it that only people, not ideas, can be dangerous. Soon afterwards he emigrated to Tibet to become a Buddhist.

I agreed to follow Penguin's suggestion, but quickly found the adaptation of the book much harder than I had foreseen. While some of its arguments fell quite naturally and profitably into a two-sided conversation, many other polemical passages stubbornly refused to budge. There was also the problem of giving the two protagonists coherent, but not too coherent, sets of views, and plausible personalities which would engage the reader without overwhelming the debates. Trickiest of all was the incorporation of the final playscript, the book's *raison d'être*. These difficulties, contending alongside everyday-life pressures of financial survival, property projects and romantic affairs, meant that it was another three or four years before I completed the conversion of the script with any degree of satisfaction.

At this juncture I believe I should mention the effects, as I saw and see them, of rendering the book's arguments, and perhaps any philosophy, in dialogue form, for, against the current fashion, I came to believe that its benefits are considerable. First, there is the 'commercial' point that it can make the substance of abstract arguments more attractive and accessible to general readers, and allow the punctuation of stretches of otherwise dry polemic by interludes, comic and otherwise, of everyday business. (I decided to set the men's exchanges in a variety of apt locations: the city's Market Square, a mental hospital tearoom, a nearby zoo-park, the physics labs, a cricket match, a roofless slum-turned-observatory, and so on.) Second, it also confers some serious, theoretical advantages: there is the common-place that there are always at least two sides to any story (or problem or question), with the truth usually lying somewhere between, or at least absorbing elements from, the choice of apparently contrasting versions (solutions, answers) on offer; and there is the more systematic reminder, close to the heart of my own particular thesis, that all of our philosophical (and scientific and mathematical) questions and justifications can only ever issue from and to *human* lips and ears, or *human* scripts and eyes.

Glossing this new human angle in the conversion of the essays into dialogue, I cast the philosopher as a young, male, broke, single, lively, sexually-hungry renegade, and the scientist as an older, quieter, well-off, politically-leftish, contentedly-married father-of-three, and allowed the personal frictions (engagements) in their relationship to rub, sometimes faintly, sometimes fiercely, alongside their theoretical disagreements. By the end of the long rewrite, I felt that these extra strands had actually enriched the book from a philosophical standpoint too: in the whole pattern of the exposition — and the order in which the arguments were presented, roughly as they had come to me, was important — there now lay a series of half-hidden paradoxes, contradictions and full-circles in the two men's positions. Not to say, I hope, that the book ends up where it begins or gets nowhere slowly, but that incidentally its two disputants personally rehearse certain interesting philosophical cycles. At this stage, the book consisted of eight chapters whose titles went: *Minds and Bodies, Causes and Effects, Freedoms and Laws, Universals and Families, Goods and Morals, Gods and Models, Physics and Metaphysics,* and *Above Olympus* (the *Electra* playscript, now incorporated into the dialogue). Interlaced with the dominant metaphysical theme, there ran also a troubled ethical debate, with both men in their different ways acutely worried by humanity's apparently inexorable tribalism, greed and march towards nuclear catastrophe (the Cold War was then at its height). As may be inferred, the scope of the enterprise was therefore very wide, beginning, I hoped, as an introduction along traditional lines that would engage the interest of any general reader, and developing, I hoped, into an original polemic. By way of a summary, I will omit the full synopsis which at the time I prepared for resubmission to publishers, and here simply quote the rewritten book's suggested (and eventual) dust-jacket blurb:

> Two strangers meet one summer's morning in a near-miss car accident; Andrew Cause is a philosopher, Malcolm Effect a research scientist. In their ensuing day-long conversation, Cause subjects Effect to a sustained sceptical attack upon the inadequacies and inconsistencies of his world-view. Traditional problems are introduced, including those of mind and body, cause and effect, free will, universals and the nature of moral goodness. Cause identifies the scientist's particle theory of matter as a crucially mistaken and hopeless metaphysics which has now outlived any usefulness. Step by step, Effect is reduced to a state of confusion and finally demands that Cause produce an alternative. In a literally dramatic climax, the philosopher invokes a new model which, he claims, *gets to the heart of things...*

The first obvious target for my new introductory material was Penguin, but predictably, by the time I returned to them everything had changed: their Victoria office had closed; Mike Dover was working in children's books for another publisher altogether; and they no longer had a designated philosophy department, so proposals like mine now fell under the aegis of their Sociology and Psychology section. A quick phonecall to the responsible editor settled the rest: "Philosophical dialogues are quite out of fashion," she explained, "there is absolutely no point in your sending it."

Thus, by early 1984 I was again back at square one. Although I felt that the book (working title by now *Making Names*) was much improved, it was arguably even less conventional than before, while I still had no reputation and no contacts in publishing. Over that year I once more trudged the well-worn treadmill and submitted the book's synopsis unsolicited to every publisher who published philosophy and to several who didn't. Apart from Granada (Paladin), whose non-fiction editor Ian Paten wrote encouragingly "I found it extremely impressive, but...," none even asked to see the script. Duplicated rejection slips arrived by return with mis-spelt entries, contradictory explanations and often totally inappropriate remarks. Sometimes the synopsis was returned unopened, its telltale hair-seal resolutely in place (I am sure many authors have conducted such tests). I tried several literary agents and they tried to be helpful, but for them any mention of 'philosophy' was the kiss of death, a subject beyond their ken and out of their 'market', the other already well-established bane-word. (Recently when I circulated London's literary agents with a one-page information-sheet about my case's legal implications, four of them — Curtis Brown, A&B, Abner Stein and Greene & Heaton — thanked me for letting them see my book-proposal, which they were regretfully unable to represent, and the latter even returned my sheet postage-due, presumably to teach importuning authors a lesson.)

That summer I myself had an Oxford near-miss. Well, no, not a near-miss, nor truly even a far-miss, but at least an exchange of sorts, with one Kim Pickin (Ms), the philosophy editor of Blackwell; a far-ms, I suppose. Her initial rejection letter was so kind and encouraging, I broke my usual rule and replied to it, prompting an apparently genuine correspondence and eventually wheedling her into inviting the script. The closing paragraphs of two of her letters are worth quoting:

> 13th June 1984: I wish I could give you more encouragement as I enjoyed the synopsis greatly. Your flair for writing suggests that you should perhaps experiment with fiction writing if you have not already done so. With a slight change of balance you may be able to marry your writing skills and your interest in philosophy in a different context. With very best wishes.
> Yours, Kim Pickin (Ms), Philosophy Editor

> 6th July: I feel that the word ['philosophy'] now turns off many readers
> who would find it stimulating and enjoyable in a more literary context.
> I am sure that Derrida would argue that philosophy is literature anyway...
> I really can't guarantee anything but if you do want to send your
> manuscript I would no doubt enjoy looking through it.
> With very best wishes etc.

Coming as they do from the philosophy editor of one of the country's
leading philosophy publishers, these remarks could surely here generate a
whoe web of digressions about philosophy and its relation to fiction, but
as she says, most readers would doubtless find such stuff off-putting, so I
shall eschew it, pausing to mark only my personal opinion that the whole
troubling point of philosophy, at least of what *I* think of as philosophy, is
that it is *not* fictional; that, from Plato to Popper, arguably, it is all about
the *distinguishing* or *graduating* of fact from fiction. At the time I did not
pursue this point, and in the end, as she apologised on the telephone
before returning it, Pickin then for two months left the script of *Making
Names* unopened on the top of her filing cabinet. But the more prosaic
truism that fiction is never a match for fact was perfectly demonstrated
seven years later, when, on the strength of our magnificently abortive
encounter, the University of Oxford decided to drag this ex-Blackwell
Derrida-disciple into court against me.

Anyway, in short, by the time I came, against my own better judgment but
at a friend's recommendation, to approach a reputedly revitalised Oxford
University Press, I was thoroughly jaded with the whole British publishing
scene and had largely lost hope of finding anyone in it willing even to *read*
my bloody book.

It is unbecoming, of course, for an author to trumpet, whisper or in any
way protest the merits or saleability of his own work or ideas. Once one
has presented them to the world, it is for the world to decide upon them,
so one should tender them tentatively, pessimistically, expecting to have
them ridiculed and rubbished, and prepared to bow to the judgments of
others, especially of such experts as professional publishers. No-one
knows a work's shortcomings and weaknesses more intimately than its
author, and no-one is, or should be, more prey to doubts than someone
aspiring to write philosophy. However, having said all of that, I do
believe, of course from an author's point of view, that one does have a
right to expect that those who wield power over a written work, again
especially such 'experts', will at least actually read it, and preferably to its
end, before passing a comment or judgment — usually the death-sentence

— upon it. It would be tempting here to launch into an analysis of the conventional wisdom on books' so-called 'marketability', on the role of editors and publishers, on the value of academic philosophy — the largely arcane, incestuous, unpurchased output of the university professionals — and on other such matters, but I fear that to do so might generate yet another unmarketable book, so again I shall resist the urge. Another debate I shall not raise, though I believe the story does eventually demand it, is the whole purpose and justification of university education in general and of Oxbridge's insufferable privilege in particular. Apart from various obviously worthwhile scientific programmes, a few learned specialists, and the occasional genuinely inspiring lecturer, do its battalions of mediocre gravy-trainers, whose talents seem chiefly to reside in the parroting of empty jargon, the concocting of bogus 'research' and the grappling of greasy poles, give good educational value for money? Is not a decent library usually a far better teacher? On these questions too, I will stay strictly silent. Besides, being myself a product, as they say, of this Oxbridge privilege, I am hardly in a fair position to complain of it, though I would ask any already disgruntled readers to note just how totally 'the system' failed in my case; surely it was only *because* I was myself an Oxbridgian that things got as wonderfully vile as they ultimately did.

Here, too, I offer another warning for incipient gruntlers. The intuitive should quickly be able sense the double-bind in which I now find myself. On the one hand this story promises to be an instructive one and worth the telling, whatever the value of *Making Names*, while on the other it is inevitably going to run the twin risks of sounding like either a long advertisment for that original book or a long lament about the way it was treated. So be it. You have been warned. Those who are susceptible to such allergies, or who would prefer to preserve undisturbed their faith in one of our country's great universities, are advised to stop reading now, before I enter its golden portals.

2

Into the Blue

IN AUGUST 1984 I telephoned OUP's philosophy editor, Angela
Blackburn, to see if it was worth introducing her to *Making Names*.
In our long (unrecorded) conversation, she, like the recent Penguin editor,
opined that philosophical dialogues "do not work nowadays", but
nevertheless invited me to submit my introductory package. This included
a four-page synopsis explaining the book's format, content and intended
market, a four-page chapter-by-chapter guide, a list of suggested italicised
running page-headlines, a rough index, an eight-line profile of myself, and
a suggested cover-design. Everything fundamental about the book except
the consistency of its style and the detail of its arguments would thus have
been evident to any publisher from a quick reading of these few introductory
pages. (Ironically, when it came to the assessment of my damages many
years later, several of Oxford's 'independent expert' witnesses immediately
pronounced the book "unpublishable" on sight of just page one of its
synopsis.) I accompanied this package with a prophetic covering letter:

> Dear Angela,
> Following our phone conversation of yesterday, I enclose herewith
> my set of introductory material to *Making Names*, which together
> should give you a fairly good idea of what the book is like and about,
> without actually 'giving away' the substance of its conclusions or the
> imagery involved in their final dramatic expression (Chapter 8).
> I realise that at first glance, *Making Names* probably seems to
> break, as you might say, every publishing rule in the book, but then
> haven't worthwhile philosophical works always broken the rules, in
> one way or another? Isn't that what philosophy *ought* to do? In reply
> to your remark about dialogue "not working nowadays", I would just
> point out that both of the recent (successful?) attempts on BBC 2 and
> Channel 4 [*Men of Ideas* and *Opinions*] to televise (i.e. popularise)
> philosophy have chosen to present it as *conversation*. In the case of
> *Making Names*, much of which started life as conventional philosophical
> essays, its transition into dialogue form has become more than just a
> change of presentation, but has actually added a number of fruitful
> new philosophical dimensions to the whole thing, as well as, I hope,
> making it more palatable to the general reader.
> I realise too that OUP's traditional market is in academic rather
> than general-readership books, but I recently met someone who works
> for the Press (in another department) who told me that it is presently
> embarking on a rather more open-minded and expansionist publishing
> policy, and that it might be worth approaching you with my somewhat
> unusual work. I very much hope that this is so and that the enclosed
> material will interest you in reading the script itself. If so, I will be
> happy to send or deliver it to you on instruction.
> Yours sincerely, Andrew Malcolm

I later discovered that at almost exactly the time I wrote the above, one of OUP's new 'young Turk' managers, a Mr Richard Charkin, was interviewed by *The Oxford Times* and said:

"The search for better, more original, more important books is now a very positive one... We don't want editors to be so commercial that they miss opportunities... The philosophy list, for example, is now stronger than it has ever been, having perhaps let slip by some of the up-and-coming authors in that field of the 1960s..."

Angela Blackburn never replied to me, but on 10th October I received this:

Dear Mr Malcolm,
Your proposal has been passed to me by Angela Blackburn, since it sounds more suitable for the General Books Department of OUP.
As you present it, the book sounds rather attractive, and I should be glad to have a chance of looking at the typescript, it you would kindly send it. Incidentally, it is not correct to say that the publication of general books is a new departure for the Press: we have always had a strong general list.
Yours sincerely,
Henry Hardy,
Senior Editor, General Books, OUP

I sent Hardy the typescript with a covering letter:

Dear Mr Hardy,
Thank you for your letter of 9th October and for your interest in *Making Names*; herewith the script. I am sorry if I appeared to misjudge OUP's publishing policy. I am also a little surprised that Angela Blackburn should have thought my proposal more suitable for the General Books rather than the Philosophy Department. I assume that this is because at present most philosophy books are not of general interest; it is my hope, of course, that *Making Names* will help to change that situation.
I would suggest that you use the previously submitted material to help you find your way about the script. I would also draw your and your readers' attention to the apology inside the front cover: the text is still in need of a good deal of work (I imagine a final six-month session locked in a room with a word-processor). There are one or two places where short passages or paragraphs are yet to be inserted; there are a number of ways in which I intend to highlight some of the sub-themes a little more carefully; and there is still a fair amount of sheer clumsiness that I must certainly polish up, particularly in the earlier and older writing. I just hope that you will make allowances for these shortcomings and that you will persevere with *Making Names* long enough to begin to recognise the ways in which its various threads weave together into what I believe to be the exciting tapestry of its climax.
Please take your time with it; I have!
Yours sincerely,
Andrew Malcolm

My *Apology* reiterated the point:

> This is only a provisionally-completed script. Although I regard the attached text as the book's final incarnation in respect of both philosophical content and literary format, there are still many passages where the writing or argument suffers from clumsiness and there is still much work to be done in terms of refining details and highlighting sub-themes. I anticipate a final six-month session with a word-processor.

Here I should perhaps mention that I had staged the encounter and day-long conversation between my maverick philosopher and his scientist quarry in one of England's historic university cities, an undisguised hybrid of Oxford and Cambridge, a setting which provided numerous opportunities to ignite the characters' personal antagonisms. When presented to OUP, the script thus already featured several ironical sub-themes which have turned out to be eerily prophetic, or maybe just self-fulfilling: the philosopher does not hide his low opinion of the academic Oxbridge cant and privilege which surrounds him, he regards himself as an outsider and all power-structures as anathemas, and he has written a book for which he has so far found no publisher. A recurring motif is a search for his book's aptest title. Certain passages from my original draft may be worth reproducing:

> at page 17:
> **Cause:** I think one has to have a name these days to get anything published, or family connections. As far as I am concerned, philosophy must have some purpose. The philosopher's job is not *just* to chart the networks of criss-crossing similarities between the instances of universals, not *just* to trace the complex patterns of family resemblance and relationship amongst our various intellectual and moral concepts. This is work for cartographers and lexicographers and genealogists, the sort of people one tends to find around this place.
> **Effect:** Yes, I know the types. Biographers too, there's another.
> **Cause:** By the way Malcolm, I have a pet argument which proves that universities, paradoxically, are the last places in the world in which to discover philosophy...

> at page 32:
> **Cause:** Remember Malcolm, before you assert that controversies are always resolved on purely scientific grounds, when rival theories are vying to explain some new phenomenon, that behind them stand rival scientists, rival laboratories, rival academics, and that behind these stand rival publishing houses, rival universities, rival governments. One must not underestimate the jealousies and powers of the academic institutions, whose interests are vested in keeping *this* theory as the accepted explanation of so-and-so or *that* model as the accepted interpretation of such-and-such or *The Other* University as the centre of bla-bla research...

and at page 48, the rather darker exchange:
Effect: (discussing Gilbert Ryle's suggestion that the *other minds* problem arises from a category mistake, illustrated in terms of the relation between the concept of a university and its various buildings): As a matter of fact, some quite long books have been written on the concept of a university. All by university men of course, and all rather different in their...
Cause: I cannot imagine a language which used the same word for 'me' and 'you'... No, a better parallel with the man who observes another's behaviour and then asks "Yes, but what is going on in his mind?" is the visitor who is shown around he university's colleges, libraries, laboratories and so on and then asks "Yes, but where does the money come from?"
Effect: Ah, but that question could be answered quite easily, quite factually.
Cause: Could it? Are you sure? Think carefully: where would the bucks stop? In the end don't we always come up against the other minds problem, or rather against the *trustworthiness* problem?

I will leave the reader to ponder the significance of these passages in the light of what follows.

Back in the real world, time ticked newslessly by, and every couple of months I telephoned Hardy or his secretary gently to ask if my proposal had 'gone to sleep'. I was assured that it had not and was being considered carefully by a referee. Since OUP's interest in the book was apparently becoming serious, as Blackwell's had previously, I began to use my answering machine to tape-record my telephone conversations with Hardy. Years later, the Chief Executive of the Press, Sir Roger Elliott, publicly branded me 'an obsessive' for making these recordings, Charles Clark states that I had made them 'carefully', while in *Publishing Law* Hugh Jones compliments my foresight. In fact, I foresaw nothing and was not obsessed at all, or at first even careful, I just wanted some record of what was said in what looked like being an important negotiation. At that time, my small basement flat had no telephone extensions, so whenever I answered or made a call, I was nearby the answerphone and could easily press its record button. Often, odd message tapes would happen to be in use, and sometimes I would simply recycle unwanted music cassettes and record over them (when a tape runs out, the machine emits a tone warning that it should be turned or changed). One nice result of this somewhat haphazard technique is that when Hardy's half-million-pound commitment is played back over a stereo system, one hears it being made to the accompaniment of Eric Clapton's version of *I Shot the Sherriff*.

The few reports of *Malcolm v. Oxford* that did get into public print all concentrated on the fact that I had made these tape-recordings, but on reflection I believe that this is probably the least interesting or important aspect of the story. All the other related precedents in the lawbooks involve publishing contracts which were oral*, and as any law student learns in his first week, it is well established that, with a few specified exceptions, the law of contract makes no important general distinction between spoken or written agreements. The chief questions about disputed contracts concern their completeness, their certainty and their solemnity. Obviously, signed pieces of paper may help in all three of these respects, but equally they can be incomplete or otherwise invalid too. In any case, tape-recordings and signed documents are only *evidence*, evidence of what has been agreed, which is normally unnecessary because normally both parties know what has been agreed and normally both parties are honest.

As Hardy's interest in *Making Names* grew, so I became more careful in all that I said and wrote, and keener to put and get everything between us in writing; it was Hardy, not I, who preferred using the telephone. I think this preference of Hardy's (several times I wrote letters to which he responded orally) may have worried me and put me faintly on my guard, but at that stage nothing could have been further from my mind than legal proceedings or the tapes' eventual importance; such thoughts only occurred much later. Looking back, actually within these conversations Hardy made several references to telephone-use which border on the Freudian, and a former OUP personnel manager later told me that there had at that time been explicit talk at the Press of deliberately using the telephone for its deniability when, for example, giving ex-employees references. As far as I am concerned, if people in positions of power choose to do their business — important, life-changing business — by telephone, then they should expect to be recorded, and certainly they should act as if they have been.

* I prefer the word 'oral' to 'verbal'. Dictionary definitions vary, but I assume that all contracts which use words, spoken or written, are, strictly, verbal. The intended distinction is between 'oral' (by mouth) and 'written'. Non-verbal contracts might be made, I guess, in sign-language (for example by tick-tack men?) or by gestures in a recognised context. In Glanville-Williams' introduction to contract law, he cites a passenger hailing a cab and the cab stopping or a purchaser selecting an apple and handing its street-vendor money as examples of implied contracts.

3

The Negotiation

THE STORY HAS ALSO been reported as though my contract with OUP consisted of just one all-important recorded phonecall, whereas in fact in legal terms it was 'contained' in a whole series of letters and conversations which took place over a period of several months, and which later comprised more than seventy A4 pages of evidence in the court file. On 18th February 1985, Hardy wrote:

> Dear Mr Malcolm,
> This is just to let you know that I have now had a response from my adviser. It is not unencouraging. Please bear with me a little longer while I look at the typescript myself. I hope to be able to write to you in substance before long.
> Yours sincerely,
> Henry Hardy

Brief though the letter was, I was not unencouraged by it. This, incidentally, proved to be not the last strange Oxford usage of the word 'encourage'. Exactly one month later, Hardy wrote again, 'in substance':

> Dear Mr Malcolm,
> In brief, we think that *Making Names* isn't by any means impossible, but that it won't do as it stands. Does this horrify you?
> We don't mind about the dialogue, though it does clank occasionally. Indeed, we agree with you that dialogue can be a useful device, and we think that you do make good use of it. What you have to say seems to us philosophically interesting too; the reader says "It makes one of the shrewdest cases for a sort of Collingwoodian Idealism that that I've read — not that it reads like Collingwood or cites him as an authority, but that its emphasis on the way we constrain the world by deciding what sort of general laws it's to follow, and what sort of explanations it's got to conform to is rather Collingwoodian.
> If we have anxieties, they are about the longish slabs of straight science, e.g. at the end of Chapter 1, and about the interpolation of the play about Electra in the last Act; they serve a purpose all right, but I think that some readers may feel they go on too long before you reveal their purpose. This connects with what is in some ways the most important worry of all — that the book is far, far too long for us to be able to give it a sporting chance at the price we'd need to charge for it to make it appeal to the kind of reader who would profit from it.
> How adamant do you feel that the book can't be made substantially shorter? That's the key question. I'm glad to hear that you are planning

to put the book on to a word processor: that will certainly make polishing easier, and my experience of using such a machine is that it makes cutting easier too. I look forward to hearing your reaction.
With best wishes,
Yours,
Henry Hardy

Here, at last, was a first, tentative, qualified expression of interest, a serious bite, although its first paragraph did convey a faint early warning that these Oxford folk were not very good at *reading* things, for example my original covering letter and *Apology*. I was cautious, but further not unencouraged. This was also, again incidentally, not the last occasion on which Hardy urged me to make the then considerable outlay on a word-processor and a re-keyboarding of the book, which in the event I decided against. Given that the script was already typed, cut-paste-and-copy was in practice to prove a far easier and cheaper option. On 24th March I replied as follows:

Dear Mr Hardy,
Thank you for your letters of 18th February and March and for the kind remarks you pass upon *Making Names*. No, of course I am not horrified that you have reservations about it, I am most gratified that you are considering it seriously.
Without burdening you with the history of the work, suffice it to say that your adviser is literally the first person in the world (publishing or otherwise) who has actually read this dialogue version of the text, the fruit of over five years of painstaking rewriting. For me it is therefore very exciting that at last someone seems to have recognised the value of some of the ideas I have been battling to express, if a little surprising that they should have been labelled 'Collingwoodian'. Now *there's* a piece of name-making if you like!
That at present the dialogue frequently clanks, I am only too well aware. The slabs of science I also realised might cause problems, and although I can think at once of certain bits that could be axed or heavily pruned, some brief form of the three key scientific accounts must, I think, remain, as they are central amongst the targets of the philosopher's attack. With respect to the anticipated objection to the book's length, besides the scientific passages, I can identify immediately a number of stretches in the book that could perhaps be cut or pruned without damaging too crucially the whole enterprise. Off the top of my head, there is a fair amount of repetition in Chapters 1 & 2, though in some cases I think it is useful and justifiable repetition. Chapter 3 could quite easily be slimmed down. Chapter 4 could perhaps be slimmed down a little. Chapter 5 could perhaps be cut by one third or more. Chapters 6 & 7 leave little room for manoeuvre, I feel. With regard to Chapter 8 and the play *The Children of Electra*, the remark that I found most worrying in your letter was the suggestion that this "goes on too long". Although more work is undoubtedly required on the play, there is a sense in which, as far as I am concerned, *Electra* is what the whole book is about. I would axe Chapters 1 – 7 before I axed Chapter 8. Chapters 1 – 7 are in

a way just the footnotes to the play-text. I could, I suppose, provide you with a more detailed 'pruning plan' if this would improve my chances of OUP publication, though this in itself would probably take me a few weeks to draw up. Whether, in the end, the cuts or changes I could agree would count as 'substantial' in your book, I am not sure. How substantial is 'substantially'? That is the key question.

I must say that, *Making Names* apart (and I think you are probably right, it is at present too long) and with all respect for your publishing experience, I do find this oft-canonised corelation between books' length, price and marketability rather depressing. Not just because it appears to succumb to a modern, simple, mass-marketing logic, but more generally (and this bears upon the philosophical arguments in the book) because it assumes far too much predictability on the part of the public and their reading-behaviour. If a 750+ page (over twice the length of *Making Names?*) pretentious, preposterous, empty monstrosity like Hofstadter's *Gödel, Escher, Bach* can become a mass-market best-seller, then surely anything can happen.

I concluded the letter with two paragraphs that should be read slowly, carefully, and at least twice; upon the first of them was to turn all of the ensuing six years of litigation:

> In conclusion then, I am adamant about nothing at the moment and I very much hope that we can agree some formula that will result in the book's publication. However, in the light of experience, one firm resolution that I have made is not to embark upon any further major polishing/ rewriting exercise, which I reckon could well take up to six months of full-time work, without first securing a firm commitment from a publisher; I feel that there is already enough of value in the text to justify such a commitment. Also, I assume that before investing money and time in any word-processing exercise, one nowadays should establish what computer system one's publisher will find most compatible.
>
> I hope that these reactions of mine still leave you not uninterested in *Making Names* and if so, suggest that our next move should be to arrange some sort of meeting. I look forward to hearing from you.
> Yours sincerely,
> Andrew Malcolm

How many thousands of weary authors, I wonder, have been here before, aching to get their work into print but wary of their umpteenth runaround? Of course the author-publisher relationship is a peculiar one by normal business standards, an unusual joint venture requiring continuing co-operation and trust, and of course a publisher should not be forced into publishing a book in which they see no merit or profit, but then, what is the slightest bit unreasonable about my above-quoted paragraphs? Would a builder build a house to his client's plans on terms that "we will pay you when it is finished if we decide we like our design"? Would a printer print a publisher's books on such a basis? How could I have been clearer or more straightforward? Where is there any scintilla of ambiguity or any want of solemnity? Am I rushing these scholarly scrutineers into an over-hasty judgment? They have, remember, already had *Making Names* for over *five months.*

Should it have sounded another warning that Hardy never responded to my suggestion of a meeting, or to my computer enquiry? Should I have been worried by the fact that, in the event, he took my last sentence literally and never wrote any reply? For a further hindsightless month I heard nothing, and so once again telephoned to leave Hardy a memory-jogging message. On 26th April he phoned back and at first tried to inveigle me into doing the revision without giving me any commitment. Again, Hardy's introductory remarks and his odd phraseology are telling; my favourite is his "I haven't just re-read your letter this moment."

> **Hardy:** I did ring you yesterday, but your line was engaged... Anyway, prior to that I have of course been somewhat negligent in not having answered your letter of 24th March... It's a very difficult one this, difficult (a) to decide what to do or say and (b) having decided it, difficult to express it to you... So I'm just going to have a shot at telling you what's in our minds and see what you think.
> **Malcolm:** You're going to have a shot now, on the phone?
> **Hardy:** Yes, if that's alright with you.
> **Malcolm:** Fine, shoot away.
> **Hardy:** First of all we obviously — well I don't know if this is obvious — but we can't commit ourselves in advance to accepting the results of a further attempt to reorganise the book.
> **Malcolm:** Uhuh.
> **Hardy:** I don't know whether you need that commitment. I haven't just re-read your letter this moment — my secretary rang you rather faster than I thought, I was going to re-read your letter — but I don't know if you feel that you need that kind of commitment in order to have the psychological motivation to turn to it again?
> **Malcolm:** I feel I need some commitment, yes. It's partly from experience. I went through putting the whole thing into the form of a dialogue on the advice of a publisher that they would be interested when it was done.
> **Hardy:** How frightful! You mean you first of all wrote it as a straight text?
> **Malcolm:** It was originally ninety percent straightforward philosophical essays... (tells Penguin story, as above)
> **Hardy:** You don't feel you were led up the garden path?
> **Malcolm:** I wouldn't have been led that far up, no, but that is why I am looking for some sort of commitment.
> **Hardy:** Understandably, very understandably.

Later, I decided that if I were ever to write an account of the affair, *The Garden Path* might serve as a good title (a cover-design involving a distant, steaming manure-heap later also presented itself). Our conversation continued with Hardy outlining, even at this early stage, his intentions for *Making Names*, explaining the economics of publishing a book of this size (500-550 pages, he thought), imagining a short print-run of a £20-£15 hardback edition followed by a cheaper paperback, and asking how much I thought I'd be able to reduce its length. He then revealed that his referee was the New College political philosopher and frequent *Times* contributor and reviewer Alan Ryan, who not only liked the book, but was also a Delegate of the Press, one of the committee of dons responsible for its affairs; in addition, Ryan at that time happened to hold the post of Assessor, a sort of roving University policeman privy to all the papers, past and present, of all the University committees. Hardy explained the role of the Delegates thus:

> **Hardy:** Well, OUP, being a university press, has a board of dons called Delegates who have to approve everything that is published. In fact I work here for a department called the General Books Department which is far freer from Delegatorial control than any other part of the Press.
> **Malcolm:** The Thought Police.
> **Hardy:** Yes, well, it isn't quite like that... Anyway, Academic editors have to submit proposals for approval by the Delegates before they sign them up. In the General Books Department we report our decisions to the Delegates *on the whole* [his emphasis]. That is why it is important that Alan Ryan is a Delegate because he has read it and he likes it very much, basically, which is good and as it were gets it over that hurdle. [Ryan's reports are quoted in full later]

Hardy was at that stage himself only half-way through the book, so towards the end of our conversation we agreed that he too should finish reading it before coming to a definite decision:

> **Hardy:** I'm temperamentally inclined to be a bit of an iconoclast and sound sympathetic to the venture, but I too feel there's a certain amount of work to be done... I think the less painful course for you [than revising the book 'on spec'] is to bear with me until I have read it.
> **Malcolm:** Yes.
> **Hardy:** Then we'll talk again if I feel encouraged by a reading of the whole thing; you know, I might be able to persuade Alan Ryan to join me in taking a more constructive line.
> **Malcolm:** If you are still reading it, obviously it's a good thing to wait for your reaction.
> **Hardy:** I know I've taken an unconscionably long time to read it.

Having had this conversation I will be that much more motivated to make it a priority... Perhaps it would be best if I gave you a ring again in two or three weeks and then we can talk again.
Malcolm: Okay.

I was also *encouraged* to learn that Hardy was himself a philosopher by training ("I'm basically a philosopher too, I have a doctorate in philosophy. I read philosophy and psychology at Oxford, so I am very sympathetic to science, in fact I wanted to be a scientist when I was a schoolboy, but suffered from a parent who wouldn't allow it"), and that he had written an impassioned plea in *The Times Literary Supplement* (26th December 1980) for reticent philosophers to go more readily into print, or at least into computer-print. Ryan, I later learnt, had read PPE at Balliol, lectured in philosophy and politics at the Universities of Keele, Essex and New York, had written a book on J. S. Mill and numerous articles and reviews for *The Times*, and was currently working on a political biography of Bertrand Russell. In 1978 he had been profiled in *The Sunday Times* as one of the new generation of 'rising star' academics and was pictured posing coyly with the obligatory clenched pipe and lapful of books.

One month later, on 20th May 1985, came the pivotal phonecall which was later to feature at the heart of the lawsuit. This time Hardy phoned me unprompted, his tone and demeanour wholly changed; he was friendly, elated, and at times almost breathless. At eight pages, our conversation's complete transcript is too long to reproduce here, but three of its key passages which were later dissected *ad nauseam* by the lawyers must be quoted verbatim, exactly as they appeared in the evidence:

> **Hardy:** ...Anyway, I have now finished reading the book.
> **Malcolm:** Oh good.
> **Hardy:** And like Alan Ryan who read it before, I feel much more warmly towards it having finished it. And we would like to do it. That is to say, I mean I know you want a commitment sufficient to take you through the last stage of revision and that's what I'm offering. I'm not offering a totally unconditional commitment because obviously if what you do seems to us to make it worse then we would write to say so.
> **Malcolm:** Of course, yes.
> **Hardy:** But we feel confident enough to say go ahead and do that.
> **Malcolm:** Oh great!
> **Hardy:** I was, I was quite gripped by the end, the last two chapters. I was reading with the kind of attention that one gives to a novel, which is not very usual with a philosophical work.
> **Malcolm:** Oh great, it's very nice of you to say that.
> **Hardy:** I think the fact that we both reacted in the same way to the later parts of the book suggests to me that...

Hardy then launched into a long, prepared catalogue of the revisions he required, the most important of which were the splitting into two of the rather rambling first chapter (the new second chapter became *Persons and Things*) and a reduction of about twenty percent in the book's overall length. This time he expressed no anxiety whatever about *Electra*, and introduced his more detailed reservations thus:

> "Certainly the book has a very careful structure, there's no doubt about that. Have you got a pen? I've got various points written down here which I'd quite like to convey to you on the telephone rather than writing a long boring monologue about them. Starting right at the top, we both feel that..."

Hardy went carefully through his list, at first discussing various alternative titles and subtitles, and at one stage suggesting, rather oddly, that the book should be called "Hmmm" (a pun, I assumed, on 'Hume', who is much-quoted by me and cited by Cause as his mentor, or tormentor). We also debated the general plausibility and timing of the conversations, and here Hardy volunteered the possibility of using the text as a 'tele-script'. His numerous points became steadily more detailed, going though words-per-page savings, coordination of the italicised headlines with page-breaks, right down to spelling mistakes and OUP's house punctuation-style with respect to quotation marks, ellipses, brackets, obliques, strokes and so forth. Needless to say, I agreed to everything. At one point he confided:

> "Both Alan Ryan and I are aware, as you must be, that this is a very unconventional piece of publishing and we're aware that we are taking a risk, but I think, you know, you've got to. Life would be very boring if you didn't take the odd risk, and it is in that spirit that I'm staying here."

He returned to the book's length and made more space-saving suggestions:

Malcolm: Oh yes, all those points absolutely taken. That is what my six months is about.
Hardy: The next thing I'm going to do this end... I mean is this a unique copy of the book that I have?
Malcolm: No, I have another copy.
Hardy: Do you want this back to work on?
Malcolm: Ermm, I don't think so.
Hardy: I can let you have it back, it's just that I would like to have it accurately cast off so I can let you know that your 180,000 (words) is right.
Malcolm: No... Keep it and cast it off accurately.
Hardy: It won't take more than a week or so.
Malcolm: Yes, yes.
Hardy: Then we can do costings and I can talk to you again about

length and then having got to that point let me revisit it and we'll talk about it some more. I mean the book has a natural length obviously and I don't want to ask for unnecessary cuts, but at the same time length equals cover price and of course...

Malcolm: Ya, ya, ya.

Hardy: I see much more having finished the book the point of the detail in some scientific sections, but the book could nevertheless bear some cuts.

Malcolm: Mm. Some of it can go. Some bits I know can go.

Hardy: At the same time I think there could be some trimming without destruction of... I wouldn't want to discourage you into making every statement a kind of grey standard length. I will let you know what the actual length is and then we'll have some costings done on the basis of the actual length and we'll talk more precisely then about what kind of saving might yield what kind of price-reduction; that again depends on whether we do it in hardback only or in hardback and paperback. I'm still wavering on that one.

Malcolm: Uh-huh.

On the subject of editing, Hardy added:

"Your language, as far as editing goes, you write on the whole very well with odd slips occasionally, which I think I can deal with. Without this basis I wouldn't have been able to accept the book, as the work would have been too great."

Our conversation concluded:

Hardy: ... Anyway, I will not go on at any greater length. I mean if you want I'll be getting in touch again when I've done the costs and cast-off and so forth and then we can, er, talk about some sort of contract.

Malcolm: Great! Fantastic news! Really good!

Hardy: It seems to me that because it's such a risky venture I'm not going to be terribly generous financially, ermm... I mean what I think we should agree is that you have a fair royalty so that if the book is a success you will do well out of it.

Malcolm: Yes.

Hardy: But I don't want to pay you in advance money that's been very riskily invested.

Malcolm: Sure, sure I wouldn't expect that, yup.

Hardy: Okay?

Malcolm: Great! That's very good. I'm just in the middle at the moment... I couldn't do anything immediately because we've got the Brighton Festival going on here and I'm involved in all sorts of things, but everything finishes in a week or two... and by then perhaps I can get down to it.

Hardy: Right. Good.

Malcolm: Great!

Hardy: Okay, well if you have any further thoughts or questions do come back to me with them. In the meantime...

Malcolm: In the meantime I'm waiting for you, you'll do the cast-off and...

Hardy: I'll write to you. Okay?

Malcolm: Splendid! Well thanks very much, that's er, that's made my day (Hardy laughs) not to say my life.

Hardy: Well let's hope it does well. Okay?

Malcolm: Okay. Thanks very much.

On the next day, Hardy wrote:

> Dear Andrew (if I may),
>
> I'm writing sooner than I thought because it would be useful to me if you could kindly fill in the enclosed Author's Publicity Form, the information in which will be invaluable to us in marketing your book. I am personally especially interested in what you offer by way of a draft blurb, since I shall base on this what I say about the book to the Delegates, but what you say elsewhere will be equally useful to other parts of the Press.
>
> I have sent the typescript off for cast-off, and will let you know the result, due in two or three weeks' time.
>
> I'm pleased that we are going to do your book and hope that it's a terrific success. As said, do get in touch if you have any queries as you work through it.
>
> Yours,
> Henry Hardy

Oxford's *Author's Publicity Form* was a glossy, six-page printed folder which began:

> "This questionnaire, which we send to all our authors, may reach you some considerable time before your book is due to be published. It would, however, be a great help to us if you could complete and return it at the earliest possible opportunity... the specialist information you can provide will help us to prepare the most effective possible marketing plan for your book."

I spent a couple of the most delirious hours possible composing Oxford's possible 50- and 150-word 'blurbs' for *Making Names*, profiling the book's possible 'target market', and typing in my own personal details. In answer to the question 'Present Position', I wrote "seated at desk". Was this possibly, I now wonder, my first possible mistake? On 30th May I returned the completed form with a covering letter:

Dear Henry,

Many thanks for your phonecall of 20th and letter of 21st May and apologies for my delay in replying. I too am pleased that you are going to do my book, very pleased. Although I have waited for over ten years for this moment to arrive, I confess that my reaction to it has so far been one more of daze than of euphoria. I think that carrying these ideas around in my head for so long has left me rather exhausted; also, there is the knowledge that there is much work still to be done.

With regard to this 'last lap', I think I should explain that for the past eighteen months or so of publisher-hunting, I have hardly looked at the book itself and have hardly picked up a pen, having been involved in a number of quite other activities. It is therefore going to take me a little while (two or three weeks?) to disengage myself from these activities and then re-immerse myself in the philosophy. To this end I am contemplating a move to the peace and quiet of a nearby country house where I will be able to concentrate wholeheartedly on the writing. Please bear with me in all this; I believe the final product will be worth the wait.

I hope I have filled in the Author's Publicity Form satisfactorily. I am not quite sure what is wanted in the blurbs. Let me know if what I have written sounds too bland or too pretentious or whatever. I would, as you can see, prefer to keep the *Making Names* and add a subtitle. I haven't yet given this much thought, but so far *a philosopher's dream of hope* is the only line that has stuck. In part this is a reference to details concerning the notions of dreaming and hoping that are due to be highlighted in the revision. How does it grab you? It would be a wonderful irony if the only pre-publication dispute between us were over the book's title, — a final argument perhaps for leaving it as it is!

I look forward to hearing your reactions.

Yours,
Andrew Malcolm

The irony certainly was wonderful. On 14th June, Hardy wrote again:

Dear Andrew,

Thank you very much for your letter of 30 May, and for the completed Author's Publicity Form. Don't worry about the delay in revising the book: it's much more important that you get it right than that we should publish it a month or two earlier. It's not as if it's tied into a centenary, after all!

I have discussed the title/subtitle issue with Alan Ryan. We agree in not going for your tentatively suggested subtitle, and also in feeling that, unless someone has a brilliant idea, it may be best to stick to *Making Names*, and let the cover illustration and blurb do whatever extra work needs to be done. So let's think in those terms for the time being, if that's OK by you. There's no hurry, anyway. The title doesn't have to be fixed until quite late on.

Yours,
Henry

So here at last it was, the jackpot: not just, after all this time, a commitment to *Making Names'* publication, but by a prestigious press, from an excited editor, and with the backing of an influential reviewer. I will leave my readers (especially any fellow would-be authors) to imagine just how all this felt. Not only, I dared gingerly to congratulate myself, had I perhaps written something worthwhile, but also as a complete outsider I had penetrated the implacable, dismissive walls that traditionally surround academe. The scale of this second achievement was later indicated by Hardy himself: "You get about one a week of the kind of thing one would classify as 'fringe trade philosophy', and one gets accustomed to rejecting 99.9 percent of it on the strength of just a few seconds' inspection, so the fact that yours has got as far as it has, out of that general ruck of stuff, shows that it's different from the others." Later still, in court, Kim Pickin painted an even sadder picture: "I was sent two or three unsolicited manuscripts every day for about three years... I would have a quick look to see if it was something I could make an instant decision about, or deal with promptly, and if I thought it was going to need more time, I would tend to put it to one side until I had a longer period of time, but, as you probably gathered, I didn't get those longer periods of time". In fact, as I wrote, my euphoria at OUP's acceptance was tempered by a dazed exhaustion, but in the face of such grim realities, could I not justifiably have then allowed myself a mighty celebration? Had not my homespun effort survived the holocaust of Pickin's wastebin and burnt its way onto the list of grandest, stuffiest imprimatur in the academic world?

4

Authors' Contracts

B UT EMOTION ASIDE, what can one now say of the legalities? Again, after even the above few quotes, what further needed to be said or agreed? In what respect was this deal incomplete? Because there was no five-page printed *Memorandum* detailing the Australian Book Club rights or the German film options? Because there was no double-signed agreement as to the UK paperback's retail price in eighteen months' time? (Believe it or not, this was later to be argued by Oxford.) Surely it would not need five years of High Court hearings to demonstrate that it is authors who write books and publishers who publish them? Besides, as Hugh Jones points out, all this law was clarified by the *Abrahams v. Reiach* case back in 1921, in which the British Olympic sprinters Harold Abrahams and Eric Liddell, who coincidentally had run for Oxford and Cambridge (and were the subjects of the 1981 film *Chariots of Fire*), successfully sued their publisher over a similar failure.

In the 1994 and 1995 editions of *Chitty* and *Treitel on Contracts*, English law's pre-eminent textbooks on the subject, *Malcolm v. The Chancellor, Masters and Scholars of the University of Oxford* (the case's official title) is accorded the honour of respectively three and six footnotes, though in the absence of a proper law report these can refer only to the short, unindexed contemporary analyses that appeared in *The Times* newspaper. This suggests that *Malcolm* is an important case not merely in publishing law, but in contract law generally, Chitty citing it with respect to lack of detail of remuneration (2-081), the purpose of an envisaged but unexecuted formal document (2-082) and the sufficient certainty of a phrase like Hardy's "a fair royalty" (2-102), and *Treitel* adding two points on damages. Outsiders reading only *Chitty, Treitel* or *The Times,* or even the full Court of Appeal judgment may be forgiven for concluding that my contract with Oxford sounds dangerously thin, and that Hardy and I had consented to very little, but of course in fact we had agreed a good deal, and certainly on everything that our context rendered important. The sole purpose of both parties to the negotiation had been to arrive at a formula — the revisions required of an already complete script — that would result in its publication by OUP, and we had discussed and agreed such a formula exhaustively. Hardy's orated "number of points I've got written down here", later confirmed in writing, ranged from precise stipulations about length-reduction to fine details of punctuation and spelling. Hardy and I had not, for example, mentioned the future book's microform edition reversion rights for they were not in our minds or in issue, but we *had* agreed on the adoption of OUP's three-point ellipses convention and when to use the oblique-stroke and how the brackets were to look. We had even, after all, agreed on the book's *title!*

Hugh Jones asserts that generally speaking a contract is complete only if it provides "some valuable consideration to seal the bargain", and that in the case of author-publisher contracts this is the author's royalty payment or advance against it. In 1921, he observes, a court held that Abrahams' "4d per copy" constituted such a consideration, and in my case, Hardy's promised "fair royalty" sufficed equally well for the 1990 Court of Appeal. I have sometimes wondered about this. Given that the whole author-publisher relationship is an unusual one, and that many would-be authors might be willing to forgo any royalty, say on their first book, simply in order to get properly, publicly into print, would a publishing contract necessarily be incomplete if no royalty were specified, or if a royalty of zero were specified (and agreed)? Would a peppercorn rate do? Some authors might argue that a peppercorn is all they get anyway. In many actual cases like Oxford's own stable of scholarly writers on obscure subjects, the author's chief reward or 'consideration' is not money but reputation, or even perhaps just satisfaction at having work approved. Besides, surely there is nothing necessarily incomplete about a *vanity* publishing contract? The basic shape of my deal with Oxford was: I will do *x* months' revision to your specifications if you will publish the resulting book. OUP's publication *was* their chief consideration. As it happens, I would have insisted on a fair royalty, for I believed (a parallel delusion) that my book might one day earn me money, but I am not certain that my contract with Hardy would necessarily have been vitiated if he had made no mention of the word 'royalty' and I had not expressly waived my entitlement to one; I guess that custom and practice might have 'filled the gap' or may in future be held to do so in other such disputes.

Another question I have often pondered is: what difference would it have made to the outcome of the case if I had failed to record the crucial telephone conversation of 20th May? The obvious, immediate answer is "all in the world", but again I am not so sure. Apart from assuming Hardy's dishonesty or faulty memory (an assumption I tried to fight off for some years, with ever-decreasing conviction), this may be to undervalue the contextual correspondence. To raise this hypothesis is, of course, also to put oneself in the position of an OUP insider inspecting their file and asking the question at the time, as someone evidently did. On memos exchanged by two other OUP editors, Angus Phillips and Adam Hodgkin, which were later discovered by the lawyers, the latter had scribbled the fateful words "Is it already under contract?" (It was never revealed what reply he got.) Indeed, although such an insider would not at the time have had transcripts of my April and May conversations with Hardy, he would, as you will learn, have had access to a number of internal OUP papers which in Hardy's own hand confirmed that he had offered me a contract. The letters we exchanged in February and March clearly set out the context of our negotiation; my penultimate paragraph of 24th March firmly stated my position; it is clear from our correspondence of May and June (whatever Hardy subsequently says) that on the telephone on 20th May he gave OUP's definitive commitment to the publication of *Making Names*; the solemnity of Hardy's commitment is confirmed by what then happened internally and in writing at the Press; and the detail of OUP's revision requirements is provided by his subsequent letter to me of 30th July. A future court, or a contemporary OUPite would find in Hardy's internal correspondence his acknowledgment that we had agreed modest royalties, together with a detailed costings sheet on which these and his other figures had been entered. I had even been sent an Author's Publicity Form, which, as Lord Justice Mustill later observed, normally only happens after a contract has been issued. In short, all that was needed to demonstrate a complete and enforceable contract was already there in Oxford's file, *never mind the tapes.*

A further, related, question is: what difference would it have made if instead of phoning me, Hardy, as he should properly have done, had on 20th May written me a letter stating his gist, say:

> I have now finished reading *Making Names*, and we would like to do it. As you have requested, I am offering OUP's commitment to its publication sufficient to take you through the last stage of revision, but conditional on you not making the script in our opinion worse. Our revision requirements are as follows (as per his phonecall of 20th May and his later letter of 30th July). I can offer no advance, but you will get a fair royalty so that if the book is a success you will do well out of it... I am pleased that we are going to do *Making Names* and hope that it's a terrific success. As said, do get in touch if you have any queries as you work through it.

If such a copy-letter had been on file at OUP, would it have made any difference to the legal position, or to Oxford's keenness to defend the action at all costs? Our complete contract would from the start have been recorded in writing, but this would have made not the slightest difference to any of Oxford's subsequent defences (that there was no printed *Memorandum of Agreement*, that the Delegates had not formally approved *Making Names*, that Hardy had no authority at OUP, that his "provided the revisions do not make it worse" condition was too subjective to be contractual, that we had not expressly agreed a print-run or the price of the paperback). All this suggests that the oral-versus-written question is the case's least important.

5

Into the Shit

IN JULY 1985, unbeknownst to me, a *third* opinion on *Making Names* was sought by OUP, when the script was sent to St. Hugh's philosophy lecturer and writer Galen Strawson (son of Sir Peter, and at that time a frequent book-reviewer for *The Observer* and *The Times Supplements*), who after reading "bits" of the script (he was given just two days) also firmly recommended its publication:

> "I think *Making Names* is really quite an attractive book. It is in no way crazy. It is very easy to read. Malcolm has a real gift for informal exposition... he is very clear and he knows what he's talking about. If it were suitably rewritten, I think *Making Names* might prove extremely effective as an introduction to philosophical problems and procedures...
> There are stylistic problems however... I'd completely forgotten that 'bird' could mean 'girl'...
> So: philosophical content, procedure etc. are fine for an introduction. The dialogue form also works well, on the whole, but needs some rethinking in its details."

From the outset I was well aware that the book was not likely to be to everyone's taste: its format was unusual, its style was far-removed from Oxford's usual scholasticism, and its content, especially in its final polemic and imagery, was, I hoped, highly controversial. Yet here I now stood, an unknown amateur, scoring a surprise hit with three out of three professional referees. I should perhaps add that, judging from their comments and reports, none of Oxford's readers saw *Making Names'* values and aims as I did, and though none sought its removal, all were at best baffled by the final playscript, which I regarded as the book's main contribution. When things went wrong, Hardy confided:

> "Obviously you may be right about the importance of what you've achieved in that play, but I don't think any of the three of us who have read it have seen the point if that's the case... We are puzzled about it, but we haven't made it one of the conditions for resubmission that the play should be eliminated. We are prepared, as it were, to accept that for you it's an indispensible part of the book."

Years later, in telephone conversation with my solicitor, Alan Ryan pronounced *Electra* "an excrescence", while Galen Strawson, interestingly, thought it "over the top". A divergence of views and interpretations is, naturally, par for the course; different people like (and loathe) the same book for quite different reasons, and authors are well used to reading reviews in which they can hardly recognise the work being criticised as their own. Later still, when I was trying to find senior book-trade figures willing to testify in court on *Making Names'* behalf, one such authority described it as "a pastiche of *Jude the Obscure*".

At this juncture it may also be worth asking: what does an unpublished author have to do? How many people does his work (again, be it literary, scientific, philosophical or whatever) have to please? Even at my most optimistic I had never expected *Making Names'* style or content to appeal to the average orthodox bookman, yet already (I later gathered) at least a dozen OUPites had contributed their pennyworth opinions. Would even a literary classic pass such a series of tests? When the legal argument got going, Oxford further claimed that the Delegates, another twenty or so, would have had to approve it too. Even if the book had formally won the Delegates' favour (as I believe it in fact did), a new set of hurdles could presumably have been whistled up. It is easy to find people ready to dismiss something, especially in England, and *especially* in Oxford. Perhaps the whole story was just another case of too many chefs.

But to resume the chronology, my unlikely three-out-of-three approval was still not enough. As Lord Justice Mustill later put it in his Court of Appeal judgment, "I then suffered a fatal reverse", or as Hugh Jones more recently glossed, "OUP then changed their minds". Curiously, for years there was no evidence that anyone at OUP did then change their mind about *Making Names*. Henry Hardy, after six years of betrayal during the litigation, wrote to me reaffirming his high estimation of the book, while Galen Strawson, despite evidently being pressured to testify in court against it, refused to modify his original favourable judgment. Nicola Bion, the junior editor who later claimed that the decision to axe the book had been hers, had not seen its first draft and had read only "bits" of its second, so did not really have much of a mind to change. And as for Alan Ryan's multifaceted mind, the reader should wait until all the evidence is, as it were, in court and then make up their own.

What actually happened was that a man who knew nothing at all about philosophy or about the book and who, according to Hardy, "had not even bothered to inquire as to its contents" intervened and, as Hardy colourfully put it "plunged us both (Hardy and Malcolm) into the shit."

(More than once he turned uncharacteristically scatalogical when mentioning his boss. A later exchange went: Malcolm: "And how is Richard Charkin, is he well?" Hardy: "Yes he hasn't tipped any buckets of excrement over me since we last spoke, or over himself. Over somebody else probably.") Charkin, the already-mentioned Managing Director of OUP's Academic and General Division, had expressed doubts about the book's financial viability, despite the "good profitability" indicated on its costings sheet, and had refused to sign an internal form authorising the necessary printing outlay. Apart from the fact that this seems to make a nonsense of the Press's supposed academic-charitable status, I have never understood how Charkin could pass a commercial judgment on a book of whose contents he was totally (and in court, proudly) ignorant, but anyway, this was the interpretation that was later accepted by Lord Justice Mustill:

> "Mr Charkin took his decision, not because he thought the book was no good — he had never seen it and the reports were favourable — but because he thought it would not sell. Let there be no mistake about it, the failure of this transaction was about money, not prestige."

The Court of Appeal, however, was not privy to a whole swathe of evidence, subsequently produced for the damages hearing, which told a rather different story.

This is one of several points in the saga where minute examination of the recorded conversations provides fascinating material not only for contract lawyers but also for psychologists and moralists, where barely audible intakes and releases of breath or the finest changes of voice-tone speak far more eloquently than umpteen pages of literal transcript. Stammered 'ifs', stuttered 'buts', throttled asides, strangled sentences and a whole gamut of emotionally revealing gurgles and gasps punctuate our recorded conversations. So far, whenever Hardy had telephoned me, he had found me in, and every time, I had more or less directly picked up my receiver. But on 18th July, by chance I was out, and when he telephoned he for the first time heard my answerphone, on which in a clearly worried voice he left a message asking me to ring him, urgently, at home. He immediately followed this with a handwritten letter repeating the request. Before our next conversation it was thus clear to me that something had gone wrong, and revealed to him that I had an answering machine. It may have occurred to him then that I had made recordings of our earlier conversations; we were both forewarned of the impending deluge.

As requested, fearing the worst but not imagining anything nearly as nasty as the truth, I telephoned Hardy on 18th July. His first question, asked in a gloomy tone, was how much work I had done on the book. I replied cheerfully and truthfully that I had planned but not yet commenced the revision, explaining less cheerfully but equally truthfully that I had just finished a spell of building work on my house with a view to letting it and moving to a secluded retreat in Ditchling to do the rewrite. In the Court of Appeal judgment the possibility was later raised of an alternative claim, on their finding of only a *quasi*-contract, for my expenses incurred and work done, literary and otherwise, between May and July as a result of Hardy's commitment. I did submit the (modest) costs incurred in preparing my house for letting, but this remained a fall-back claim which I never needed to test. Other authors, however, in appropriate circumstances might find this area of law useful; Mustill LJ refers to *Goff & Jones on Restitution*, 3rd Edition, Chapter 18, and another good starting-point is William Lacey Ltd. v. Davis [1957] 1 W.L.R. 932. Hardy's second, rather edgier question was how much I remembered of our previous conversation:

> "I'm hoping that you've got a good memory... I remember drawing your attention to the fact that the contract has a clause in it which specifies that the typescript as delivered must be acceptable, a let-out clause... Again I remember telling you that we have a procedure here which involves filling in a form which has to be signed by a man who... This form has not yet been signed... In telling you that we were going ahead I was jumping the gun..." so forth.

These were transparent lies; Hardy had said no such things and had no memory of saying such things, for of course if he had, they would have made a complete nonsense of our entire negotiation. Interestingly, later, whenever I reminded him of this nonsensicality, he would turn instantly tetchy, like an irritable horse trying to twitch the flies from an inaccessible sore. I believe that Hardy's absurd reinvention of the history was also a test; not only of how I would react to the obviously imminent bad news, but also of his uppermost fear, that I had kept notes of our conversations, or perhaps even taped them. Even now I can remember clearly the racing of my brain through those split seconds as the stench of dissembling and betrayal wafted unmistakably from the earpiece. My first emotions, of course, were despair and anger, my first impulses protest and denunciation, but as he stammered on through his charade, a quieter, steelier instinct took over: "I'm being fucked over here, that's that; there's no point in making a scene, no point in confronting him with recordings, he'll only go defensive and clam up. No, stay calm, play dumb, and you may learn what's happened." So, I stayed calm, played dumb, and sure enough, Hardy talked.

When he had satisfied himself that I was not going to erupt into rage and that I had not recorded our previous conversation, so leaving him free to rescript it, he audibly relaxed and his emotions freed. During a series of exchanges, the truth, and the true source of his tension, emerged: his job was on the line. Charkin had served him with a 'Stage Three Warning Preparatory to Dismissal' because of some alleged 'jumping the gun' with me, and had written me a letter reneging on OUP's commitment. Hardy was therefore very anxious to talk to me — to sound me out and calm me down — before I received Charkin's letter. He knew that if I were to react with anger, or a writ, as I had every right and cause to do, Charkin would then be able to give him the sack. The upshot for me ("the dirty end of the stick", as he put it) was that *Making Names* was being shafted not because of anyone's low opinion of it, nor even, as the Court of Appeal years later concluded, for financial reasons, but because of an entirely unrelated feud going on at the Press. This was not exactly the sort of intellectual controversy I had had in mind for the book, as Hardy gradually revealed: "It has become a pawn in this power-struggle thing between him [Charkin] and me... It has become a matter of personal pride... He would lose face by now accepting it and he's not someone who will lose face... There's an element of personality in here which has nothing to do with your book... It's not going to get a fair hearing here now that it has been treated in this way... He wouldn't want to give me the satisfaction of the book going through... Charkin has been trying to get rid of me for some time and it has been suggested that he's using this as an excuse..." And as Charkin later relishingly admitted in court: "The key thing was that it was a Henry (Hardy) book... It would have been one more nail in his coffin".

It transpired that for several years Charkin and Hardy "had not seen eye to eye" and that Hardy had been responsible for a number of OUP books of which Charkin had disapproved. One notorious Hardy project was *London After the Bomb*, a demolition by a group of scientists and doctors of the *Protect and Survive* manual and of (Tory) Government estimates of the likely casualties and effects of a nuclear attack upon the capital. The book had large sales but incurred the wrath of the Home Office, provoked questions in Parliament, and sparked a ceremonial burning of copies on the steps of Wandsworth town hall (its cover depicts the central pages of an *A-to-Z* on fire). It began to seem as though my book too was being thrown on the fire, the fire of these two men's vendetta. Every time Hardy mentioned Charkin's action against him, his normally even tone would explode into a splutter: "it was *totally ludicrous*," he exclaimed, "*totally ludicrous!*" Indeed, he added that his support for *Making Names* was actually strengthened by Charkin's treatment of it: "I made a commitment to you which I think we should honour collectively" he pronounced. "Yes" I mumbled, and he thanked me for not being crosser. On 19th July I received Charkin's letter:

> Dear Mr Malcolm,
>   I am writing with what I imagine may be very disappointing news. Your book proposal came to our editorial meeting with Henry Hardy's full support. I am afraid that we were not convinced enough to ask for a contract to be issued. There were doubts about the market and worries about extent and content. I know that you propose working on the latter, but we would have to see the finished typescript and have it fully refereed before committing ourselves to publish. Even then, there would be considerable commercial and sales problems and I cannot hold out much hope that we would publish.
>   I would quite understand if you felt unable to undertake the revision without a firm commitment from us.
>   I must also apologize on behalf of Oxford University Press for the unnecessary raising of your hopes of publication.
>   Yours sincerely,
>   Richard Charkin
>   Managing Director, OUP Academic and General Division

After all my and Hardy's painstaking discussion of *Making Names'* required length, structure, timing, style, typography, page-layout, punctuation and countless other matters, suddenly there was no point in my making any revisions to it whatever. Charkin's summary flourish rendered our whole year's careful negotiation a complete waste of time. In a phonecall on the same day, Hardy confirmed that *Making Names* was a dead duck at Oxford, and we discussed alternative possibilities; the transcript of our long conversation now reads like a condensed course in book-publishing. Observing again that my first-draft script would need very little editing, Hardy offered to publish it himself under his own small imprint (he mentioned a medical text written by his father and a book of epitaphs: "I've been lucky in one or two cases and got the odd review in things like *The Tablet* and *Country Life*"), while I offered to put up the money (his overall figure for production and promotion was £10,000), but we both agreed that an unknown imprimatur on a book's spine (his example was "Neasden Groupies Inc.") gave it a far poorer chance of success than OUP's. He suggested Harvester or Blackwell, but I explained that I had already tried the former and got no request for the script, and then read him my futile correspondence with Kim Pickin. We went back over the detail of the Penguin story, and I told him of even earlier experiences I had had with TV comedy scripts being unreturned and their ideas ripped off. "People are shits aren't they!" he exclaimed, with no detectable trace of irony. He went on presciently to explain the difficulties involved in self-publication and distribution by mail-order, at one point suggesting that I should go round the country's universities and polytechnics putting up fly-posters. Perhaps, I mused absently, I would do that some day, but where I wondered, would I start?

In this and our previous conversation, Hardy revealed his former intentions for *Making Names*, the details of which were later to assume some significance in the damages assessment. He explained that he had planned to "put it through first as a hardback alone, costing about £15, in order to get it approved, and then at that point to get different costings for doing it simultaneously in hardback and paperback, which is the way I would like, er, I would have liked, to do it." The price of the paperback, he estimated, would probably have ranged from £5.95 to £8.95. On 18th July, "just to cheer me up", Hardy had read out OUP's third referee's favourable report, and now he identified its author as Galen Strawson, simultaneously admitting that he should not be doing so: "There is a general rule in publishing that you don't reveal the names of your referees... because that stops the author going out and murdering them". However, when I asked him for copies of Ryan's and Strawson's reports so that I might show them to other publishers, he declined. He then, long before the legal tango began, did send the latter's, but anonymised, and with an odd handwritten and presumably uncopied postscript drafted as though he had not already revealed the name. None of this was helping to get *Making Names* published elsewhere, but it was, it later transpired, providing much valuable information and ammunition. Then, actually during our conversation, someone entered Hardy's office and delivered his formal notification of his disciplinary appeal hearing.

In our next conversation on 22nd July, which featured our most intimate mutual revelations, Hardy explained that Charkin's Stage Three entitled him to lodge an appeal which entailed both men going, on the following morning at 9.45, before a panel of senior OUP executives to argue it out, and that these proceedings involved the drafting of formal charge and defence documents. During this explanation, the realisation dawned not only that my book had been dumped arbitrarily, but also that I was now being *used*, by both men. From what Hardy said, I inferred (more or less correctly, as it turned out) that Charkin's charge against him would state that Hardy had committed OUP to the publication of *Making Names* without having got Charkin's signature on some internal form, and that Hardy's defence would admit this but claim that it had been necessary to do so if I was to go ahead and revise the book as he required. In other words, the one thing they were likely to agree on, in writing, was that Oxford was committed to the book's publication. I for my part, whilst apologising for its present draft's roughness, reaffirmed my belief in the value of *Electra*, despite my and her latest batterings, and confided to him that I still regarded the idea it attempted to express as the most important I was ever likely to have.

Hardy admitted that my reaction to Charkin's dumping of *Making Names* would greatly affect his position at the Press, which he now regarded as very precarious, and he said that he fully expected to lose first his appeal and then his job. At one stage, he dictated an acquiescent letter he wanted me to write on his behalf to ameliorate his situation, and he even asked me to send him a copy of Charkin's rejection, which he himself had not been allowed to see. That afternoon I complied with his second request, but accompanied it with a rather different letter of my own, later described by Mustill LJ as 'dignified':

Dear Henry,

As you are no doubt aware by now, I have recently received from your colleague Richard Charkin what has to rate as the single most disappointing letter of my life, rejecting my proposal *Making Names*.

By rights I know that I should be extremely angry at this setback after all your interest and encouragement, not to mention your firm written commitments to the book's publication, especially as although I have not actually begun the final revision (I was just about to), I have made a number of arrangements, some financial, in the light of OUP's apparent acceptance. In fact however, my disappointment has so far been tempered more with resignation than with anger. I suppose that all along I have known, not so deep down, that it would be too much to hope that a philosophical work as evidently controversial as mine would ever be published by a press as respectable and as 'safe' as yours. All I can say is: thanks for your faith in the book and for your efforts on its behalf; I hope that they have not landed you in too much trouble yourself.

On reflection, I think that I may return to the work after all and try to improve some of its least satisfactory passages, if only for my own gratification; I have nothing much else to do at the moment. From the tone of Mr Charkin's letter, there is clearly no point in returning any revised version to OUP. It seems that it would not matter if I had written the most important philosophical text since *Language, Truth and Logic* (which if I may be forgiven the arrogance now that all is lost, I think perhaps I may have done), it will not even get considered. However, since you have taken a personal interest in the project, I hope that you may be interested to read any major revisions that I make, and perhaps even to help me to find an alternative publisher. Any assistance will be greatly appreciated.

Yours,

Andrew Malcolm

In short, with a few wind-ups and a clear warning, as one is supposed to do in such circumstances, I thoroughly washed my hands of Oxford and its perfectly poisonous press.

This, one would have thought, should have put an end to the miserable affair, but no. On the day of his disciplinary hearing, Hardy telephoned to thank me for my letter and to tell me that he had 'won' his appeal, kept his job and had Charkin's warning erased from his personnel record. Obviously, this had made Charkin's behaviour look vindictive and excessive, and the latter was now keen to 'mend his fences'. Charkin had read my letter, "admired its fighting spirit, being a fighter himself", and then *instructed* Hardy (Hardy's emphasis) to write to me and say that, after all, OUP *would* now like me to revise the book as originally agreed. Hardy proceeded to try to persuade me, against my better judgment and despite all their foregoing duplicity, to undertake the six months' work I had originally envisaged. I was very reluctant to have any further Oxford dealings, but he persisted, giving me several new guarantees and undertakings, though now stopping short of his previous clear commitment. He promised, for example, that he would remain editorially responsible for the book and be the sole person with whom I would discuss its contents and cuts. I also warned him that if I went ahead and Charkin later trotted out a routine rejection citing 'marketing worries' or some such, then I *would* sue; he said he quite understood and assured me that Charkin "could not possibly get away with that". Finally, I agreed to go ahead if he would send me all of OUP's revision requirements in writing.

On 30th July, Hardy sent me a two-page letter "summarizing the changes that seem to us to be required". His summary precisely confirmed the various points he had made to me in writing on 18th March and on the telephone on 20th May: a length-cut of twenty percent (his first-draft cast-off was 500 pages); splitting the first chapter into two; a reduction of the characters' use of each other's first names; an improvement of the timings; some pruning of the book's scientific passages; elimination of non-conversational abbreviations such as 'i.e.' and of bracketed asides; observation of house-style conventions like the use of three dots, not four, for ellipses, and of single rather than double quotation-marks; and again, even details like my misspellings of 'discrete' and 'discreet'. On the subject of *Electra* he wrote:

> All the readers, as you know, have been worried about the play. We have discussed this at length on the phone, so all I will say here is that anything you can do to make its role in your drama more accessible, and its performance of that role more effective, will be worthwhile. Knowing that you regard the play's contribution as central, we are not asking you to remove it — just to make it work.

His letter ended: "Now, I guess, you just have to get down to it: but let me know if you need anything further before you start." Hardy asked my permission to make and keep a photocopy of my first draft before returning its original to me for my forthcoming cut-and-paste exercise. In August, with a vague feeling of being thoroughly armed, and faintly aware of the tape-recordings' impending significance, I started work.

By October I had completed the splitting of the first two chapters and thought it would be politic to keep Oxford abreast of my progress. I telephoned Hardy and was informed that he had been transferred by Charkin against his wishes out of General Books and into another department, Academic Sociology and Politics, where he no longer had any control over *Making Names*, and, as he said, "was no longer in a position to publish any interesting books". Instead, I was now to be 'handled' by a non-philosopher assistant editor by the name of Nicola Bion. Yet again the writing was on the wall, and yet again I felt myself beginning to go up it. Nevertheless, I asked Hardy if he would read the new first two chapters to see if he thought I was on the right track, as per his caveat of 20th May. He agreed to do so, and in November he replied:

> Dear Andrew,
>   I have now read the rewritten chapters (*en route*, perhaps appropriate-ly, from Oxford to Cambridge!). My opinion has of course no status in the matter any more, but they seem to me to be fine. I wasn't comparing them directly with the original version, so it may be that they seem better partly because I am coming at the material for a second time; but I don't think that can be a very large ingredient. Certainly it is better now that this section is split into two, and the style and level seem much more even. I congratulate you on cutting the length: I can't see that this has any untoward side-effects. It certainly makes the material more digestible.
>   Nicola will try to read the chapters soon, and will then write to you if she has anything to add.
>   Yours,
>   Henry

Nicola wrote and added nothing.

6

The Bionic Pan

IGNORING HARDY'S ominous second sentence, I ploughed on for five more exhausting months, relieved only by a spell in the beautiful Spanish city of Salamanca. I completed the revision and fulfilled or exceeded all of Oxford's requirements, most importantly cutting the book's length by twenty-six percent. Partly for amusement and partly to test any new refereeing, I had also added one or two self-v.-Oxford-referential touches (some of Hardy's own lines to me, a scatological allusion to his boss, a comment on Strawson's sad "bird" confession and so on), but no-one at Oxford ever picked up on them. The final chapter incorporating the verse play, though improved, was still in need of more work, but in February 1986, with my digestion shattered (partly by Madrid salmonella and partly by Oxford anxiety), I felt ready to resubmit the script. I telephoned Hardy, who at once referred me to Bion, saying that he was "anxious not to get involved with the book again", and that it should now "automatically go through". In case it would speed up this 'going-through', I had prepared two copies of the second draft and offered to send him one if he would return his duplicate of the first; a nice moment came when he agreed to do so, but only if I would send him £30 for the photocopying.

Bion asked for the two copies and assured me that "it would not take more than a few weeks for two or three people to read them". Getting no acknowledgment of the scripts' receipt, I phoned a week later to check that they had arrived safely (they had), and was told that "Oxford's couple of readers shouldn't take more than three weeks". Over a month passed silently before I phoned again, now to be told that Alan Ryan had taken the script with him on holiday to Canada and that Bion was "still hoping to send it to someone else". Two weeks later she told me that Ryan was not due back in Oxford until May and that "he did not want to rush it". Finally, on 12th May, I received this:

> Dear Andrew,
>   I've now had the reports on your revised typescript and discussed them with colleagues. The news is not good, I'm afraid.
>   Despite the fact that the cuts and amendments you have made are undoubtedly an improvement, we still don't feel that it <u>works</u>. There

are a number of reasons for this. First, it's still too long: I know that you've made substantial cuts, but it's not so much a question of the actual extent as the feel of the thing. And it feels too long. You have to be particularly careful about this when writing for a lay audience.

Secondly, there are quite a lot of places where it would need to be made brisker and livelier (and I have to say I don't like the sexist aspects either). Something could of course, be done about that, but it would require a great deal of editorial input from OUP. We do unfortunately have to take into account the overhead costs of every book we sign up, and in this case we feel that the editorial work would be disproportionately expensive,

Another problem, from our point of view, is what we perceive to be a gradual change of climate in trade publishing... OUP is moving away from what we see as the more 'peripheral' areas of publishing... Trade philosophy books have always been difficult to market (with a few notable exceptions) and they are becoming more so.

Having weighed up all these factors we have decided, extremely reluctantly, that we cannot make you an offer of publication.

We did feel that there was the seed of a book there — otherwise we obviously wouldn't have been able to encourage you at all... It would be very unwise — and unfair — of us to encourage you to continue the time-consuming and agonizing business of further revision without any firm prospect of publication.

I wish I could suggest a positive way forward... I would be happy to send the typescript to Harvester with a covering note.

Yours sincerely,

N. Bion

By this farrago OUP contradicted or ignored virtually every single judgment, observation and undertaking made to me about the book by the editor who had now for over eighteen months been exclusively discussing it with me, who a year earlier had knowingly and on file contracted it, and who had expressly assured me that he would remain editorially responsible for it. The very "marketing difficulties" routine of which I had carefully warned in July, and which in any case should have been settled by two minutes with the book's 1984 synopsis, was trotted out almost verbatim. The one bit of good news was that with Bion's "undoubtedly an improvement" concession, Oxford was admitting in writing that I had satisfied Hardy's only condition of publication: I had fulfilled my side of the original deal. Into this tortuous and tortious rejection Hardy had inserted a postcard note:

"Andrew, I am, of course, terribly sorry about this... With hindsight I would prefer, of course, not to have offered you any encouragement in the first place... so forth."

Years later, it turned out that from its very first sentence, the Bionic flushpaper was, er, rather misleading. Oxford's discovered evidence suggests that the second draft of *Making Names* was never read by anyone, and certainly OUP obtained no readers' report on it. Bion stated in court that she took the decision to reject the book, yet she was a junior editor with no knowledge of philosophy, she had not read the first draft, and she clearly had no sympathy with the second. Okay, so editors change their minds about books, and staff are hired and fired. So publishers are taken over, fall on hard times, or adopt new policies, and the climate in trade bookselling blows hot and cold. So contracted and uncontracted projects are routinely trashed for countless specious reasons. But how often, I mused, can an author have fallen foul of such protracted, intricate, mob-handed bad faith as this, as I began to toy with Oxford's DIM, pseudo-Latin motto *Dominus illuminatio mea*. I say *pseudo*-Latin, for as with much Oxonian, '*illuminatio*', I learned, was a post-classical invention.

I sometimes wonder if I should have declared my telephone tapes and their truth back in July 1985, as soon as things went wrong first time round, and should have threatened to sue then. During the lawsuit, several of the OUnuchs cited my failure to do so as evidence of the absence of a contract, almost as though thoughts of being sued or threats of litigation were for them commonplace; as though the dance-routine was familiar. The ugly legal acuteness betrayed by such comments is, of course, matched only by their ugly legal dullness: (a) had nobody read my 'dignified' letter of 22nd July, carefully recording and reserving my rights? and (b) what could I then have sued *for*? (I had done little revision work, and my only expenses had been on the preparation of my house for letting). Obviously, if at that point I had turned litigious ("jumped up and down" as Hardy had put it at the time), all that followed would have been different, but what good would have come? Some foul air would have been cleared, but Hardy would probably have been sacked and *Making Names* would certainly have been a gonner. As is so frequently reiterated, the author-publisher relationship is one of mutual trust and co-operation, not of coercion, and as Hardy himself had advised in apparent sincerity, while there was still a chance of turning the situation around in a civilised manner, that was by far my best option. With the publisher holding all the cards, the only thing the author can do is to grit their teeth and keep playing the game politely.

I am not, or at least then was not, by any stretch a litigious person. I had absolutely no knowledge or experience of law or of litigation. At first, all I felt was an immense sense of injustice and a deep, consuming anger, an emotion which as it happened is examined obliquely in *Making Names*; it surfaces in the opening chapter when Cause's car gets a parking-ticket, initiating a discussion of behaviourism, and re-emerges at the climax (of the first draft), when the two protagonists come to blows. In my first pre-litigation response, I gave Oxford the references: "In my letter of 22nd July I stated that my disappointment had so far been tempered more with resignation than with anger. My disappointment is now tempered with anger." Exactly what I had predicted against all of Hardy's assurances had happened, and as he himself had insisted, Oxford "could not be allowed to get away with it". If this was normal, acceptable practice in the gentlemanly world, it was time it was exposed and stopped. I also knew that I was at the end of the road with writing generally. Even if there had been worthwhile publishers untried, I no longer had any desire to try them. Needless to say, no-one at Oxford helped in this respect, and I was not even allowed to use their referees' favourable reports. Traditional, humble, script-in-hand subservience was no longer tenable: I could not continue listening to editors' various gimcrack opinions while the boil of Oxford's two-year poison remained unlanced. If I *had* found another publisher interested in *Making Names*, I simply would not have trusted or believed anything they said and certainly could not have acceded to their obligatory litany of suggestions ("why not recast it as a series of essays in plain text...?") No, an interesting new career was beginning to take shape; perhaps a new mission; or perhaps just something to do.

But even after OUP's second-draft rejection, I for a while persisted with a stoical civility. Before taking any expensive and confrontational legal steps, I thought I should first write to someone at Oxford who was senior to both Charkin and Hardy and therefore above their vendetta: surely there must be some decent man in the hierarchy who would be appalled when he learned what had happened and who would do the right thing and honour Hardy's original, well-documented commitment? Hardy had said that Charkin's senior was Robin Denniston, who held the post of 'Oxford Publisher' and who, he had added, was sympathetic both to Hardy and to *Making Names*. In July I wrote Denniston a careful letter marked *Personal and Confidential* which recounted the essential elements of the story, outlined my legal position as I saw it, and mentioned the five-plus hours of tape-recordings, from which I quoted verbatim. To my surprise, I received no reply from Denniston, but two from Charkin, the first sentences of which read: "I have been passed your letter addressed to Mr Denniston. As it seems that I am the cause of your anger, I feel I should reply..." (This strange intervention later chimed with a remark made by Charkin in an interview for *Publishing News*: "It's true, at OUP I didn't get to see *all* of the incoming mail, but I did used to sniff around the post quite heavily.") He went on to state that the decision to dump *Making Names* had been made not by him, but "by the Delegates of the Press". After a second letter from me in which I warned of the affair's becoming "a turning corkscrew", Denniston himself finally responded, with a single line: "I have read the correspondence but have nothing further to add." I was now fully *encouraged*, and decided to talk to lawyers.

At first, most of my lay or semi-professional advice (like, I imagine, most of the OUP staffers' non-lawyerly reactions) was that without a formal, signed *Memorandum of Agreement* I had no contract. I could never understand this view, which seemed to be based on either an elementary misconception of contract law (which I was now beginning to read), or a careless digestion of the evidence, and in particular of the key sentence of my letter of 24th March 1985 around which the whole deal had revolved: "In the light of experience, one firm resolution that I have made is not to embark upon any further major rewriting exercise without first securing a firm commitment from a publisher." It was true that I had been expecting OUP's *Memorandum* and had not received it, but I knew full well (from a friend with one) that its opening sentence reads: "The Publisher shall subject to his approval of the finished typescript publish...", a let-out clause that would have invalidated the very premise of my negotiation with Hardy. If Hardy had sent me such a *Memorandum* and declined to amend its opening clause appropriately, I would have refused to sign it and would not have revised the book. In a funny way, I felt that I was better off *without* such a document.

Other would-be authors (and negotiating editors) may here wish to pause to consider the lessons so far, some of which are immediately clear. As Hugh Jones advises it is obviously best to be as unambiguous as possible, preferably in writing (in correspondence and in any formal contract or schedule or synopsis attached to it), about what constitutes 'the work' to be published. If, as in my case, a completed text is submitted and the question to resolve is what cuts or revisions are required by the publisher, get them spelt out in detail. If the book is unfinished (accepted perhaps on the strength of the first chapter or two) or unstarted altogether (accepted merely on the basis of a synopsis or the author's track-record), clarify its ultimate form and content as precisely as possible beforehand, again either in correspondence or in a schedule or synopsis attached to the contract; at the risk of being prolix, every letter from you about your intentions, even if unanswered by the publisher, could later provide them with a headache. The more detail that is agreed (and fulfilled), the less easy will it be for the publisher, *x* laborious months down the line, to wriggle out of the deal. If you are worried by an OUP-style opening clause, try to get the publisher to agree to its deletion or amendment. The fact that it is printed means not a jot; most completed OUP *Memoranda* (and by now I have quite a collection) carry many crossings-out and typed or handwritten insertions. Every negotiation, situation and book is different.

Agents' agreements, of course, are drafted more favourably for authors, and different publishers use different standard forms, not all of which insist on the extremely wide powers of rejection afforded OUP by its *Memorandum's* opening "subject to our approval of the finished script" clause. However, a first-time author may not be in a position to drive a hard bargain and may not wish to antagonise those who are taking this precious first interest in their work, so it may be that some such blanket let-out will have to stand. If so, detailed, approved synopses will still help in the event of any dispute, and the publisher's vetting of the final script will have to be exercised *bona fide*, that is in good faith. In my Oxford encounter, *bona fide* was obviously a commodity in zero-supply: not only was there the evidence of my own long and treacherous garden path and the well-documented feud and disciplinary battle between Charkin and Hardy, it was clear that Alan Ryan, and by the end even the Delegates, had been deceived too. I believe that if the issue in my case had been the *bona fides* of Oxford's rejection of my revised script, it would have been rather easier for me to win than it was (although it would have to have been pleaded differently and would have relied on a quite different array of evidence): there was, for a start, Hardy's telltale invocation on 18th July of an imaginary escape clause, and the absence of any reports on the second draft. My experience, however, was obviously exceptional, and most authors would probably have a hard time proving to the satisfaction of a court that a publisher had rejected their script in bad faith, unless, of course, they had, as I did for a brief while, an aggrieved editor on their side and ready to talk.

The recent phantom case of *Chris Patten v. HarperCollins and Rupert Murdoch* (1998) here prompts a quick digression. According to the news reports, when HarperMurdoch refused to publish Patten's Hong Kong memoir *East and West*, Patten sued for breach of contract, but as I pointed out in a letter published in *The Daily Telegraph* (2nd March), although it seemed clear that Patten had had a contract and that it had been breached, if he had gone to court with such a claim, he would have been unlikely to win any damages. Firstly he had sustained no financial loss, for his book had immediately found another publisher (Macmillan); and secondly he had suffered no loss of reputation or publicity, which if anything was greatly increased by the episode. I suggested that Patten's more profitable suit might instead lie in an action for defamation or defamation of goods (in which actual loss does not have to be proved) on the grounds that HarperCollins' publicly-stated reasons for rejecting his script ("does not match up to outline... failed reasonable expectations... boring..." so forth) had been revealed and admitted as bogus. This exposure of HarperCollins' *mala fides* in turn resulted from the unusual circumstance of a whistle-blowing and subsequently departing editor Stuart Proffitt, who himself sued HarperCollins for constructive dismissal. One so far unremarked side-effect of the affair was thus the confirmation of the suspicion, common amongst authors, that the reasons given by publishers for the rejection of their work, contracted or otherwise, are routinely phoney. It was later reported that in rapid out-of-court settlements Murdoch conceded Patten's £125,000 advance plus a bonus of £20,000, and that Proffitt too managed to negotiate a six-figure deal. Lucky for some, although it was nice to see a powerful publisher being *set up.*

7

The Spoiling

DOWN AT THE OPPOSITE end of the global power-heap, during my early searches for legal advice in 1986, I was introduced to an experienced High Court litigation solicitor who had worked as a London barrister but who was now in the process of setting up his own practice in Brighton. Richard White was himself an Oxford man and had at one time even worked for the printing division of OUP, so although he was not a publishing contract specialist, he knew the general territory and had one or two Oxford contacts. On studying the correspondence and the transcripts, he, like me, thought that in my original exchanges with Hardy up to July 1985, I had all the essentials of a contract, whose arguable bareness (most obviously the lack of a formal *Memorandum*) was probably evidentially counterbalanced, for example as to Hardy's intentions and solemnity, by OUP's likely internal documents, which Oxford would be obliged to produce. Further, the 'merits' of my case were greatly strengthened by all of the scandalous detail surrounding OUP's breach. White's quick grasp of this detail impressed me, his analysis was convincing and gave me odds, and so, with my heart in my mouth, and my chequebook in my hand, I went with him. One of his first pieces of prophetic advice was that I should re-read Dickens' *Bleak House*, or *Bleak Hut*, as it soon became known to us. I began transcribing the answerphone tapes.

It might be interesting to digress here on the general nature of the relationship between a solicitor and his client, and on our particular relationship as it developed over the next few years, but I guess this might generate yet more unmarketable stuff, so I will again desist. Suffice it to say that such a relationship has a logic all its own, something like that between a jockey and their horse in a steeplechase, with it sometimes being unclear who is the jockey and who the horse. I was not eligible for legal aid, to which in any case I am temperamentally averse, but I did have a small reserve of money left over from the sale of a Brighton maisonette which I had converted. White, after a free initial examination of the evidence gave a properly cautious assessment and left it to me to decide whether to go ahead. He described himself as "a heavy front-end loader" by which he meant that he needed a lot of work and cash in advance so as to be in complete command of all the evidence and case-law before considering any first moves. I am certain this is absolutely the correct policy, but of course it does mean that from the start the client has to be reconciled to losing money; the "is this good after bad?" question arises early. Who, on the other hand, would trust a cheap lawyer, or one who gave his opinion after only a glance at the file?

Another thing to remember is that very few people, I guess, who embark upon litigation remotely imagine that they will actually end up in court. I certainly did not. Although one never wants to make threats one does not intend to execute (early on Richard Charkin warned that Oxford would fight the case to the House of Lords), and one must beforehand carefully weigh all the possibilities in the awful event that it does go the distance, yet, certainly to start with, one expects the first solicitor's letter or two to do the trick. With this in mind, and aware that so far we had failed to penetrate the OUP hierarchy above Charkin's level, White composed a very careful (and, as it turned out, very prescient) 'letter before action' to George Richardson, who was then the Secretary to the Delegates, OUP's equivalent of Chief Executive. While threatening legal proceedings and carefully listing many of the classes of documents Oxford would be obliged to produce, thereby indicating just how much we knew about what had happened, White's letter still held out the hope that OUP's publication of *Making Names* presented everyone's best way forward and repeated my invitation to discuss any textual changes they might wish me to make. Yet again Oxford's reply, in September 1986, came from Charkin, and yet again it was flatly uncompromising. No reason was ever given for the book's rejection and no failure to meet any of Hardy's requirements was ever specified. Charkin concluded with the perfect non-sequitur:

> "We repeat that no contract exists. Even if it had done, it would of course have been subject, like all our contracts, to approval of the finished typescript."

This magnificent, glaring logical and legal blind-spot, and that March paragraph of mine on which no Oxford eyes could focus, were to obscure all clear reasoning from their perceptions for the next five years.

Richard White's other preliminary steps included writing to Hardy and Ryan in the hope of interviewing them, and inviting the latter to read a further-revised version of my Chapter Nine. Tellingly, the iconoclastic editor replied "my instructions are to decline to be interviewed", while the successful sociologist turned in a New College corker:

> "Although I understand that if matters proceed so far I may be required to appear as a witness, I cannot see my way to volunteering any information whatever about this business and I must therefore decline to be interviewed. I cannot think that your client believes that I

can give a dispassionate assessment of his revisions to chapter 9 under circumstances such as those he has now created; I therefore return it herewith. I am sorry to disoblige you."

Shortly afterwards, Ryan took up a post at Princeton, U.S.A. One year later, in September 1987, White had a telephone conversation with him in which he talked of having been "at cross-purposes with me", an odd observation that was to recur; in fact of course, I had never exchanged a single word with the man about the book, or about the revisions, or about anything. Odder still, at around the same time, a mutual acquaintance who knew the story asked Ryan why the book had been ditched; Ryan explained that he had always wanted to do it, but that "they [the ever-evanescent ones] had not allowed him to." We also contacted the Society of Authors for help and advice, but Mark Le Fanu, its secretary and himself a lawyer by training, was pessimistic about my chances and could offer no support to a non-member; I, of course, could not join the Society because, Catch-22, I had not had a book published. The Society of Authors aspect of the story reappears interestingly later.

At that time I had only a very vague idea of what legal argument would attend the question of whether I had a complete and enforceable contract. My main thought was: OUP cannot possibly fight this because when Hardy and his superiors are confronted by a recording of what he actually said on 20th May 1985 (as opposed to what he may have told them he said), his only viable personal line would be to re-run the defence I (correctly) guessed he had used at his own disciplinary hearing that July. I imagined a courtroom scene featuring Charkin and Hardy testifying against one another, with the latter being on my side in respect of both the contract and the book. Hardy had seemed totally sincere in his belief in *Making Names'* merits, and had even said that his commitment to it had been strengthened by Charkin's sabotage. I did not see how Oxford could conceivably defend any argument with its own two key witnesses in such open and well-documented mutual dispute. Some form of this view persisted with me for a long while, despite Hardy's instructed silence, through his long lack of help, and even after my receipt from him in January 1989 of a mendacious affidavit (a court-admissible statement sworn on oath). It was still just possible that he was reserving for some suitable dramatic moment an honourable and decisive intervention. Only with my receipt of his pathetic witness statement three years later did that assumption-turned-hope finally evaporate.

This puts me in mind of another strange aspect. No-one at Oxford seemed to have the slightest interest in what Hardy had actually said to me. It would have been obvious from their file of correspondence, had anyone bothered to skim it, that a crucial and probably contractual conversation had taken place on 20th May 1985, yet no-one ever asked to hear my recording of it. Surely this was the first thing any decent manager at the Press should have done at the outset, if only to get the facts straight? I had declared the tapes in July 1986 and would willingly have sent copies to anyone. When the lawsuit began, they were formally transcribed and listed by February 1987. But still no-one at Oxford asked for their key evidence. It was a further two-and-a-half years before they requested a transcript of the conversation and over three years before they asked for a copy-tape. How can solicitors and Counsel possibly assess or begin to defend an action before hearing the opposition's primary material? The only conclusion can be that as far as Oxford and its lawyers were concerned, it did not matter what Hardy had said to me in that or in any other conversation, they did not care. They were absolutely confident of winning the case, whatever the facts, presumably because they had limitless money, had countless tricks up their sleeves, and simply, well, *were Oxford.* Three years and tens of thousands of pounds went by before they deigned, or dared, to listen to a few minutes' worth of contractual exchange.

By the Autumn of 1986 it was time to work out how to plead the case and draft the writ. The way a case is pleaded is all-important, and although one wants to leave oneself room for manoeuvre, complete changes of tack made once proceedings are underway are bound to look to a court like weaknesses or failures (Oxford made several such tacks). Our problem was this: my negotiation with OUP from August 1984 arrived, on 20th May 1985, at a complete contract which was then confirmed by our correspondence of May and June. By the time I seriously began the revision, in August, Hardy had told me the whole scandalous inside-story of his disciplining but had expressly back-tracked on his original clear commitment. Obviously, I wanted to expose the full *mala fides* of Charkin's rejection, but this would mean relying on *all* of my communications up to the end of July, which included Hardy's re-writing of history and about-turn caveats. Although in neither fact nor writing had I done so, it might be argued that in going ahead with the book's revision I had *prima facie* accepted OUP's rescission of the contract. I needed to introduce the scandal, but withhold the tapes in which it was revealed.

The solution was to plead that OUP breached the contract twice, first by Charkin's letter of 18th July 1985, sent before I had started the revision, and second in May 1986 by their rejection of the revised text. The law grants a litigant privilege (that is, privacy, the right of non-disclosure) in all documents (and tapes) drawn up with a view to taking legal proceedings, so by pleading that OUP's first breach was Charkin's first letter, I could truthfully argue that from that moment I was contemplating legal action. Strangely, this argument was never put to the test by Oxford's lawyers, at least not until much much later when I started to rely upon parts of the privileged conversations which were relevant to the question of damages. So far, so good; but how could I now introduce all the very damning evidence about the Charkin-Hardy power-struggle? The solution, we decided, was to name Richard Charkin as a second, individual defendant, and to state a claim against him under a tort of 'wrongful interference in or procurement of a breach of contract'. This putative secondary action justified us in setting out the whole grisly story in the writ, whilst preserving privilege for the post-July tapes.

What was at stake? The remedy sought at the end of my claim was 'specific performance', that is a court order that OUP publish *Making Names* and additionally or alternatively, pay damages and interest. But what, I can hear it being asked, is the point of having a book published by a reluctant or even hostile publisher? Couldn't they just print a few dozen copies and throw them off Barnes Bridge, or leave them in their warehouse unpromoted? Wouldn't this be locking all one's authorial rights in jail? What I originally envisaged was Oxford being ordered to fulfill the print run of hardbacks planned by Hardy, the details of which I knew he had entered on the internal costings sheet, and then either Hardy being put back in charge of the project (in which case he would have a personal motive to vindicate his judgment and turn it into his "terrific success"), or the books then being handed over to me. I assumed that if I won the case and the latter were ordered, firstly these OUP editions would become valuable and secondly I could then get *Making Names* properly published elsewhere.

One nightmare scenario did cross my mind. Suppose I were successful in demonstrating a contract; could not Oxford, already famous for its 'changes of mind', then turn around (perhaps under a new M.D. with different alleged 'values' or with a high opinion of *Making Names*) and say "well, we therefore have the sole rights, as envisaged in May 1985, in this now-celebrated work." After the author had been forced into litigation by the publisher's intransigence, the publisher might lose the lawsuit and yet end up in a good position to make huge profits from their defeat. Such fears were quickly allayed by the assumption that any court would surely rule that by its original breach and repudiation of the contract, Oxford had irrevocably renounced its rights in the book. Nevertheless, one could imagine some crafty legal manoeuvres here.

As to the damages, in itself another complex area of law, the writ left the quantum unparticularised and unspecified, seeking simply "additionally or alternatively [to specific performance] damages for breach of contract". For a long while we made it clear in correspondence that OUP's printing of Hardy's originally planned 2,000 copies, at their own estimated cost of £5,000, would have sufficed to get me off their backs. Oxford did not request quantification of the damages I was seeking until October 1989.

One question which any litigant and their lawyers must decide before issuing a writ is in which jurisdiction they wish to fight their action. Normally for a civil claim of breach of contract such as mine, the choice is between one's local, County Court and the High Court (Queen's Bench or Chancery Divisions) in London. The County Court has obvious logistical advantages, and can prove a cheaper arena in a number of ways (small claims are automatically heard at County level), but its judiciary and administration are likely to be less senior and efficient than those of the High Court, and claims filed locally inevitably acquire a certain perceived triviality. Our peculiar circumstances also afforded us a third alternative, an ancient, obscure Oxford court actually presided over by the University's Vice-Chancellor, but the daredevil attractions of this option were out-weighed by the procedural chaos we would probably have encountered in a court that had not sat for fifty years or so, and used to do so mainly on matters like the gating of high-spirited undergraduates. We decided to plump for the gravity of the Chancery Division.

The writ was issued and served on Oxford (but not yet on Richard Charkin) on 23rd December 1986, not so much to spoil any Oxford Christmases as to ensure my full enjoyment of my own. Having had it issued in London on the last working day, I travelled to Oxford personally to serve it on their solicitors, a local firm amusingly named Dallas Brett, who had been warned of its delivery and were staying open specially. By the time I reached the front door it was evening, but the lights were still on and I could see movement through the net-curtained windows. I took a deep breath of the cold night air, and was just about to insert the fateful document into the large brass letterbox, when suddenly from within there came a tramping down the hall, the lights went out, and a tall, slightly hunted-looking man opened the door and walked briskly off down the road. I went into instant passer-by mode, with the writ back under my overcoat, and assumed the man to have been their senior partner Hugh Brett, waiting in to read it. I guessed he would now have to wait until after his Xmas break.

Here I should perhaps correct a mistake of potentially important detail in Hugh Jones' account of the case, which is headed *Malcolm v. OUP*. In fact, because OUP is wholly owned by Oxford University, the word 'Press' was struck by the Court from the original writ, where it had been bracketed "trading as..." literally on Day One of the proceedings. It never formally reappeared, and as I have mentioned, the case's full and proper title reads: *Malcolm versus The Chancellor, Masters and Scholars of the University of Oxford*, or, for short *Malcolm vs. Oxford University*, and even shorter *Malcolm v. Oxford*. This is no mere pedantry, for the case's true title, that is the accurate identification of its defendants, will eventually become an important feature of the action's settlement.

I will not tire the reader, as Oxford tried to tire me, with the technical detail of its solicitors' opening responses to the writ, all of which consisted of routine spoiling tactics: applying to have the claim struck out as being "frivolous and vexatious", lodging complaints about the form and wording of the writ, an allegation that it was "an abuse of the process of the court" and so on. However, one scene from those early, frivolous days does stick in my memory and is perhaps worth recounting. Every case in the Chancery Division is allotted a Master to adjudicate in the preliminary, interlocutory hearings, and we were entrusted to a Master Barratt, himself an Oxonian, but an unfailingly pleasant and courteous man. It was not until some way into the action that I realised that he was a very brave man too: he had lost the use of his legs and got around the court buildings entirely on crutches. Later, for the more important hearings, and for the trial and the appeal, it was stipulated that special non-Oxford courts had to be convened, for strictly interpreted, I was suing almost half the High Court judiciary (Oxford graduates count amongst its 'scholars'), but in the early proceedings, and in the final assessment of damages, nearly all of the adjudications were made by Barratt.

In one of these early hearings, Oxford's solicitor and barrister, in their different ways both rather oily gentlemen, were arguing against Richard White that the statement of claim on our writ was over-detailed. As required by the Supreme Court rules, we had quoted the key 'commitment' passage from my 20th May conversation with Hardy verbatim, and I had been absolutely scrupulous in my transcription of the recordings, including every hesitation and interruption, every 'um' and 'er', many of which seemed to carry Freudian or other telltale significance. (I was gratified to note that, even in Hugh Jones' abbreviated account, he saw fit to quote Hardy's wonderful use of 'er' before the word 'contract', though with the benefit of the tape I have added its commas.) As a consequence, the quoted exchange, though still only a third of a page, contained some exclamations and interjections which occasioned much pompous scoffing and chortling from the opposition. Master Barratt ordered us to replace this verbatim paragraph with a summary and to retranscribe the conversation omitting all of its irrelevances and hesitations, with the costs of the operation being awarded to the grinning oilymen. (It subsequently appeared that Barratt's ruling here was wrong; the judges all requoted our deleted passages, even including their 'ers' and 'ums'.) Years later at the appeal, when Oxford's umpteenth bogus defence had at last collapsed, the ultimate straw at which they clutched was to seek the reimportation into the cleaned-up transcript of various different versions of a sliver of a remark that I had haltingly started but then swallowed when I had realised, even in those heady, pre-legalistic days, that a complete bargain had already been struck. How gratifying it was to watch the oilymen floundering as the court out of hand dismissed it from their final, feeble, greasy grasp.

To be fair, Oxford's oilyman barrister, Mark Warby, was proper, civil and correct with me throughout our steadily-increasing contact, and especially when I later began acting in person. He was a youngish, elegant, rather good-looking man with a quietly impressive, understated delivery. His only weakness, I think, was that his perpetual tan looked rather phoney, perhaps more the result of lying under UV lamps than of frequent holidaying in Barbados. To start with, of course, he went through the ritual of gently, patronisingly pooh-poohing my chances of success, but as the action gradually looked more and more serious, and, I think, he became more and more frustrated with his own clients' repeated changes of tack and story, perverse discovery and inept, mendacious witnesses, his demeanour towards me became steadily more respectful and polite. By the run-up to the appeal, he clearly realised he was on a loser, and more than once, when some crazy new Oxford move or unlikely Oxford statement yet again pulled the carpet from under his current line of argument, his eyes would flicker to the heavens and he would shrug resignedly not to his own solicitors, nor even to the judge, but to me.

8

Diversions

WHILE THE LAWYERS were engaged in their preliminary nose-thumbings, I began researching into OUP. There has been printing at Oxford since the fifteenth century, but it was not until the 1630s that it was brought fully under the University's control by Archbishop Laud, who obtained a Royal license to print 'all manner of books', including Bibles. Oxford's rare royal license to print Bibles was, effectively, a license to print money, and provoked an expensive legal battle against the Stationers' Company in London. In 1678 a compromise was reached, and Oxford began flogging the holy book, quickly building up a large business and amassing huge sums with which to fund what became known as 'the Learned Press', which by 1850 was churning out a million Bibles a year. OUP has therefore always been something of a hybrid organisation, a heavily commercial operation on the one hand (with dictionary and ELT publishing today roughly filling the former role of Bible-printing), and an academic vanity-press for the University dons on the other.

It is generally assumed (and was in 1986 by me) that OUP enjoys the privilege of charitable status, and thereby exemption from taxes and rates, by virtue of its ownership by the University, whose colleges are automatically unregistered educational charities. However, recent research (see page 251) reveals that this is in fact not so, and that OUP's true tax situation is rather more precarious. Unlike ordinary charities, the university presses, of which OUP is the giant, are also exempted from registration or provision of a formal 'governing document' which could lay open their policies and practices to public challenge. (An interesting exception here is Yale UP UK, which, being American-owned, has to register and cites as its charitable purpose "to foster promote maintain and advance the education of the public.") OUP's tax breaks are, naturally enough, widely resented by its marketplace competitors, especially when they see it regularly reporting huge so-called 'surpluses' (charities are not allowed to make 'profits'); the figure for 1994 was £27 million. On the other hand, OUP also enjoys an uneasy relationship with the University: in 1996, for example, it donated only £4 million of its £21 million 'surplus'. This unease surfaced in 1987, when a proposal to sell a 49 percent stake in the Press was floated in *The Times* by a group of dons who felt that it was not contributing enough to the University's finances, which were then in serious deficit (Robert

Maxwell was their mooted buyer). In 1989 it was reported that Margaret Thatcher too wanted to sell off the Press, for £44 million, as part of her government's privatisation programme.

Another curious fact I learned in 1987 was that the would-be charitable Press had registered as no fewer than *thirty-five* different limited companies at Companies' House, most of which were non-trading 'dummies'. It seems that around 1984 some rival entrepreneurs had set up a publishing business in the city also using the O-word, and OUP had bought them out, along with any other similarly tempting names, in order to protect the exclusivity of their own. An odd, legally vacuous rigmarole recently to appear on the frontispieces OUP books goes: "Oxford is a trade mark of Oxford University Press". 'Cattle crossing', I suppose, just doesn't have the same ring to it.

I also researched other OUP contract misdemeanours in the hope of enlisting allies or assistance, and unearthed several interesting precedents. In 1981 maverick lawyer and historian Anthony Mockler had a book on Haile Selassie's war in Ethiopia accepted by OUP provided he cut its length by forty percent; he spent a year doing so, only to find it then rejected for 'financial reasons'. Mockler, who had journalist friends, conducted a publicity campaign against the Press, which eventually relented and honoured his contract. I copied Mockler's opening move and advertised for help in *The Spectator*. Another author, Peter Hill, had a similar story and got his revenge by lampooning "the old women of Walton Street" in a thriller based on the deportation of Alexander Solzhenitsyn called *The Cuban Connection*: his description of OUP's rejection of Horace Muir's contracted *Illustrated History of English Literature* after he had spent nine months working on it sounded like an exact rehearsal of the *Making Names* affair. Then there was the delightful story of the bribes paid in 1985 by the Russian embassy to get Oxford to rewrite various ELT dictionary entries in its Russian editions: for a few dollars cash, *Socialism*, for example, had become "the first phase of communism, a social system based on public ownership of the means of production which is now replacing capitalism." This 'definitions for hire' sideline of the DIM-squad Gulag was later to feature in my own Siberian case.

Further entertaining relief was provided by an OUP party held in January 1987 at Dillons' newly-refurbished bookstore in Gower Street. I had been in touch with an OUP author who had been invited but did not fancy all the Oxoniana; as many of the players in my drama were going to be in action, we thought it might be rather amusing if I went disguised as him and mingled, if only to get some close sightings of the enemy. With obligatory corduroy jacket, gold-rimmed jam-jars, crazy hair and lapel nametag, I blended in nicely and lunged blindly with the best of them for the Sauternes and canapés. Hardy, Bion and Denniston were all circulating hard, and the latter made a heartwarming speech, but Charkin, unfortunately, was absent. An instamatic snap of la Bion being furtive with another corduroy and a sliced orange still graces my pleadings file.

Although my recording of Hardy's phonecalls was not in any way obsessive, my prosecution of the lawsuit, I freely admit, soon became so. Any individual who has pursued litigation with right on their side will know just how addictive the quest for justice can become. The urge to be heard, to be vindicated, to expose the bogus reasonings and outwit the cynical ploys, *to prevent them from getting away with it* quickly becomes all-consuming. And of course in no time at all the addiction has become an investment too, a grand financial gamble, a game of poker, a dare of see or raise in which the lawyers are the only steady winners. One's morale, one's career, one's solvency, and one's very faith in life and other people, all come to depend upon a successful outcome of the action. In short, one becomes obsessed. Oxford, too, became obsessed, but in that frustrating way of large organisations for whom money does not matter, nor what is said, nor when, nor by whom, so long as responsibility is periodically shuffled from these shoulders to those, the papers passed forever unread from this desk to that. Lord Justice Mustill later observed "Nor does the course of the litigation give any reason to suppose that the Press had any interest but to resist the claim, no matter on what grounds, so long as they succeeded." As Oxford's statements lurched from one unlikely avowal to another, my first suggested translation of their cod-Latin motto became "Oh God, what do we say now?"

The law soon became a fascination for me too. Academically, it bears strong resemblances to analytical philosophy: it often involves the minute explorations of words' meanings, and their different meanings in different contexts; its logic of commitments, conditions and undertakings is as clear as syllogism; its ceiling-high corridors of precedents that form the law libraries present an endless balancing of one moral principle off against another, centuries of argument establishing a hierarchy of rights, prohibitions and obligations. Even in its arcane, at times apparently absurd rules of procedure, every provision has a reason, every obstacle a purpose. It is, I suppose, as near as one can get to moral philosophy in action, ethical debate whose conclusions *cost money*. There's the rub, of course, for the expense of enforcing the law can soon overshadow the remedy being sought, distorting all judgments on all sides and turning a noble cause into a ruinous folly. Thus it is that, at the hands of professional lawmen and determined litigants, a five-thousand pound dispute can easily end up costing half a million. Litigating is not a career for those of an ulcerous constitution.

Back with my early experiences amongst the hired quill-pushers, Oxford's spoiling tactics could not continue for ever, and at length the University was obliged to recognise that it actually had an action to defend. In reply to my detailed and perfectly accurate statement of claim, OUP's formal defence pleading had been woefully thin, consisting, as Lord Justice Mustill put it, of "a bare traverse", that is, of a simple denial that OUP had made any commitment or entered into any contract, without any explanation as to why this might be so. In the manner of Charkin's non-sequitur of September 1986 (see page 48), its central paragraphs 4 and 5 went:

> "In the premises it is denied that any agreement was concluded as alleged [on 20th May 1985] or at all, and it is denied that the letters [from Hardy] of 21st May and 14th June confirm or evidence any such agreement. Alternatively if, which is denied, any agreement for publication was concluded then it was an agreement whereby the Defendants agreed to publish the work subject to their approval of the final revised version, which the Plaintiff was to produce."

Again, the hypnotic blind spot; was no-one at Oxford, not even their counsel, not even now, capable of reading my pivotal paragraph of March 1985? There was another surprise. My statement had carefully pleaded all of Hardy's revision requirements, itemised as (a) to (k), claimed that I had fulfilled every one, and asserted in particular that I had achieved a twenty-six (as opposed to his required twenty) percent cut in the book's length. I had assumed that Oxford's lawyers would be keen to challenge these claims and would try to rest their defence upon their detailed, and potentially very lucrative dissection, but in the event they were never questioned. I think the OUnuchs felt it beneath them to (re)open the script, and that to have done so would have been to shift the fight to 'my ground'. This lack of detail in their defence also suggested to us (that is, to Richard White and myself) that, as we had hoped, Hardy was at least declining to cooperate with whoever was conducting the Press's case. So *encouraged*, we decided in February 1987 to serve the writ on Richard Charkin. With Oxford's pleading so weak and Hardy onside, this could all be over by Spring.

Charkin, who had originally specialised in medical textbooks at Pergamon Press, had learned his publishing skills, I was warned darkly, under the tutelage of Robert Maxwell. He had recently been hired by OUP as one of their new generation of aggressive young managers, and had already had a public legal spat with Margaret Drabble and her agent over some illicit repackagings of her *Oxford Companion to English Literature*. I heard from many sources that Charkin had rapidly acquired numerous enemies at the Press, and when a mutual friend told an OUP employee he knew that I was planning to sue the man personally, she excitedly volunteered to help, described him in highly colourful terms, asked to be put in touch with me, and offered to provide copies of any Oxford documents that I might need. By this stage, voices both in and outside my head were suggesting that Hardy's use of the telephone had been a deliberate policy of OUP editors, and was perhaps even stipulated in a confidential memo, a copy of which would quickly settle the case. Unfortunately, it appears that my would-be mole's careless tongue then earned her a dressing-down from Charkin, a flurry of costly lawyers' letters ensued, her offer of help was withdrawn, and the incriminating memo remained a myth. Her father, it emerged, was an Oxford don with books in print at the Press. This incident served also as an early demonstration of how easily litigation can poison personal relationships: as in war and espionage, the world quickly divides into allies and enemies, with every source of help also affording an instant route of betrayal. An iron curtain comes down too on even the simplest of information: at one stage I was warned by the University Offices that the statutes relating to the Press were confidential. Fortunately, Brighton's excellent reference library was at once able to provide them.

In April 1987 Oxford made a 'without prejudice' offer to settle of £1,000. ('Without prejudice' correspondence has to be kept strictly separate from the normal 'party-party' procedural stuff and generally goes unseen by the adjudicators.) Since I had already spent over five times this figure on the litigation and Oxford's lamentable defence had made us bullish about a result, this seemed more like an insult than a realistic tempt and was duly rejected. Instead, assuming Hardy's non-cooperation with his bosses, we decided to beef up the claim against Charkin and to plead this aspect of the story more carefully and in more detail. The secondary suit was starting to look like a runner, so we deliberately raised the stakes and ran it.

At this point there occurred an incident which, though quite unrelated to the lawsuit, I feel I should recount, for it may subconsciously have fuelled any tendency in me to paranoia and thereby have strengthened my general resolve. On the evening of 30th May, while I was away in London, my Brighton flat was broken into. The intruder(s) had been very persistent, smashing three windows before successfully forcing an entry, and cutting themselves badly in the process; a good deal of blood was sprayed around the walls, floors and furniture. Oddly, nothing was stolen, despite numerous obvious and portable temptations: an unlocked cash-tin containing about

£200 still sat openly on the kitchen table (the takings from a local jazz club which I was running at the time); cameras, mini hi-fi and a gold watch lay untouched in an opened drawer. Even a prominent bottle of gin remained undisturbed. Instead, some of my bank and building society records had been removed from my filing cabinet and lay scattered around the floor. The police took statements (a neighbour had seen someone lurking suspiciously), preserved some blood samples and fingerprints, and found a fine shoeprint on the wallpaper (the intruder had evidently had to clamber back out through the jagged hole left in the part-glazed front-door), but as nothing had been stolen the police did not investigate further. With hindsight, I suppose it is possible that from a psychological point of view, the coincidental timing of this break-in may have affected some of my ensuing decisions, but at the time I paid it no mind.

9

Discoveries

IN AUGUST 1987, Oxford repeated, but did not increase, its settlement offer, but by now its lawyers were well behind schedule with their obligatory discovery of the Press's internal documents, which we obviously needed to see before considering any next move. My documents and tapes had been listed in February 1987 and remained unrequested; Oxford's were not listed until over a year later, and were then declared piecemeal. Even their very listing was inadequate: one is supposed to note all the documents' senders, addressees, dates of posting, whether they were originals, carbon copies, photocopies and so on, with different lists for the papers once but no longer in one's possession, still in one's possession, and those known to have been lost or destroyed. Oxford's first list was demonstrably incomplete and made no distinction between originals and copies, so their solicitors were obliged to make a second, more detailed inventory and have its completeness and accuracy verified on affidavit by "some responsible officer of the Press". The responsible officer they chose turned out to be one Ivon Asquith, an editorial director (humanities) who himself had had nothing whatever to do with *Making Names*.

When Oxford's first batch of documents did at last arrive, it included much important ammunition we had expected (of whose existence we had evidence) but also several surprises and absences. Alan Ryan's report of 11th February 1985, which as Hardy wrote, "had got the ball rolling", can now be quoted in full:

> "I've now read Andrew Malcolm and have surprised myself by changing my mind [that phrase again] about it. I think it's rather good. It's variable, and it looks to me as if it is vastly too long as it stands, but I'm rather keen that we should have a go if it's possible. It would, I think, be a plausible general book, and it might do well as a sort of introduction to philosophy for people doing 'A' Level philosophy under the new dispensation and people doing Open University courses.
> It's philosophically rather good, I think — it makes one of the shrewdest cases for a sort of Collingwoodian Idealism that I've read — not that it reads like Collingwood or cites him as an authority, but that its emphasis on the way <u>we</u> constrain the world by deciding what sort of general laws it's to follow, and what sort of explanations it's got to conform to is rather Collingwoodian. I like the dialogue style; it clanks

occasionally, but generally it is rather fun, and the two protagonists are distinct personalities — to say the least.

If I have anxieties, they are about the longish slabs of straight science, eg at the end of chapter 1, and about the interpolation of the play about Electra in the last Act; they serve a purpose all right, but I think that some readers may feel they go on too long before the author reveals their purpose. Perhaps the right thing now would be for you [Hardy] to try it and see whether you'd feel like putting in the effort, then ask Malcolm if he would be willing to think how he could cut it down to a size which would give it a sporting chance at the price we'd need to charge for it."

On 18th July, *after* Charkin's intervention, Ryan had sent Hardy a second, even keener report:

"I've had a word with Richard Charkin and things don't seem too bad at all. As you know, I should have been pretty irritated if I had thought he was second-guessing my view of the intellectual merits of the book, but he was emphatic that he wasn't doing that, and said that he thought there was every chance of its being perfectly publishable when it came back. He said that he was going to write to Malcolm in those terms himself. [Readers might like to compare Charkin's actual letter to me, of the same date, at page 34.]

As you know, my feeling about the book is that it is well worth doing, both because it is interesting in itself, and because it's a bold attempt to do philosophy in an unusual literary format — most dialogues fall terribly flat, but his seems to me to stand up very well for long stretches, and to need only a small amount of tinkering to be wholly readable throughout. I do think it belongs among general books rather than academic philosophy partly because it ought to appeal to people with a general interest in science on the one hand and literature on the other, and partly because its dialogue form would get in the way of an academic reviewer's appreciation of it, but would very likely count in its favour with an Encounter-ish sort of reviewer.

Of course it might do badly, but every so often books like Colin Wilson's *The Outsider* or Hofstadter's *Gödel, Escher, Bach* (which I don't like at all, to tell you the truth) do exceedingly well, so a bit of boldness is in order. So, I hope Richard Charkin is as cheerful as he sounded on the phone, and that we can gallop ahead as he suggested we could. It would be nice to take a chance and win, and the so-called 'downside risk' isn't too drastic if we don't."

Here was not only an extra rave about *Making Names* (at that time, remember, still in its first draft), but also evidence that Oxford was thinking of it as a possible bestseller. Furthermore it clearly documented Charkin's deliberate deception and *mala fides*.

Next there came the costings document ('Academic and General Division Publishing Proposal Form' or PPF for short), two pages dated 18th June 1985 which carried, as I had inferred, all the detail needed for a specific performance order: net royalties of twelve percent (UK) and ten percent (US & export); an initial printing of 2,000 hardback copies; expected sales in the first year of 2,000; a chosen format option of 400 pages at 216 x 138 mm case-bound; two-colour jacket; UK price £15; a net line value of £9.15; an average discount of 39 percent; a gross profit of £5.033 per copy, or 55 percent; cash-flow projections over the first 12 months; 'green' for good profitability and payback; and first costs of £2,515 plus manufacturing costs of £3,616, making an initial production total of £6,131. The commissioning editor was entered as Angus Phillips, pp. Henry Hardy (who was away on holiday). A managing editor was appointed (Will Sulkin), a marketing manager (Martin Cowell), and production and publications officers (initialled CEA and LAB). How much more *specific* would a court wish to be?

Then (oh joy!) came Charkin-n-Hardy's formal disciplinary charge and defence documents (yes, after a while they did begin to appear in one's imagination as a comedy double-act). Sure enough, both men confirmed that Hardy had committed the Press to the publication of *Making Names*. On 18th July, Charkin had written:

Dear Henry
Further to our discussion of 17 July 1985, I am writing formally to confirm the gravity of the situation whereby you gave a written indication to an author that OUP would publish his book without having gone through our editorial procedures. In failing to observe these procedures, particularly with a book in philosophy and which has been rejected by Penguin, you have shown distinct lack of editorial and commercial judgement. You have committed the Press to an investment of £10,000 for which I am responsible [incidentally, an instant doubling of Hardy's figure]. You have overstepped your authority and you have wasted my, your, and others' time.

In the light of all this, I have no alternative but to give you this final written warning under Stage 3 of the disciplinary procedure. In the event of any repetition or similar occurrence this will lead to most serious consequences.

You have the right to appeal within three working days and this should be in writing and copied to Personnel (Clive Moody).
Yours sincerely,
Richard Charkin
(copies to George Richardson, Ivon Asquith, Clive Moody)

Hardy had replied by return with this long, sad, painstaking defence:

Dear Richard,

In reply to your letter of 18 July. It is true that I indicated to an author, before a PPF had been signed, that, subject to satisfactory revision, OUP would publish his book. I acknowledge that this was not in accordance with our official procedures. But since exactly this breach of procedure is in practice a frequent occurrence, at least in the General Books Department, for which I was working at the time, you will I think agree that the central issue is my judgment of the book.

The typescript had been read by a Delegate, Alan Ryan, who thought well of it, with reservations. I read it too, and agreed with him. Both he and I had been too hard-pressed to read the long typescript quickly, so that the author was understandably becoming anxious for a decision; and I did not want to keep him in suspense for longer than necessary. The typescript had to be cast off before a PPF could be completed and submitted (so that I had an accurate basis on which to ask for cuts), and I was advised that this process would take a matter of weeks. I did not anticipate any problems at PPF stage.

In these circumstances I decided, with the agreement of Alan Ryan and Will Sulkin (my then head of Department), both of whom I kept fully informed at all stages, to tell the author we wanted to publish his book, so long as he revised it satisfactorily – and I made a point of stressing that this would be an essential condition of publication. The reason I spoke in terms of a contract, rather than simply a willingness to consider a revised typescript, was that the author estimated that the revisions we sought would take six months' solid work, and did not feel able to undertake this work without a provisional commitment on our part. This is understandable, especially since he had already radically rewritten the book once on the basis of informal encouragement from an editor at Penguin, only to have it turned down by a different editor.

The production investment is £5,000. Though of course there would be additional overheads, I do not understand how you arrive at your total of £10,000. I told the author there would be no advance and only modest royalties.

I dispute your assertion that I have shown marked lack of editorial and commercial judgment. It is possible that I am wrong about the book – we all make mistakes. But this is not a case of offering a contract out of the blue for a book that happened to take my unconsidered fancy. It had the support of a Delegate; I had read it all through myself, and as a trained philosopher I am not unqualified to form an opinion of it; it has subsequently been reported on in generally positive terms by another philosopher, Galen Strawson (though he too has reservations similar to Alan Ryan's and mine). The fact that the book has been rejected by Penguin is of very marginal relevance, if any: lists differ.

I have worked for the Press for eight years now – most recently as joint acting head of Department for eighteen months – without reprimand. It is even possible that I have made some positive contribution to OUP's activities – though this is for others to say. Anyone who knows me will confirm that I am a responsible and reasonable person. Neither my temperament, nor my record, nor the gravity of my alleged misjudgment merit such high-handed treatment. It would have been quite sufficient for you to tell me informally that you wished me to observe the procedure more scrupulously in future; I would of course have accepted this, and acted accordingly. Your reaction is quite out of proportion, and I am genuinely at a loss to understand why you consider it appropriate.

Yours, Henry

I too am genuinely at a loss, a loss to understand why on earth Oxford continued defending the action with these two wonderful items now openly in the arena; obviously they provided a lawyers' field-day (keen students may wish to practise their highlighting techniques). Here were at once removed any doubts as to the certainty and gravity of Hardy's contract. (It is entertaining to compare his above letter with the transcript of our phone conversation of the previous day.) Here was recorded fairly accurately and with utmost seriousness the importance Hardy knew he had attached to his "decision". Here was documentary evidence of Hardy's good, reliable memory, and even of his undertaking to me on royalties. Here it was demonstrated that both men *knew* that OUP was committed to my book's publication; as I had anticipated, it was the one thing upon which they were agreed. Indeed, Hardy's commitment to me was regarded as having been so solemn that it warranted his virtual sacking. Charkin's charge-sheet concluded with an uncharacteristic understatement:

> "You have raised the hopes of an author who may well cause us embarrassment and adverse publicity, and who will be very upset by the letter I shall have to write him."

Finally there was a document about *Making Names* described in Oxford's list as a "Delegates' Note". This paper was dated 16th July 1985 (the day *before* the book had come to Charkin's fateful attention), was headed "TO ALL DELEGATES" and "General Books", and included a selection of Ryan's and Strawson's most glowing comments. An apparently rubber-stamped panel at the sheet's top right-hand corner was divided into five sub-boxes in which had been typed the following entries: TOTAL INVESTMENT FOR FIRST EDITION £5000, LIKELY YEAR OF PUBLICATION 1986, RED/AMBER/GREEN (profitability), with red and amber crossed out, leaving green for good, EXTRA INHOUSE TIME left blank, presumably meaning no editing required, and FLEXCAT. General Philosophy. At the bottom left of the sheet, *Making Names'* estimated length was entered as 400 pages, proposed printing number as 2,000, and proposed price as £15.00. This Delegates' Note was credited to Nicola Bion but had been dictated, it was later revealed, by

Hardy. Ivon Asquith's affidavit confirmed that copies of this Note had been circulated to all the Delegates on 16th July. Hardy's 'blurb' for them went as follows:

> "*Making Names* is an introductory philosophy book, but one which also has substantive theses to air. Cast in the form of a day-long dialogue between a philosopher and a scientist, it is written in plain language and aimed at the general reader. Traditional problems are introduced, including those of mind and body, cause and effect, free will, universals, and the nature of moral goodness. Special emphasis is given to a radical critique by the philosopher of the belief that science supports a metaphysical materialism. The philosopher offers an alternative metaphysics in the form of an allegorical playscript, which the disputants read through together at the end of the book."

The discovery of this Delegates' Note came as quite a surprise. I had understood from Hardy that the book would have been "reported to" the Delegates, and that Ryan's high opinion of it "had got it over the hurdle" of their approval, but I had not expected to be given definitive, documented proof that such a process had occurred. We knew that, according to the University statutes, the Delegates met fortnightly during term-time on Tuesdays, with other meetings scheduled as necessary, and a major one in the summer vacation. 16th July 1985 was a Tuesday in the summer vacation, so it looked as though this was an agenda paper for a meeting on that day at which my book had formally been presented. If so, where were the minutes recording the Delegates' response? If it turned out that way back in July 1985 the Delegates had raised no objection to the book, or had even formally approved its first draft, then Oxford's whole defence, along with Charkin's, at a stroke collapsed, based as it was on the assertion that the book had been rejected. It was common ground that there was no higher authority at the Press than that of the Delegates. Case solved.

Oxford had taken almost two-and-a-half years to cough up these few, incomplete documents. What was supposed to have been a routine preliminary process, a laying of cards on the table, so as to enable both sides to assess each other's 'hands' before risking more serious money, had already cost several thousands of pounds. Many lawsuits, and defences of them, naturally collapse at this discovery stage. Unless a great deal still hangs on the testimony of witnesses or there remains some fine and moot point of law, cases are usually then either settled or abandoned, for although both sides' lawyers have livings to make, they do also share the same lawbooks and precedents according to which, from hereon, the case is likely to be decided. Nothing, however, about *Malcolm v. Oxford* was going normally, and the University showed no sign of yielding, even with this arguably fatal and certainly very damaging evidence now face-up before us. As it turned out, another two years of expensive proceedings would have to elapse before I was to hear it whispered by excited clerks on the eve of a seven-witness, five-day trial, "it's going to be decided on the paper, it's going to be decided on the paper!" In the even more bizarre event, the 1990 Court of Appeal was to find a complete contract solely in this common preliminary material, which Oxford's lawyers had held since February 1987 and its staff since July 1985. My natural elation at the receipt of these apparent clinchers thus became dulled by the gradual, sickening realisation that Oxford nevertheless intended to fight on, that the battle was inexorably descending beyond the province of reason, or even of financial self-interest, into a kind of *madness*, and that this, of course, was precisely what all the lawyers had been hoping. Someone at Oxford, perhaps someone with whom I had never exchanged a word, let alone a greeting, must now be taking this thing very very personally.

The struggling artist or author who, in favour of some perceived cause or calling, rejects the conventional world of secure, salaried careers, yet remains resentful of their consequent deprivations, is, of course, a familiar cliché. Less well known, I have heard it said, is the special, complementary sort of jealousy that their office-drudge-bound counterparts can sometimes feel of those who aspire, even misguidedly, to creativity or to some mission. I began to sense this now. The OUnuchs' further pursuit of the fight was beginning to demonstrate a terrible and unexpected truth: that beneath all their obligatory Oxford polish and politeness, there runs a streak in these people that really *hates* authors. Years later when Richard Charkin protested his sincerest concern for authors' welfare, the fact that he did so unprompted, mockingly, on expenses, and from across an acrid courtroom would vividly confirm the bleak diagnosis.

Although Oxford's first dose of discovery completed some key areas of the jigsaw, it also left some gaping holes and created some new uncertainties; a number of documents were obviously still missing. One surprising absence was of any reader's report in 1986 on the revised draft of *Making Names*. On the telephone Bion had spoken of two or three readers, and in her rejection letter had written "I've now had the reports on your revised type-script and discussed them with colleagues", so I had anticipated that on discovery I would find two or three new reports, presumably negative. Instead, there was nothing, nothing at all analysing the book or comparing it with the earlier draft, nothing at all to suggest that anyone had checked whether or not I had fulfilled any of Hardy's requirements. The only clue was an elegant, ten-line, hand-scrawled slip from Alan Ryan, dated 3rd May, advising Bion how to draft her rejection:

Nicola, I think something v. near the truth is the way. Can you say we've read it, like it as before, but (i) think it's still a good deal too long to risk as a trade book – and n.b. that the idea of a trade philosophy book gives nightmares to salesmen, marketing managers etc, (ii) that there are quite a lot of places where it would need to be made brisker and livelier and this would, sadly, take more editorial time than the Press can afford. (iii) We don't really know what to suggest he should do – he requires a small publisher and a keen editor and we haven't one to hand. We needn't say that on second reading the yobbish and sexist aspects get on one's nerves a bit.
Ever, Alan

This would not have been a *bona fide* evaluation of a submitted picture-caption, never mind a 400-page book that a year earlier Oxford's keen senior editor had knowingly contracted. Ryan's scrawl ended with another of the case's classic lines: "Will that do?" As I later suggested to the trial judge, it would not. The copy of *Making Names* which Ryan was supposed to have had for three months and to have taken with him on holiday to Canada was subsequently returned to me and later exhibited in court: it was absolutely pristine, with its uncreased binding and fine, crisp pages apparently unopened. The revelation that the second draft had never been read demonstrated that the whole volte-face, "please Malcolm, spend six months revising it for us after after all", had been no more than a cynical charade acted out to smooth various ruffled Oxford feathers. It was clear too that nearly every Oxford person involved (Hardy, Ryan, Charkin, Bion) long before any litigation had got going, had been less than generous with the truth, both to me and to each other. Ryan's glorious opening sentence, complete with its telling abbreviation, became my new DIM-squad favourite.

Other documents were demonstrably missing too: there was no trace or account of the potentially decisive, and evidently carefully-prepared telephone notes, perhaps headed "offer contract", from which Hardy had been dictating to me on 20th May 1985; there were no minutes of the "Publications Committee" meeting of 17th July at which *Making Names* had been rejected by Charkin, or of the Delegates' meeting of 16th July at which it had apparently been presented. There was no documentation either of what had happened at or after Hardy's disciplinary appeal hearing. In June 1988 we therefore issued a summons for specific discovery of these classes of still-missing documents, and on 8th August won a hearing before Master Barratt, who ordered their production in full, with costs. This order winkled out various new papers including the withdrawal of Charkin's disciplinary warning, which revealed that the Hardy's appeal panel had been chaired by Bill Andrewes, OUP's Finance Director, and included Clive Moody (Personnel Director), Will Sulkin (Head of the General Books Division) and Ivon Asquith. Apart from these crumbs though, Oxford produced not one of the other documents that the court had ordered.

Instead, the University's response provided one of the many notable moments in the affair at which its degradation sharply crystallised, or took a further, jolting, quantum-lunge. Barratt's carefully-worded order had specified, obviously enough, that Henry Hardy himself should depose as to the whereabouts of the prepared notes from which he had been dictating in his contractual phonecall of 20th May. However, in the event, who should step forward, once again, but the hapless Asquith, cunningly changing Barratt's wording from "for" to "during" and swearing, with his hand touching a Bible, that Hardy had made no notes *in the course of* that now-famous conversation. Oh how clever! Oh tee-hee-hees! Asquith also swore that there were no reports on the second draft of *Making Names*, no minutes of the Publications Committee meetings, no minutes "of the Delegates' meeting of 16th July 1985" and no minutes of any other such meetings. At the time I was using some unusually sinister post-it notes with a picture of a spade and the legend, in red: IT'S STARTING TO GET DEEP. Asquith's eloquent affidavit was soon covered in them.

10

Enter the Delegates

B ESIDES IN THEIR role of book-approvers, the Delegates were hoving into view in another aspect of the case too. Master Barratt had ruled in January that Richard Charkin be struck out of the action, on the undertaking of Robin Denniston to write a letter to my solicitor "for and on behalf of the Delegates stating that Charkin had acted at all times *bona fide* within the scope of his authority at OUP". Mention of the Delegates threw Oxford's lawyers into alarm. This was typical: on the one hand, when there was bad news to impart, the Delegates were invoked or blamed (remember that in his letters of 1986, Charkin had stated that it was they who had rejected *Making Names*); on the other, there was panic at the prospect of the Delegates being informed about the lawsuit. On 20th January 1988, as reported to Richard White by Master Barratt, Oxford's solicitor had telephoned Barratt to say that it would be difficult to obtain the letter as agreed because "the Delegates are a body of distinguished old gentlemen who meet only once a year". Obviously Barratt, like us, knew this to be untrue. Denniston, needless to say, never wrote his letter as ordered to White, but Charkin was nonetheless struck out and early in 1989 was allowed £1,219 taxed costs. At about the same time, Charkin made a public speech in which he expressed fears that the impending collapse of the Net Book Agreement would invalidate most author-publisher contracts, so I suggested donating his costs to the Society of Authors. Despite his concern, Charkin declined my offer and in April I had to pay his costs. In a sense though, the secondary claim had by then served its purpose: the scandal was now well and truly exposed and the Delegates' interests were now, as Lord Justice Mustill was later to say, "directly in suit." The argument had moved upstairs, and surely the Delegates, this most august body of senior academics, many of whom were Fellows of the Royal Society or British Academy, were proper, responsible, honourable men? Surely they would not let this crazy travesty continue?

In February, as was becoming the pattern, Oxford's lawyers carefully twisted the terms of Master Barratt's order, leading me to suspect that the Delegates had not in fact ratified Charkin's actions in any way, or even been informed of the affair. I therefore decided at the end of March to write to them all myself and obtained the current list from the University Calendar. It seems that each year the composition of the roughly twenty-

strong committee changes, usually with two or three arrivals and
departures and with the University's Vice-Chancellor, Assessor and two
Proctors being Delegates *ex officio*. Behind the Delegates there also stands
a nominating committee of thirteen, whose composition seems to change
almost completely from year to year, with the Vice-Chancellor and
Proctors again being *ex officios*. The 1988 roll-call ran impressively:
Professor J. Barr, Christ Church, a Hebrew scholar, who, I learned, had
been one of the world's few recipients of the sensitive material from the
Dead Sea Scrolls; Professor J. Boardman, Lincoln, the distinguished classical
historian and archaeologist; Professor D. J. Weatherall, Magdalen, an eminent
medic and expert on haematology; Sir Roger Elliott, New College, of
whom more in a while; Professor Ian Brownlie, All Souls, an international
human rights lawyer, who in preliminary hearings defended the two
Libyans accused of the Lockerbie bombing;. Professor Sir Richard
Southwood, a zoologist, chairman of the National Radiological Protection
Board, in 1989 Oxford's new Vice-Chancellor, and subsequently head of
the Government's investigation into BSE; Sir K. V. Thomas, Corpus
Christi, the distinguished historian and critic; Doctor A. J. P. Kenny,
Balliol, a Catholic philosopher, and author of several books; Professor Sir
Peter Hirsch, St. Edmund Hall, a metallurgist expert in electron
microscopy; Doctor G. A. Holmes, St. Catherine's, an authority on English
and Italian history; Professor R. J. P. Williams, Wadham, a research
chemist; Professor L. Weiskrantz, Magdalen, a psychologist and neurologist;
Doctor G. Marshall, Queen's, a constitutional and political theorist; I. C.
Butler, Christ Church, a lecturer in English; and P. M. Oppenheimer,
Christ Church, an economist and BBC radio and TV presenter.

Amongst these, Thomas, Kenny, Brownlie, Butler, Weiskrantz and Elliott
(chairman since 1975) have all also served on OUP's all-powerful inner
Finance Committee, which consists of roughly half senior Delegates and
half senior management, plus two external business advisers (in 1988 Sir
Gordon Brunton, listed as Chairman of no less than twelve major companies,
and Sir Martin Jacomb, Deputy Chairman of Barclays bank, Chairman of
Barclays De Zoete Wedd and a Director of the Bank of England). The
Delegates as a whole had been characterised to me as "an academic book
committee", but in reaching these Finance Committee members I was
directly addressing the people ultimately responsible for Oxford's legal
decisions. I made my letter as polite as possible, and asked three simple,
factual questions: (1) Was their solicitor's "distinguished old gentleman
who meet once a year" description a fair one, and if not, what was? (2)
Had they, as unconvincingly suggested by Denniston, ratified Charkin's
actions over *Making Names*? and (3) Had they, as stated by Charkin, taken
the decision to reject the book? Surely this most eminent panel of the

nation's senior intellectuals would object *en bloc* to their lawyers' "once a year" calumny, and surely one or two of them would ask to see Hardy's file on the affair, or check on the approval question? Apparently not. In reply, one did show some concern and telephoned me decently and at length, but most did not respond at all. Two or three sent evasive acknowledgments, and Brownlie wrote, tellingly, "I have absolutely no knowledge whatsoever of the matters to which you refer in your letter, which I was very surprised to receive." He invited me to write instead to Messrs Denniston and Charkin. However high up one went, it seemed, the buck (book?) continued to be passed.

Two months after I wrote to the Delegates, Charkin unexpectedly resigned from the Press. A year earlier, George Richardson had announced his intention to retire, and it had generally been assumed that Charkin would succeed him as Chief Executive. Instead, to many commentators' surprise, in May it was announced that the chairman of the Finance Committee Sir Roger Elliott, not Charkin, was to get the job (by coincidence, Elliott was also the chairman of the selection panel which made the appointment). Charkin resigned in disgust and evidently amidst some acrimony; I gather that his departure speech was highly colourful, especially in respect of the Delegates. That July he joined Paul Hamlyn's burgeoning Octopus conglomerate (later sold to Reed International) as head of its paperback imprint Mandarin, where he quickly went on the rampage. A celebrated purple press release penned by him to plug Michael Jackson's "smash-hit autobiography" *Moonwalk* and other such "chart-toppers" caused much hilarity in the trade. In January 1989 Robin Denniston also left OUP and took up the office of Rector of Great Tew, a charming country church near Oxford where I later had the honour of being blessed by him during a moving service of nine lessons and carols. In a valedictory interview, Denniston remarked: "Publishing's proper function is to provide a limited and comparatively humble means of access of authors to readers." Well amen, at least, to that.

Back in Walton Street, the Press, to much comment, was now being run not by a professional publisher, but by a quondam physicist who had specialised in the magnetic properties of the lanthanide metals. However, although not a book-trader, Elliott was certainly a professional committee-man, having served as Secretary of The Royal Society, on the Atomic Energy Authority, on The University and Research Council's Computer and Advisory Boards, and numerous suchlike bodies. In April 1989 he was elected to the Council of the Publishers' Association and went on to become its President for two years. In 1991, Charkin's Reed cancelled its £100,000 subscription and withdrew from the PA, which it claimed had grown too large. This may be an appropriate moment to note that in 1982 the PA had agreed a code of practice for dealings with authors which included the following relevant points:

> "Failure to accept the guidance in this Code without good reason is clearly likely to damage the standing of individual publishers and of publishing generally...
> 5   The publisher must give the author a proper opportunity to share in the success of the work. In general, the contract should seek to achieve a fair balance of reward for author and publisher.
> 6   The publisher must handle scripts promptly, and keep the author informed of progress. At least a progress report should be sent by the publisher within six weeks of receipt of the script.
> 7   The publisher must not cancel a contract without good and proper reason. In any such case the publisher must give the author sufficiently detailed reasons for rejection. A change in the publisher's circumstances or policies is not a sufficient reason for declining to publish a commissioned work without compensation... Depending on the grounds for rejection, the publisher may be liable for further advances due and an additional sum may be agreed to compensate the author."

Would Elliott perhaps now read his association's code and honour it?

OUP was undergoing other upheavals too. In February 1989 it announced the closure of its historic, 500-year-old printing business, despite having invested over £1 million in it over the previous two years; from now on, its 'P' was to stand only for 'publishing'. The loss of the 250 jobs was greeted with dismay and anger by the unions; and the loss of Oxford's unique collection of ancient typefounts, and of its royal Bible license (one of only four ever granted) was lamented by many scholars and historians, who in a flurry of letters to *The Times* accused the Delegates of academic vandalism. Another storm broke in April, when it was revealed that despite the *fatwa* on Salman Rushdie, OUP had decided to break the worldwide embargo of the Tehran Book Fair in order to maintain its Iranian textbook sales. This provoked castigation from many prominent OUP authors, from the writers group P.E.N. International and from much of the serious press, especially in America. In justification, at around the time he was personally issuing his own *fatwa* against *Making Names*, Elliott stated: "We are interested in the free circulation of books, whatever the regime." Three years later he put his signature to a PA letter to *The Times* deploring the attempted assassination of Rushdie's Norwegian publisher William Nygaard. My own eventual publisher expressed his dismay at this hypocrisy in a letter in *The Bookseller* magazine of 17th December 1993.

11

Contempt and Contumely

BACK IN 1988 with another silenced author in Chancery Lane, the magisterial university's tactics had descended to the level of kindergarten games, or mocking teases, and its catalogue of court-order infringements was steadily growing, especially in respect of document discovery. From the start, Oxford's submissions had smelt of evasion, but the reek from Asquith's second affidavit was now overpowering. All in all, Richard White thought that we might be able to bring the action to a comparatively swift conclusion by issuing a motion for Oxford's contempt of court over these various contumelies and failures, a move which would at last allow us to lay the mounting scandal before some senior non-Oxford judge. Having decided on this course, there arose two problems: first, as we knew, under the archaic rules we would now have to incur the extra expense of briefing a barrister to do the courtroom laying; second, unforeseen, the Chancery Division's Malcolm-case gearbox suddenly went into neutral, or seemed spontaneously to choke on its own cogs.

We had already encountered numerous bureaucratic slips at the hands of the various court offices with which we had had to deal: there had been muddles over hearing dates, mistakes on summonses, and delays and errors in the issuing of orders. These problems had been unsurprising in such an evidently old-fashioned, overburdened and complicated system, but the impasse we now hit in trying to get our contempt motion (or more accurately, motion*less*), lodged and listed was altogether different: it was total. Like a faulty British Rail machine, however Richard White inserted the requisite paper, it refused to issue a ticket. It had not escaped us, of course, that in suing the Chancellor, Masters and Scholars of the University of Oxford I was technically suing not only roughly half the High Court judiciary, but also many of the senior court administrators, listings clerks, registrars so forth, but it had never for a second crossed our minds that this would have any effect on the case's procedural mechanics. During the prolonged issuing of this motion, however, even the determinedly untroubled White decided to start tape-recording his conversations with the various officials, and was then sufficiently moved to assemble all their baffling contradictions and false denials into a carefully logged, transcribed account, intended for later submission to the courts' internal complaints bureau. (In the event we agreed that such a submission would be perfectly pointless: to whom can one complain about a court? We were in the position of the man who discovers that his mail is being intercepted, but who then wonders to whom he can usefully write.) Meanwhile, in an attempt to save money and to restart the action, I myself travelled to London several times and began to acquaint myself with the bureaucratic labyrinth in which our motion had come to a halt.

Most people are probably familiar with exterior of the sprawling Victorian-Gothic pile sandwiched at the Aldwych end of the Strand between Kingsway and Chancery Lane, whose front entrance frequently, sometimes daily, provides the backdrop to legal stories on the evening television news. With its rambling facade of intricately ornamented archways in pleasing white stone, its first impression is of a European cathedral manqué, or perhaps of an Oxford College travestied. (Amongst my collection of curiosities there is an OUP language-teaching magazine on whose cover, as either a joke or a mistake, the Royal Courts are seen posing as a casual DIM-squad scene, with a couple of wigged and gowned lawyers presumably thought to pass well enough to foreigners for your average Oxford dons.) Often when I arrived hot-foot from the Temple tube, I would find myself brushing shoulders with celebrities addressing pavement camera-crews, or having to thread my way through knots of demonstrators carrying placards and distributing leaflets, rubs which ignited in me the foolish notion that here was where the action was, where people came to do serious business, where one could get properly *stuck in*. Once up the steps, through the doors, and past the makeshift security checks, the terrain becomes less encouraging, and hopefully less familiar to all but my professional lawyer readership. The initial cathedral illusion is maintained by the Courts' high, vaulted Central Hall, on whose fine mosaic floor stand the notice-boards advertising the day's hearings. However, once one has recovered from invertigo and ventured from this echoing vault into the warren of passages, stairways and occasional derelict-looking lifts that radiate from it, any illusion of grandeur, let alone of religious inspiration, is immediately lost as the dingy maze takes on the oppressive atmosphere of a pseudo-antique private school. I remember that one of my regular routes took me past some wonderfully neglected, unlit display-cases of bygone judicial robes, whose mothy, faceless wigs I more than once caught laughing drily in the shadows. The windowless 'cafeteria' must have been one of the gloomiest rooms in London.

Needless to say, the complex was permanently undergoing 'modernisation', with offices frequently being relocated or in temporary quarters, and whole areas suddenly being roped off or returning to use. This ensured that, in the best traditions of supermarket layout or one-way-traffic-management, as soon as one had finally discovered where everything was, the plan was changed and one's bearings were lost. As often as not, once I had at last navigated my way to the necessary forbidding door, the office inside would be brightly lit, computerised and staffed by youngish clerks, doing their best to be cheery and efficient with their steady stream of litigants and lawyers. Given the pervasive public-school atmosphere, there were surprisingly high proportions of Asians and Afro-Caribbeans (usually girls) amongst the office staff and of cockney sharp-boys amongst the queues (mostly barristers' clerks, I guessed), giving rise to much good-natured sexual banter and often relieving the long dreary waits. A couple of times on these missions, I encountered the chilling spectacle of the compulsive plaintiff, some or other unfortunate soul who, longer ago than anyone could remember, had entered this dark warren, doubtless in a once-worthy cause, and never managed, or wanted, to extricate themselves from its endlessly self-generating procedures. "See that old bloke," I was told, glimpsing a hunched figure beetling off down a deserted passage with a sackful of files on his back, "mad as a box, practically lives here; for the past thirty years, he's never had less than ten applications on the go at once." On another occasion I witnessed a fiery dispossessed-dowager-type ranting non-stop but quite unattended in the corner of a summons-issuing office, and heard it whispered that she was "a regular" there. Oh God, was this now *my* destiny, I reflected, or was this perhaps *already me*, as I harangued an anxious girl for the third time about my stalled motion, confronting her with bits of Richard White's transcript or an extract from the Court's "White Book" practice notes. At last, her alarm must have communicated itself sufficiently clearly to the central gearbox operator, for our motion finally got moving; it had taken over four months to do so.

In the end, a date for the hearing, before Justice Morritt, was fixed for 6th March 1989, and prior to it, several remarkable things happened. Hardy at last swore an affidavit, stating that he had not, after all, been dictating from notes on 20th May 1985 (that he had therefore lied to me on the telephone in 1985). Clive Moody, OUP's personnel officer, swore that there were no further documents relating to Hardy's disciplinary appeal. And Oxford's *solicitor* Mr Shaw was wheeled in to depose to a revised version of the events that were supposed to have passed, over a few days four years earlier, at OUP offices whose inmates themselves had long since forgotten. His new account was pure hearsay and therefore virtually value-less, but evidently the weight of Oxford inconsistencies was becoming too heavy even for Ivon Asquith to bear, and Shaw had been deputed to swear an affidavit contradicting *both* of Asquith's previous two. The trial judge later dismissed all of Hardy's evidence and concluded that Asquith had "calculated to mislead". Later still, when the Court of Appeal's triplicate files were returned to me, I found that all three of the judges had removed their copies of Asquith's and Hardy's three affidavits, presumably for closer examination. Whether these ever found their way into the bottomless vault which I am assured lies under the Department of Public Prosecutions, or whether they just ended up in their Lordships' private rogues' galleries, I have no idea.

Dallas Brett had from the start *delegated* a number of junior or middle-ranking staff to handle the case, of which Mr Shaw was by far the longest serving. His oilyness was of a different grade from Mark Warby's, being more of the pallid skin and greased hair variety; he was one of those people who, one imagines, already looked middle-aged when they left college and had perhaps even been born wearing a shiny suit. He was slightly short, slightly rotund in face and build, and slightly seedy, but was always perfectly pleasant with me and just got on and did his job. He had a habit, I remember, of dropping his final 'g's, and one particular piece of advice he gave in some court corridor or other became one of our favourite lines: "I think you should be considerin reamendin your pleadin."

Shaw's revised version of the history was that the Delegates' 1985 summer vacation meeting had been held on not the 16th, but the *23rd* of July – the same day as Hardy's disciplinary hearing – and that the Delegates' Note for *Making Names*, despite being listed as a photocopy, had been *prepared and dated* on the 16th, but, oddly, and in contradiction of Asquith, had then not been copied or circulated to anyone. He gave a new timetable of Charkin's rejection, and repeated the unlikely assertion that OUP's editorial meetings went unminuted. This new account posed at least as many questions as it answered, so an appropriately-tweaked version of our motion went ahead. Then, in the courtroom during the hearing itself, came another of those quantum-lunge revelations: over Warby's shoulder, I noticed that his xerox of the increasingly interesting Delegates' Note carried some extra writing that must have been erased from the xeroxes sent to us: in what was recognisably Hardy's hand, it read: "for Delegates 23rd July". For the past year Oxford had passed off its most contentious document as a fraudulent copy.

Theoretically, if our motion had been wholly successful, it could have resulted in the arrest of Oxford's Chancellor, the Right Honourable the Lord Jenkins of Hillhead, so just in case of such a delightful outcome, I had prepared for the cameramen of the court steps a news-sheet with a masthead 𝕿𝖍𝖊 𝕯𝖆𝖎𝖑𝖞 𝕮𝖑𝖆𝖗𝖊𝖙, and a picture of a grimacing Roy under the headline WITER STWANGLED, MAN APPWEHENDED. Sadly, in the event the hearing proved indecisive and the poster remained in its roll. The motion did, however, help in two important respects: first we now had the aid of a barrister, whose wisdom and kindness later proved invaluable; and second it edged our juggernaut further up OUP's hierarchy. Shaw's new version of the history required Oxford's production of the agenda and minutes of the Delegates' meeting of 23rd July 1985. The agenda paper featured just a bald heading "General Publications", but in the minutes, the corresponding entry read:

> "The proposal for *The New Oxford Book of Modern Verse* was deferred for further consideration. On the Concise Dictionaries of Physics, Chemistry and Biology the Delegates requested that steps be taken to control overlapping. The other titles tabled were approved."

The obvious next question was: okay, so what were these other titles? Oxford was providing no list or record of the General Books the Delegates had evidently approved. Although Justice Morritt was sternly, and on reflection I guess rightly, against us on some points, he made no mistake about this one, and as we requested, ordered that Sir Roger Elliott himself, the Secretary to the Delegates, should personally testify as to the missing list. Once again, the opposition lawyers went into panic-mode as it became clear that Elliott was becoming involved, and in trying to dissuade Morritt from making such an order, Warby gave yet another novel characterisation of the Delegates' role: "they are like the shareholders in a company," he explained. "Don't you mean the directors?" "Nope, the shareholders."

Earlier on, given the calibre of Oxford's witnesses, it might have seemed feasible to ascribe some of the discrepancies to muddle or incompetence, but not any more. There were now just too many plainly false affidavits, too many obvious trickeries of wording and too many directly conflicting accounts. No-one obscures parts of photocopied documents or changes a court's "for" to "during" without, literally, having things to hide. Soon after the hearing, I therefore visited the office of Oxford's solicitors to inspect, as is one's right, OUP's file of original evidence, and for good measure I took a camera with which to colour-photograph any new revelations, of which there were several. The Publishing Proposal Form (PPF), for example, turned out to be a double-sided cardboard sheet which had been completed in at least four different coloured inks and which bore heavy layers of correcting fluid under the royalty rates. As originally listed (but logically denied by Shaw's new account), the Delegates' Note in their file was itself a photocopy. Inspection of its typing had shown that the original must have been corrected with tippex or some such fluid, and so would be definitively identifiable; my colour-photograph of their tippexless photocopy later became an exhibit in the court file. Hardy's handwriting was also in photocopy. So where was the original Note and why was it not in the file? Did the original carry the extra 23rd July date and if so why? Why had this vital date been obscured from the copies sent to us? Why were so many different copy-versions in circulation (by the end I identified at least four, each with differing photocopied marks)?

We had had no knowledge or evidence of the Delegates' Note's existence, and Richard White had not mentioned it in his letter-before-action list. If its original had not been copied or circulated, OUP might even have been able to argue that it was within the legal rules to omit any mention of it. So why did Oxford's virtuosos of denial declare the troublesome paper in the first place? The only plausible answer was that its non-discovery would have been too risky with twenty or so Delegates in possession of duplicates. In short, Oxford's very declaration of the Note demonstrated that it must have been circulated. Hardy was now saying, in the new history, that the original was produced on his instructions but was never copied or sent to anyone and never left his file, which he surrendered early in the litigation; yet his original was now missing, the copies used early in the litigation did not bear his handwriting, and the different xeroxed versions were starting to breed like lies. So began our hunt for Hardy's original 'top copy' Note: we hit the tippex trail.

The hunt also began for the missing list of General Books approved at the 23rd July meeting. Yet again a long telltale wrangle broke out, this time over the precise wording of Justice Morritt's order and of Elliott's required deposition, of which several unexceptionable drafts were rejected by Oxford's lawyers. To cut this particular tiresome story short, in July 1989 Elliott eventually swore that:

> "Save for the [already produced] documents, there is not now and to my knowledge there has not at any time been in the Defendant's possession, custody or power any document listing titles of General Publications tabled at the meeting of the Delegates of The Oxford Press held on 23 July 1985 or otherwise indicating what General Publication titles were approved at that meeting."

If my 'commitment' paragraph of 24th March 1984 was the OUnuchs' unfocussed blind spot, this unlikely oath from Elliott became their sharp spike, a barb upon which all their subsequent testimony became twitchingly impaled. Several senior personnel in one of the most self-evidently bureaucratic publishers in the world had testified that minutes were not kept of the decisions made at their editorial meetings. Now its chief executive was insisting that no lists were made or records kept of the General Books approved by their Delegates. I must be careful what I write here, for Elliott has sued for libel over this before, but, well, really...

At this point, an astute reader, or a lawyer may well ask: yes, yes, but what has the Delegates' approval (or non-approval) of your book got to do with the existence, or not, of your contract? What has it got to do with you? How would it help your case if you could prove it? Isn't all this just an azure herring? There are several answers to these questions, which I did frequently ask myself at the time. First, as later observed by Mustill LJ, demonstration of the Delegates' formal approval of *Making Names* would at once demolish Oxford's defence that this contractual condition had not been met. Second, it would provide a solid basis for a court's order of specific performance, that is for the printing of the planned 2,000 copies (the PPF had not been signed, but the Delegates were OUP's highest authority). Third, if it could be shown that Oxford had been dishonest at *Delegate* level, then surely they could not honourably continue *any* defence. And fourth, well let's just say: if you think you've seen a truth...

Obviously though, the question of whether or not the Delegates had in July 1985 (or whenever) formally approved *Making Names* was strictly irrelevant to the existence of a contract concluded between myself and Hardy in May and June; authors cannot have to ferret around amongst their publishers' ancient internal committee papers (or lack of them) in order to confirm that their contracts are valid, so in a sense I was here treading my own irrelevant and expensive legal garden path. The fascinating thing was that Oxford followed me down it. Typically, when they sensed that there might here be an historical circumstance which I could not absolutely prove, they started to rely upon it themselves. As we shall see, during the trial and right up until a month before the appeal, Oxford even chose to rest its whole defence upon this very point, however ridiculous the implications of such a ploy would have been; regardless, for example, that it would have invalidated all of its own formal *Memoranda of Agreement*.

Plunging ever deeper into the dark blue labyrinth, my next research was to try to trace back all the Delegates from 1984/5 to see if any of them could remember any mention of *Making Names* or had kept their papers from the period or would be willing to tell the truth about the listing of General Books. One problem, of course, was that current Delegates who 'overlapped' already knew of the litigation from my letter of March 1988 and so were unapproachable. However, several others were not, including: Sir Geoffrey Warnock, Hertford, former Vice-Chancellor of the University and distinguished moral philosopher; Sir Michael Atiyah, St. Catherine's, the eminent mathematician who later became President of the Royal

Society and Master of Trinity College, Cambridge; David (D. F.) Pears, Balliol, the Wittgensteinian philosopher and monographer; Amartya Sen, All Souls and Harvard, a political economist and author of numerous books on economic development; Doctor R. H. Lonsdale, Balliol, an English literature don; Mrs. Ruth Deech, St. Anne's, a lawyer, Senior Proctor in 1984/5 and currently the chairman of the Human Fertilisation and Embryology Authority; and Doctor Glenn Black, Oriel, an English literature fellow, the Junior Proctor in 1984/5, and current (1999) chairman of the Proctors' Committee. The discovered minutes recorded that Elliott, Deech, Black, Ryan, Pears, Lonsdale, Weatherall, Thomas, Holmes, Weiskrantz, Williams and Brownlie had all been present at the fateful 1985 meeting. Surely one of these would have kept their records of the books they had approved?

12

The Dele-gate Tapes

IN ADDITION, I made phonecalls to officials at the Proctors' offices and to the University archivists who might have held copies of the missing papers, and I had an interesting conversation with the University Marshal on the "difficult and delicate" relationship between the University and its touble-prone Press. Of the Delegates, Sir Michael Atiyah said he vaguely remembered *Making Names*, repeatedly confirmed the existence of lists, and believed that he had kept all his papers, which he thought I was entitled to see. He kindly invited me to put in writing exactly what I wanted, assuring me that he would do his best to find it. Five weeks later, he wrote back to apologise that his files had, after all, been disposed of (in one of several such odd circumstances, his letter arrived already torn open). Of all the Oxford people I approached, I think Atiyah was the one most genuinely concerned and troubled by OUP's conduct. Amartya Sen, in a call to America, also vaguely remembered my name and the book's title. Doctor Lonsdale could not remember particular books, but categorically confirmed the existence of General Books *lists* in 1985 (his emphasis), as did Glenn Black and Ann Smallwood, the Vice-Chancellor's secretary. David Attwooll, in 1985 an OUP director working in New York, said that he had heard about the *Making Names* affair through the *minutes* he had received of the editorial committee meetings. Perhaps the most interesting case was that of D. F. Pears, the co-translator of Wittgenstein's *Tractatus Logico-Philosophicus,* who in our first conversation emphatically confirmed the existence in 1985 of *lists* of General Books, and clearly remembered my name and my book's title, and that Alan Ryan had been its advocate at Oxford. Then, in a second conversation a few weeks later, Pears beat a hasty and ill-tempered retreat which I think is worth quoting:

> **Malcolm:** Hello. I phoned you about a month ago in the States about a problem I'd had....
> **Pears:** Yes, and I told you I wasn't at the meeting and I had heard about your book. I advised you to try elsewhere...
> **Malcolm:** It seemed a simple matter of fact to discover whether or not the Delegates had approved the book at a certain meeting.
> **Pears:** Yes, well it is of course a matter of fact, if it was taken as an item on the agendas of the meeting. Since I wasn't there, I don't know.
> **Malcolm:** Well one thing that has transpired is that we have got the minutes of the meeting and you are listed as being present at it.

Pears: Good heavens! Really? I assure you I'd completely forgotten. But if you have the minutes, then you've got your answer.
Malcolm: But the minutes are incomplete. [Explains the missing General Books list, the date obscured from the Delegates' Note *et cetera.* Reveals that the dispute is the subject of litigation.]
Pears: Let me ask you a question: are you taping this conversation?
Malcolm: (Unhesitating) Yes.
Pears: And you taped my last one?
Malcolm: (Unhesitating) Yes.
Pears: Without telling me?
Malcolm: (Unhesitating) Yes.
Pears: Okay, no more help from me then! That's not the way to behave! I was treating you with sympathy and kindness. You are being led up the path in bringing a legal action... It only enriches lawyers... [Surprisingly, he did not then hang up but continued for some time, repeatedly but unsuccessfully trying to explain his lapse of memory over his attendance at the meeting.]

I fancy that this exchange, like Hardy's of 18th July 1985, might make a rich discussion-text for students of psychology and moral philosophy. What is it with these people, and what *does* Oxford do to them, I was beginning to wonder, and what *was* the proper way to behave? Obviously it was not to conduct a careful, open, year-long negotiation, or to try to get everything unambiguous and in writing. The steady multiplication of cavalier lies was beginning to echo the programme at the heart of *Making Names* itself, in which the philosopher Cause sees it as his mission systematically to strip away the fibs, fudges and fallacies that underlie many of Effect's scientific assumptions and theories, and to claw his way closer to some more sustainable, if less precise certainties. Similarly, here I now was, sentence by sentence, affidavit by affidavit, lie by lie dismantling the barrages of illogic and falsehood with which Oxford was continually trying to block the judicial path. Though pinching myself against such delusions, I could never completely silence the thought that these people are the *authorities*, the experts who hand us down the truths of physics, philosophy, ethics and the rest. Students take notes of their lectures on the structure of matter, the meaning of meaning, the origins of the Universe and the sources of morality. Some of them are even in charge of the nation's plutonium. Yet how can they be trusted on such grand and weighty matters as these if, when something in real life is actually at stake, they err on the simplest trivialities of lists, meetings, dates, or what they said last week? My allusion to plutonium, by the way, is no hyperbole: as a member of the Atomic Energy Authority, Sir Roger Elliott was one of the men secretly entrusted with the task of publicly misleading the nation over the economics of civil nuclear power generation in order to facilitate the military stockpiling of its weapons-grade 'by-product'.

Another amusing phone-taping incident occurred when I telephoned a senior Oxford left-winger and ex-Delegate who, I had been advised by a friend who worked for the Labour Party, might be sympathetic to my cause. After a few minutes of rather frosty conversation, there was a series of clicks and buzzes, and I heard, as he mistakenly thought on another line, a lady with a 1940s GCHQ, Cholmondeley-Warner voice trying to explain to him how to make a recording of the call. He need not have bothered, for I would happily have sent him a copy of mine. He was not, incidentally, the slightest bit interested to hear what had happened over *Making Names*, and stated that he would automatically side with the Press, whatever the facts. This strangled exchange, though trivial in itself, did reinforce the impression that now I really was entering the bunker. This seemed an Oxford far removed from the parade of fine stone gateways and courtyards basking in the admiration of the tourists, from the droves of students swotting in their libraries and spilling beer over their pool-tables, and from the spacious sitting rooms adorned with ancient knick-knacks, where genteel folk with reedy voices and manicured grammar extolled the beauties of Marvell's poetry, of Arabic calligraphy, or of Persian carpets. No, here I was entering Oxford's clandestine basement, where grey steel cabinets of electronic equipment hummed monotonously, and radiating corridors of cables warned doorless offices around the country of trouble above ground. It was just another silly fantasy of course, but by that time I had amassed quite a file of strange telephone phenomena. How foolish of me to have so intruded, to have so *importuned.*

While the proceedings rumbled on, I placed the transcripts of some of my conversations with the Delegates in evidence, and at about this stage Richard White advised me to start acting in person: by now the detail of the case had got very complicated and expensive, and my grasp of the requisite procedures and techniques had become, he thought, reasonably thorough. I followed his suggestion, retaining him and my barrister as advisers. At the end of July 1989 the Summons for Directions was heard and a timetable fixed for the action to go to trial. The contract question, it was agreed, was to be settled separately from any damages assessment. In August 1989 the action was set down — that is, entered into the High Court's bureaucratic machinery. A countdown was now ticking, and I think someone at Oxford may at last have realised that perhaps this claim would 'go the distance', that perhaps they really were going to be dragged into court to justify themselves. I learned from OUP insiders of people "burning midnight oil" on the case, and of the top management being summoned to weekly briefings on its progress. In October, Oxford for the first time asked for a quantification of my sought damages. By now I was armed with Ryan's marketing suggestions citing A-Level and

Open University courses and his ambitious mentions of *The Outsider* and *Gödel, Escher, Bach*, and on the basis of the then-available (and as it emerged hugely conservative) figures for those books' sales, I filed a speculative claim for about £100,000. Then, at last, for the first time in three years, Oxford asked to hear the recording of Hardy's contractual commitment.

Also in October, witness-statements were exchanged; Oxford's line-up included Elliott (amended once), and Hardy, Charkin and Bion (all amended twice). They contained nothing much new or unexpected, but certain odd points should perhaps be noted. Elliott described the functions of OUP's Finance Committee, but omitted to mention that he had been chairman of it since 1975. On the matter of the recording of the Delegates' decisions he stated, presumably because his previous attempt sounded so implausible, that the 1985 procedure of not listing General Books had since been changed to one of listing them, although he did not say when this change had occurred. Hardy, as by now had become sickeningly clear, was denying absolutely everything — his commitment to me, his responsibility for *Making Names*, the reliability of his memory, the authenticity of the tape-recordings, and even the content of his own disciplinary defence. Charkin's statement contained several choice nuggets, including a blunt opening sentence "Editors commission a book", an interestingly evasive line on the Delegates, and a fine declaration of his publishing ethos ("I use three criteria to decide on books: profitability, quality and author."). And Bion stated, own-goal fashion, that in 1985 the top copies of the Delegates' Notes were sent to a Mrs Margaret Goodall, the, wait for it, secretary to the Secretary to the Delegates. In reply to all this, I served a single unamended statement, my own.

The hunt for the original Delegates' Note, indexed as document D19, continued. Numerous notices were served, but D19 was still nowhere to be found at Oxford. Then, as a result of the multiplying riddles concerning the Delegates' meetings, Margaret Goodall was ordered to swear an affidavit explaining her procedures. In this she admitted that in 1985 she had been responsible for collating and distributing all of their agenda papers and minutes, but said nothing about the missing list of General Books. She attached a set of subsequently computerised 'investment statistics' on which, surprise surprise, *Making Names* did not appear, but as these were deletable printouts they were inadmissible; their production did, however, then require Elliott to swear a second affidavit contradicting his first. My lawyers were evidently not the only ones becoming increasingly cynical about Oxford's testimony on these points, and in a pre-trial hearing on 12th February 1989 Master Barratt ordered that all six of Oxford's witnesses and deponents, including Goodall, would have to appear in court for cross-examination. It was only when Goodall was approached by the lawyers and her affidavit filed, that Oxford finally unearthed, after more than three years of litigation, the top-copy of Delegates' Note D19, the paper that was supposed never to have left Hardy's file. It was produced by order at the hearing, and, sure enough, carried the definitive tippex correcting fluid and Hardy's definitive handwritten second date. Hardy's explanation of this in court was later to become one of the case's great comic scenes.

The trial was scheduled for Monday 12th March, again with the court's stipulation that it must not come before an Oxonian judge. Realising that the Oxford Six were all preparing to say in court that no records or lists were kept of the General Books approved by the Delegates on 23rd July 1985, I decided to serve subpoenas on some of the Delegates and other Oxonians who had told me differently. In February I had a selection of subpoenas issued at the Royal Courts in London and on 3rd March I travelled to Oxford to serve some. Luckily, I found several of my target recipients at home, and in a variety of silly sketches, managed to insert the necessary bits of paper into their several perplexed fingers, informing their owners that they were commanded by "ELIZABETH THE SECOND, by the Grace of God, of the United Kingdom of Great Britain and Northern Ireland and of Our other realms and territories Queen, Head of the Commonwealth, defender of the faith, to attend before... *et cetera, et cetera.*" Mathematician Sir Michael Atiyah lived in Shotover on the edge of Oxford in a pretty country house unfortunately overlooked by a scrapyard; as in our previous communications, he was polite and gentlemanly, and seemed to regard the matter with some gravity and shock. Glenn Black, the English Fellow and Proctor, lived in a pre-war semi; he had been pleasant and talkative on the telephone and seemed to want to continue on the doorstep, but I asked him to save it for later. Anne Smallwood, the Vice-Chancellor's secretary who had handled the Delegates' papers for years, lived in a modern North Oxford flat; she indignantly grabbed the subpoena, as if expecting it, and slammed the door in my face. I had wanted to serve one also on D. F. Pears, but his wife told me that he was away in America. The final turn was a *duces tecum* version for Charkin, who lived in a red-brick Victorian terrace nearby the Press; he was already ordered to attend, but the subpoena obliged him also to bring for inspection his business diaries of the period. Memorably, his wife answered the door visibly quaking, as though they were regularly confronted by unannounced and threatening visitors, and when Charkin heard who I was, he promptly appeared from behind the door and started blustering. Not wishing to stay for tea, I stuffed the paper firmly into his hands and departed, at last able truthfully to utter the words "see you in court".

The week before the trial was frantic. To add to the expected rush of preparation and study, Oxford's lawyers had evidently seen in my subpoenas a chance to lard on some nice fat costs. Atiyah instructed a different set of solicitors to get his subpoena set aside (annulled) on the grounds that he no longer possessed any of the relevant papers and that from 12th to 14th March he was to give three mathematics lectures in Geneva. In view of his Swiss engagement I agreed to the setting-aside, but his solicitors nevertheless pressed ahead with an application for a special hearing before Master Barratt that Friday. Glenn Black and Anne Smallwood then instructed yet another set of solicitors to apply similarly and to attend the same hearing, resulting in an absurd swarm of lawyers (each had a barrister too) descending on the court on the last working day before the trial. In his affidavit, Black contradicted what he had previously said on the telephone and denied that in 1985 lists of General Books were drawn up, while in hers, Smallwood swore that since my phonecall she had discovered that her confirmation of such lists' existence was, after all, mistaken. In the by now obligatory tell-tale slip, her typed "I have since ascertained that..." had been deleted and replaced by a handwritten "I understand that..." Was there no-one in Oxford prepared to admit the obvious?

On the strength of these affidavits, Master Barratt duly set aside the three subpoenas with costs, and the new Oxford solicitors duly sent me their bills: in three days they claimed to have notched up just £8,624.67. The pretence that they were acting for clients independent of the University was soon exposed when one of the solicitors inadvertently let slip on the telephone that he was "awaiting instructions from Walton Street". The University itself later tried to base its application for security of costs of my appeal upon these supposedly independent bills. Tim Heald, who at the time compiled the *Pendennis* column in *The Observer*, had got wind of my subpoena-serving antics and took an interest in the story, publishing in that Sunday's edition a colourful piece headlined "Platonic labours lost, and no love". Flatteringly, he puffed *Making Names* as "a modern Platonic dialogue" and the action as "a connoisseur's case". It was some consolation for the lost subpoenas, and I was pleased to see that Mark Warby brought a copy with him to court on the Monday; no doubt he had scrutinised it carefully for libel.

On Wednesday March 7th, Margaret Goodall served an eleventh-hour witness-statement giving a new, perfectly Alice-in-Wonderland account of her paperwork and procedures (something about compiling lists and then throwing them away), the main intelligible point in which was that at some time since 1985 (again, she did not say when) they had changed. Her one other intelligible revelation was that, in contradiction of her statement of a month earlier, in 1985 she had after all *not* taken the minutes of the Delegates' meetings (again, she did not say who had). There was by now no time for further investigations or applications; Oxford's kindergarten games had continued right to the courtroom door.

13

Malcolm and the Trolleymen

ON THE EVENING of Friday 9th March I was informed that, provided I had
no objection, the case would be assigned to Gavin Lightman Q.C., then a
deputy judge of the High Court, who as it happened lectured on law for
two days a week at Merton College, Oxford. (Soon afterwards, it was
Gavin Lightman who conducted the investigation into Arthur Scargill's
handling of the NUM's finances.) I was asked by the court officers if I had
any problem with this (the alternative was postponement), and on being
advised that he was a very sharp and thorough lawyer, said no.

I should perhaps break off here to describe the physical circumstances in
which I now found myself. The barristers who normally do the High
Court talking of course all have fine chambers nestling tight around the
Strand, chambers equipped with case-law libraries, computerised
networks, colleagues, clerks, copiers and coffee machines; the quantities of
massive files and books which have to be at their disposal are humped
around the miles of corridors and stairways by solicitor and clerk
underlings. I, thanks to the generosity of my friends and barrister, enjoyed
some of these blessings, but still had to do a fair bit of heavy file-humping
to, from, and around London. Even an action as small as mine had generated
a set of five courtroom files each containing about 100 pages, not to
mention the quantity of lawbooks, authorities, Supreme Court Rules and
so forth with which one needs permanently to be armed. Further complete
file-sets had to be provided for the opposition, the judge and the witness-
box. For the appeal, another 100-page file was added to each set and
everything had to be in triplicate for the three judges, and by the damages
hearing, the mass of paper was probably doubled again. I soon discovered
why the minions wheeled the stuff around on carts. I conducted both the
trial and the appeal in a pinstripe suit specially purchased (an excellent fit)
from a Brighton Help the Aged shop, some ancient white shirts, a new silk
tie and a pair of Polish (but unpolishable) rubber-soled shoes; my only
concession to style was a red-and-black Dennis badge pinned inside my
lapel bearing the motto "Who menaces wins". If I were ever to write a
film-treatment of the story, I think I'd suggest, Grisham-style, that it be
called *The Suit*.

Three memorable things happened on the opening morning of the trial. I and my girlfriend Liz arrived after a nerve-wracking taxi ride from our Hampstead bolt-hole hot-foot at the courtroom high in the modern Thomas More Building toward the northwestern corner of the Strand site. We were both seriously weighed down with bags of books and files, and I was anxiously trying to remember all the things I was supposed to be anxiously trying to remember, when we were greeted by a wonderful, gawky young Chancery clerk, who had evidently been studying the judge's papers. "The bastards, the bastards!" he whispered conspiratorially, "but don't you worry Mr Malcolm, you'll get 'em. *Planchè v. Colburn, Planchè v. Colburn, quantum meruit,* don't you worry... The bastards!" *Planchè v. Colburn* turned out to be a case from 1831 in which an author was commissioned to write a volume on Costume and Ancient Armour for a periodical series called *The Juvenile Library;* the author did a lot of work but then the publisher axed the series and the author never completed his volume as there was no point. The author sued successfully for his full fee, despite never delivering his manuscript. Not a bad try for a casual well-wisher, yet none of the lawyers had heard of the case. Dickens would have been proud of this barmy clerk, who became a strange source of morale throughout the trial.

The second odd encounter was with Henry Hardy, who was hovering around with Oxford's lawyers. I had seen him in Dillons and so recognised him, but he had never seen me. "Oh gosh, I always imagined you as tall and dark!" he exclaimed, stumping me completely. I think my reply was an apology for disappointing him (I am, or was then, medium and medium), but in my mind chimed Quentin Crisp's sad, gay "But there was no tall dark man". Hardy himself was of medium height and light-medium build, with a neatly-trimmed beard and moustache and gold-rimmed spectacles; I guess that if I had not previously seen him, he too would have presented a surprise, nondescript mismatch with his pleasantly distinguished telephone-voice. The third surprise was that after my opening remarks and Lightman's confirmation that the question of remedy, if any, should be decided separately, Mr Warby at once announced that Oxford was applying to scrap the defence it had been running for the past three years and to plead instead that Hardy had no authority, either actual or ostensible, to bind the University or its Press to any contract.

This, of course, amounted suddenly to tossing three years and fifty grand's worth of litigation up into the air as if it were just so much confetti. "Okay, so perhaps Hardy did seem to agree a contract with you, but if so it was a personal, fraudulent one that does not bind Oxford. Go on, sue him instead." This, I think, was the gist of their new suggestion, made at about 10.30 on the opening morning of the trial. As the confetti settled around the courtroom, the purposes of the move became clear. Their first intent, obviously, was simply to wrong-foot my ignorance of the wholly different area of law that would now be raised: master-servant relationships, warranties of authority, passing off, fraud, and God knows what else. On the afternoon of the first day, Oxford's honourable, professional, gentlemanly Mr Warby handed me the references (just the references mind, not the authorities themselves) to various obscure cases culled from some ancient Lloyd's shipping reports, the chief of which, as I recall, had to do with the sale, subject to a satisfactory survey, of one of the River Thames' bulk quicklime barges. Fortunately some dusty, late-afternoon legwork in the Lincoln's Inn law library unleashed the requisite slurry of paper.

Oxford's second purpose was to turn the whole long betrayal into a purely personal one perpetrated by Hardy (not far off the truth, as was by now clear) and to let the mighty University and all else who sailed in her slimy barge off my firmly-embedded anchor. Again, a frantic telephone-session with Richard White in the luncheon adjournment returned me to the courtroom unfed, but armed with the necessary precedents and authorities. I pointed out that if there had been any validity in this line, Oxford had had over three years to raise it, that it still had not settled the form of its proposed new defence or testimony, and that if these were allowed, I should be granted an adjournment at the University's expense to make the necessary preparations (this would have meant Oxford paying virtually all of my costs of the action to date). The University duly balked at the prospect of an adjournment with costs, and on the second morning Lightman duly dismissed its application to run its new defence. Round One to me.

Oxford's failure to get its new defence on the rails did much more than simply waste most of the first day of the trial and lose its costs. It looked, for a start, like a tacit admission that there was a contract here of some sort, but one which failed, at least against the University, for alleged *technical* reasons. Also, it demonstrated to Lightman exactly what I had been up against for the past three years. Besides the absurd, disreputable lateness of the ploy and its obvious desperation (it looked an exceedingly unpromising line in any case), this new defence would stand a chance of working only if the congenitally-forgetful Hardy suddenly, three years late, had an entirely fresh and detailed recollection of some newly-asserted phantom exchange with me. He now had to testify that he had *told me* that he had no authority, and that the Delegates would have had to approve the book, or whatever it was that the new defence required, adding that he had only just remembered the fact. Warby explained that Hardy would be amending his statement accordingly, and further admitted that Hardy had also suddenly at last remembered that he had at some point (he could not remember when or how) *lost* his 20th May telephone notes, thereby rendering his 1989 affidavit perjured. The judge expressed amazement, and from the outset Hardy's witness-value was zero.

Paradoxically, Oxford's new defence depended heavily too upon a very peculiar interpretation of my pre-contractual telephone conversation with Hardy of 26th April 1985. Far from arguing that there was no contract because our key exchange was on the telephone and not in writing, Oxford was now suggesting the exact opposite, and to boot relying on telephone evidence — the earlier tape — that *I* had supplied. Another odd consequence was that it suggested *prima facie* that the Delegates had approved *Making Names* back in April or May, so Lightman at once had to order the production of yet more Delegates' agendas and minutes, which later proved revealing. So there, on the first morning, were Oxford's key witness and its lawyers scrabbling around with cobbled and recobbled bits of testimony, odd paragraphs and sentences, trying to fit bits of paper into their statements this way and that so that the new defence might run. To Warby's mounting irritation, various bungled drafts were actually tried and abandoned in the courtroom, but none even began to make sense and Oxford's move inevitably descended into farce. I can only guess what impression this spectacle made on Lightman.

More seriously, it seemed eloquently to illustrate Oxford's whole approach to the action. No-one ever asked what was actually true, what had actually been said, written, meant or committed. Their questions were always of the form: how can we present so-and-so? Or: what if we claimed such-and-such? Suppose we argued that he meant this here, and that she meant the other there? They saw the evidence, the key passages of conversation or correspondence, merely as so many bits of text to be idly cut-and-pasted around a computer-screen, regardless of their chronological order or logical sense, as if they were just the items dealt out for some detached word-play exercise. It was, by turns, eerie, chilling and rather sad, like witnessing a stroke victim's gradual loss of linguistic coherence.

In a bizarre correspondence years later, I asked Hardy if anyone at OUP or his own solicitor had at the time explained the consequences for him personally if Oxford's attempt to run its new defence in conjunction with some new version of his witness-statement had been successful. (Lightman had publicly explained the implications for me and had pointedly asked Oxford's lawyers if they really were sure they wanted to pursue it.) Hardy replied that nothing of that sort had ever been explained to him, or at least that he could not remember such an explanation. Yet as I understand it, if the University's move had worked, the whole of my claim and its costs would (a) probably at once have succeeded, at least in principle, and (b) have fallen entirely on Hardy's shoulders and would almost certainly have bankrupted him, job, North Oxford house, Volvo and all. The cynicism and vindictiveness of Oxford's scheme to pit me against my chief convert were almost as breathtaking as Hardy's lame naïvety in acceding to it.

Tactically, it seemed an odd move too, for it would have thrown the question of whether or not the Delegates had approved *Making Names* right into the centre of the legal stage. Although Oxford sensed that this was the one point which I might never be able absolutely to prove, the new defence would inevitably have introduced all the witnesses and evidence that their lawyers were most anxious to keep out of the frame, that of the Delegates themselves. The subpoenees who had been spared appearance in court, the numerous Delegates' transcripts confirming the existence of *lists* of General Books, the subsequent bundles of new evidence, perhaps even the Vice-Chancellor of the University, all would have been dragged into the spotlight. Here we see also the systematically ambivalent role of the Delegates becoming OUP's fundamentally crippling problem: one moment their staff and lawyers regard and pass them off as "a body of distinguished old gentlemen who meet once a year" or as "the shareholders in a company", the next they cast them as being responsible for every publishing decision.

Another point to make is that if Oxford's application and defence had both succeeded (that is, if it had been allowed to plead its new defence and this had later been upheld by the court), the precedent that would thereby have been set would, again as I understand it, at a stroke have invalidated most if not all author-publisher contracts in existence. I can't imagine that there are many authors or authors' agents who when they negotiate with publishers do not do so with editors of some sort. It may be that when formal contracts are issued, they are signed by higher level officers, managing or finance directors or whomever, but all the negotiations about what the published book is to be, the terms which give any contract its specificity as to "the work" commissioned, can only be with the publisher's editorial staff. If Oxford had successfully argued that its senior General Books editor of eight years standing had insufficient authority in law to bind his press, then hardly a contract in the land would be worth tuppence. Again, did no-one at Oxford stop to ponder the implications of this preposterous line? Or did they just not care, so long as they kept me at bay for another month or two, and kept my money running out to the lawyers?

14

The Trial

O N THE SECOND DAY, once Oxford's new defence application had been dismissed, I returned to the analysis of my contractual exchange with Hardy, and in the afternoon, as my own only witness, I took to the box to be cross-examined by Warby. Like all the witnesses' testimony, mine was tape-recorded by the court, but tellingly, when the case went on to appeal, Oxford ordered the expensive accredited transcription not of *my* evidence but of only its own, so for years afterwards I had no official record of what I said, only Liz's abbreviated notes. Recently, by chance, I learnt that some time *after* their Court of Appeal defeat, Oxford, with its customary perverse extravagance, *did* order the transcription of my evidence, but without ever telling me or using it. I have now obtained a copy of the transcript, and reading it seven years later is a strange, unnerving experience, like viewing an old, previously unknown film of oneself. The general tenor of the exchanges confirms my own hazy memory of Warby being completely flummoxed and having no useful questions to ask, but in a strange way, by its very emptiness, this documentary record of his long, limp, futile effort perhaps provides the case's most chilling read of all.

I had recounted the whole story accurately and truthfully in my statement, and Warby cross-examined me on hardly a single aspect of it. His main question was how long it took to turn or change an answerphone cassette when it ran out. The answer was a few seconds, as demonstrated by the virtually continuous flow of the transcripts, but his only hope was to try to insert into one of these chinks Hardy's mythical, freshly-recollected exchanges about his non-authority. This was another legacy of Oxford's aborted defence-switch: having re- and re-re-drafted his statement on the opening morning to try to fit it in with OUP's new line, Hardy could hardly then retract his changes when the application was disallowed: Warby was stuck with them, like an embarrassed juggler. But the recordings were obviously complete, our deal was confirmed by the correspondence and by OUP's internal documents, and Hardy's fresh 'conditions' would anyway have made a perfect nonsense of our original negotiation. (Oxford must have realised this, for no-one ever bothered to inspect the tapes.) Warby's feeble line of attack was soon cut short by Lightman.

Warby's only other attempt was to argue that Hardy's "provided the revised script is no worse than the original" condition could not have been a contractual one because all opinions about a written work's quality are entirely *subjective*. What an extraordinary line for any publisher ever to take, I mused, let alone for Oxford to be taking here, as I tried dreamily to extrapolate its legal consequences. (I imagined a snowstorm of shredded literary criticism and exam papers blowing bleakly over the rubble of the University's dynamited English faculty buildings.) In fact, as I pointed out, most of Hardy's requirements — the twenty percent length-cut, the conversations' accurate timings, adherence to OUP's house-style — were thoroughly measurable, *ob*jective criteria, all of which I had fulfilled. I don't think Warby had expected his new 'too subjective' defence to meet with much resistance, and when it did so he quickly speeded it aside, but now perhaps it deserves a moment's more attention. The transcription confirms it: at this point in their historic defence of academic integrity, the legal representatives of Oxford University solemnly, publicly argued that *all opinions as to writings' merits are subjective and therefore idle.*

Presumably this would extend to all music, to all fine art and sculpture, to all novels, plays and poetry, to subjects like history, sociology and politics, to philosophy (of course), and perhaps even to the very sciences. So was the University by this extreme subjectivist philosophy now going to legislate itself out of existence and finally admit its city to be no more than a grand souvenirs shop? Besides, where would this new dogma have left OUP's own *Memoranda's* opening "subject to our approval of the script" clause, or its current defence that *Making Names* had failed some imaginary test of further approval? I had by this time come fully to accept that the opinions of great intellectual arbiters like Alan Ryan could legitimately change and back and change again all within a coffee-break, but now even such momentary 'evaluations' as his were apparently formally to be conceded worthless whims. Well, I suppose it made a kind of sense: this was Academia after all, where ideas are only *toyed with*, and where all other notions — fairness, honesty, the truth — had so far proved very 'subjective' indeed. Anyway, whatever the latest campus fashion, by the end of the afternoon Warby had scored nothing but own goals, though I should add that this is not to say that he was in any way incompetent, or that any other barrister could have done better. What had become abundantly clear was that Oxford had never had a proper argument to raise.

The next day, Wednesday, was set for my cross-examination of Oxford's six-strong task force. I had passed a largely sleepless night in Hampstead going over their reams of implausible and conflicting statements, amendments and affidavits. It had been accepted that they should be questioned in each other's absence so that they could concoct no impromptu corroboration, but I had no say as to the order in which they were to appear, which was at Oxford's lawyers' discretion and at the various individuals' convenience. This made it rather hard to plan a strategy, for what one asked one witness would often depend upon the answers previously extracted from the others; the best I could do was to prepare various floating lines of inquiry and leave the rest to improvisation.

Liz and I arrived at the court, as usual file-laden and breathless, to find quite a knot of people on the landing. Besides the lawyers and some of Oxford's witnesses, my parents had arrived for the show, along with one or two friends and supporters who popped in and out during the day. We overheard that there was consternation lest Sir Roger Elliott and Richard Charkin should meet, and that logistical manoeuverings were being planned so as to prevent their paths from crossing; it seemed that having me as a common enemy was not effecting any reconciliation between these two doyens of British publishing. Charkin arrived huffing and puffing about time being money, him being so busy, important meetings to attend, how inconvenient it all was, so forth. "Oh bad luck" I replied, whilst flicking through his strangely empty diaries.

To Oxford's chagrin, the 'no-conferring' ground rule was confirmed and its witnesses excluded from the room to await their turns, though Lightman did order that since Ivon Asquith's affidavits related only to document discovery, he should stay in case needed, but be admitted to one of the side benches. The parade began. It was decided that first up would be Sir Roger Elliott himself, hustled in, aCharkinwise, wearing an outfit of traditional academic chic: heavy green hessian jacket, shiny olive tie, huge bushy eyebrows and undisciplined wire hair. From the start, his demeanour and body-language spoke as though he and Lightman were natural allies jointly facing a hoodlum. He used an exaggerated, waffly Oxford drawl with the occasional final-vowel flourish music-hall comedians used to use when lampooning toffs; he obviously thought he sounded immensely authoritative. Lightman, I was pleased to observe, was not noticeably impressed, and remained even-toned and incisive throughout. I had not expected Elliott to appear first, and logically his testimony fitted last, so all I could do, having established that he must know all there was to know on the subject, was to plunge straight into the arcane questions about how the Delegates' decisions were recorded. Elliott had already filed several implausible statements, and it had come down to a question of when the procedure of not listing General Books had changed to one of listing them. I had assumed that he would have a well-rehearsed answer to this obvious first inquiry.

To my amazement, he did not. Instead, he denied any knowledge of when the procedure had changed. Immediately, this was quite absurd: how then did he know that it had changed at all? How did he know that it hadn't changed *before* 1985? His second answer was still crazier: he knew by looking at the minutes. *But the minutes of 1985 repeatedly referred to lists of General Books; studying just the minutes revealed no procedural change of any kind!* Within a few opening exchanges, and without even having tried, I felt as though I had the magnet man on the ropes. For some moments he was gasping, his bottom jaw wagging but emitting no sound, his eyes blinking uncontrolled from behind their shrubbery. Obviously these are subjective memories and impressions which go unrecorded on the transcript, but I have several witnesses to them. His cross-examination descended into farce:

> **Elliott:** General Publications were then [in 1985] listed and dealt with...
> **Malcolm:** You just used the phrase "listed and dealt with".
> **Elliott:** Yes, well, the answer is they were not listed.
> **Malcolm:** So in fact by the word "list" you were not meaning "list",
> you were meaning "bundle of papers"?
> **Elliott:** That is right.
> **Malcolm:** And bundles of individual sheets are described in the agenda
> paper as "lists"?
> **Elliott:** That is described, as you point out — perhaps not entirely
> appropriately — as "a list." I think we are getting slightly confused about
> the nature or the meaning of the word "list." I honestly do not think that
> this matter of whether it is called a list or not is significant... so forth.

Impaled on his listless hook, Elliott had to go on to say that *never* in 1985 did the minuted word 'list' mean list, under whichever agenda heading it appeared, be it General Publications, College Publications, Educational and ELT (English Language Teaching) Publications, or OUP (USA) Publications, despite the fact that the words 'list' or 'listed' occurred no less than *eight* times in the 23rd July minutes alone. I was about to release him from further questioning, when suddenly I remembered that Oxford had been ordered to bring to the courtroom the Delegates' original typed minute book, a huge leather-bound volume which included all of their meetings up to 1988. I had a hunch and asked for its production, rapidly skimming through the later entries. Sure enough, the most recent minutes used exactly the same terminology, with equally frequent use, and occasional absence of the word 'list', as the 1985 minutes, indicating absolutely no change in the procedure, and certainly no change evident just from inspection of the minute-book. Elliott's testimony was demonstrably worthless, even on the subject of the Delegates' practices. Lightman immediately got the point and ordered that the recent minutes be photocopied and added to the evidence file.

Lightman then himself asked Elliott to clarify the distinction between the Academic Publications, which individually had to be approved by the Delegates, and the "listed but not listed" General Books like *Making Names*, which were only 'reported' to them. Elliott had evidently been waiting for this one and came out with a long jargon rigmarole which featured the intriguing new concept "retroactive scrutiny"; despite Elliott's heartiest, breathiest upward flourish of its final vowel, this splendid phrase hung in the courtroom air stubbornly undigested, entering only our own private language of treasured Oxfordese. More semantic muddle ensued over what Elliott meant by the word 'list', but whatever it was, he was absolutely emphatic: "Nothing is ever listed in any other way!" He also admitted that he could not at this distance remember what decisions were made with respect to individual books, and Lightman at once pointed out that therefore he could not himself testify as to the fate of *Making Names*, one way or the other. Elliott conceded that this was the case, and it became apparent that no useful, or even intelligible testimony was ever likely to issue from the lips of this grand custodian of our language's great dictionary. Lightman then embarked on some polite interrogation of his own which yielded perhaps the most revealing exchange of the day:

Lightman: Sir Roger, if you heard that some responsible officer of the Press had given a commitment to an author that the Press would publish his work, would you feel concerned if, at some later date, that commitment having been given, it were withdrawn?
Elliott: Editors are not allowed to give such commitments.
Lightman: Supposing the individual in this case had the authority to do so, would you be concerned about it?
Elliott: Well, I would be concerned if he had given such a commitment since he had no authority to give such a commitment.
Lightman: And that would be the basis of your response?
Elliott: That would be the basis of my response because all our editors are quite clear that, while of course they must enter into negotiations with authors about their books and they must obviously be encouraging about the books, they are not in a position to enter into a commitment or sign a contract. They have to get Delegates' approval and the contracts are signed by the head of the division after that approval has been given.
Lightman: Now Mr Malcolm's case is that he received a commitment. There is in fact, on the pleadings of this case, no defence raised that the individual concerned did not have the authority; that is not an issue in the case. It is accepted that if Mr Hardy did in fact enter into a contract with Mr Malcolm, then there is a contract irrespective of any absence of authority. Against this background, would you feel concerned if a commitment were given by Mr Hardy to Mr Malcolm that he would publish and was subsequently reneged on?
Elliott: Well, I would be concerned of course, because it would be a serious breach of discipline within the Press.

Lightman: And also a serious injustice to the author?
Elliott: (long pause) I can see that it could be an injustice to the author; it would depend upon how long it was before the matter was put straight.
Lightman: Thank you. Are there any further questions you want to ask?
Malcolm: No, my Lord.

During this choice little exposé I felt a gentle surge of satisfaction as Lightman's incisive questioning quietly took over from my own. As Elliott, eyebrows awag, sank inexorably and quite unwittingly into his dark moral mire, all became released; I had been waiting for something like this to happen for over three long years. It was, I suddenly also saw, that special sort of moment which justifies all the expense and paraphernalia of actual courtroom proceedings. Elliott's blithe, unrehearsed blundering, his deafness to Lightman's thrice-repeated prompt, was as dramatic and unexpected, in its way, as the unlikely witness-box confessions frequently wrung from accused murderers at the dénouements of cheap American thrillers; I guess that if I had seen it on TV, I would have judged it too implausible to pass for real life. When the room's disbelief had settled, Warby disconsolately re-examined his paymaster on the new puzzle revealed by the recent entries in the minute book mentioning 'lists', but OUP's Chief Executive, longest-serving Delegate and ten-year Finance Committee Chairman could of course explain and remember nothing. He apologised and left.

Next came Margaret Goodall. She was a large, middle-aged impressive-looking woman, but appeared almost rigid with fear: her walk was stiff and halting, her jaw clenched, her teeth chattering and her delivery stilted. She must have wondered how on earth she, a secretary quite uninvolved with this pestilential author-person, had ever have come to be trapped into this ghastly courtroom grilling. The reason, of course, was the ever-murkier mysteries of the Delegates' Note and book-approval system, mysteries her own affidavit and witness statement had only deepened. Her testimony was little more help: the procedure being alleged to have applied in 1985 was by now so complex and absurd I doubt if anyone in the courtroom, including Goodall herself, any longer had the remotest idea even of what it was *supposed* to be; Warby was looking steadily blanker and blanker. The only certainty, repeated *ad nauseam*, was that, despite the minutes' frequent use of the word 'list', there were no lists, and that all General Book approvals went unrecorded.

We did at length learn the identity of the man who had, after all, taken the Delegates' minutes in 1985, a retired editor by the name of John Cordy. Goodall explained that he used to write the books' titles and decisions in longhand on the top-copy agenda paper. I at once asked Oxford's lawyers to produce some of the pre-July top-copies ordered by Lightman, and, sure enough, although these carried handwritten notes about which Delegates had been present, there was not a single mark on them about any book decisions. Again Lightman ordered photocopies to be added to the evidence, and again a further twist was added by the increasingly tense Goodall to her already impossibly tortured story: this time it was something about there being different sets of top-copy or 'master' agenda papers, some of which were thrown away, others not, and so on and so on. It was a palpable relief when, released from her agony, she almost ran from the courtroom; I imagine that once outside it she must have wept bitterly. But for all of Oxford's copious bureaucracy, and its witnesses' acres of testimony, the court still had no way of ascribing any meaning to the now-famous entry "the other titles tabled were approved", and was no closer to discovering whether these "other titles" numbered one, three hundred, or ten thousand, let alone to identifying any of them.

It was the turn of Nicola Bion, who had been characterised to me by another OUP author as "captain of hockey". I had seen her, of course, in cahoots at Dillons, so I was expecting her stern, almost aggressive countenance; what I was not expecting was to find her marching up to the witness-box heavily pregnant, I guess by seven or eight months. She was clearly angry and affronted at having to answer to this troublesome unknown, but made a great effort to stay cool and steely in her responses, with her pregnancy somehow adding to her air of self-righteousness. Her first interesting admission was that OUP's editorial meetings *were*, after all, minuted, at least in respect of the decisions taken at them; this had repeatedly been denied in Oxford's affidavits, so seemed at once to indicate yet another important failure of discovery. At this point in her cross-examination though, there was some frantic semaphore from Oxford's lawyers to my left, and Bion began to back-track and waffle that only *some* of the decisions were recorded. She then gave an account of the stormy 17th July meeting at which Charkin had axed *Making Names*; she could remember clearly some aspects of what had happened but was curiously forgetful of others. Bion, Charkin and Hardy all gave differing accounts of this meeting, even in respect of who had attended it and who had presented the book. Bion then reiterated her own-goal assertion that she had seen the top-copy Delegates' Note in October 1989, when in fact it was not discovered at the Press until January 1990. An examination of this point demonstrated to Lightman the relevance of Ivon Asquith's first affidavit which had verified that it had been sent to the Delegates *before* Charkin's intervention, and also the significance of its elusive top copy. There was more surreal lexicographical confusion:

Malcolm: The date of posting of the Delegates' Note has been verified
on oath by Ivon Asquith as 16th July 1985.
Bion: Posting?
Malcolm: The date of posting.
Bion: Posting where?
Malcolm: So the meeting [of 17th July] took place *after* the Delegates'
Note had been posted.
Bion: Could you make it clear what you mean by "posting"?
Malcolm: Could *you*?
Bion: Put into the post?

At this point, Lightman decided that, after all, Asquith should testify on
these matters, and he was ordered from the courtroom under the no-
conferring rule. As he was escorted to the door, head-shaking and fretful,
he muttered testily to Oxford's lawyers, Oliver-Hardy-style, "*Now* look
what you've got me into!" Lightman then asked to see the top copy of the
Delegates' Note. Mr Shaw duly scrabbled for it in his file, but at first
passed me only another photocopy, bearing no correcting fluid. When I
rejected this, he actually had to switch it, in front of Lightman, for the real
thing, which Lightman then passed on to me for confirmation. Lightman
promptly stamped a special court label on the troublesome paper and had
the clerk lodge it, once and for all, on the court file, where I trust it still
remains. Having at last reached the end of the tippex trail, Lightman asked
Warby to explain all the D19 anomalies to me during the luncheon
adjournment; Warby began "I don't expect you to believe this, and I don't
understand a word of it myself, but my instructions are that..." After the
trial I requested Dallas Brett to commit these 'instructions' to paper; their
resulting letter is another of the case's obscure little delights.

After lunch, I turned to Bion's rejection letter, inferring from Oxford's
gaping lack of such evidence that its opening sentence "I've now had the
reports on your revised typescript and discussed them with colleagues"
was simply untrue. I invited Lightman to inspect the pristine, unopened
script (he said he had already studied it), and Bion rose angrily out of her
seat in protest, demanding a right to retort to my slur upon her integrity.
Then, in a delicious twist, Oxford's own Mr Warby re-examined her and
asked her to confirm that the letter still expressed her *bona fide* opinion of
Making Names. Her righteous indignation by now at full throttle, she
repeated emphatically that it most certainly did, not realising that she was
thereby also confirming that my second draft was "undoubtedly an
improvement" and so irrevocably closing off Oxford's last remaining
'condition-precedent' escape-route.

Asquith returned. He was a tall, lanky man with long lanky arms, dangly hands and a long, gaping sort of face with a receding chin. He looked something like a deep-water lantern-fish, only without a lantern. His voice and delivery were of the 'Oxford imperious' school, though on this occasion his fidgeting, grey-suited form looked anything but magisterial; he was obviously in extreme discomfort, and when questioned on the reliability of his affidavits, he quickly reddened. He had first been dragged into the litigation, remember, to verify Oxford's second list of documents, and had been required to distinguish between their originals and photo-copies, dividing roughly fifty-fifty. Asquith had initially sworn, correctly, that the Delegates' Note was a photocopy, and that its original had been posted [by inference to Mrs Goodall] on 16th July and then copied and circulated to all the Delegates, but his story had since changed. Warby and Lightman took up the challenge:

> **Warby:** Do you understand that the original of the document listed at D19 was at the date of this list no longer in OUP's possession?
> **Asquith**: I would not know whether the original was in OUP's possession, because that particular Note to the Delegates was not sent to the Delegates.
> **Lightman:** How do you know it was not sent to the Delegates?
> **Asquith:** By all the accounts, and...
> **Lightman:** You have no direct knowledge?
> **Asquith:** I was not at the editorial meeting.
> **Lightman:** I see. You are really only concerned to answer questions in relation to matters within your direct personal knowledge... What you are really being asked is why you say you had a copy as opposed to the original. Is that right, Mr Warby?
> **Warby:** Yes, my Lord. I am grateful for that assistance.
> **Asquith:** I do not know why, my Lord, it would be a copy rather than the original.
> **Lightman:** Did you go through the schedule with your solicitors?
> **Asquith:** Yes, I did.
> **Lightman:** Did you see item D19 referred to as "Copy letter to all Delegates from Nicola Bion?"
> **Asquith:** I am afraid, my Lord, that I was not distinguishing clearly between what was a copy and what was an original at the time.
> **Warby:** At the time you swore your affidavit, did you have any knowledge of your own as to whether the Delegates' Note had or had not been posted?
> **Asquith:** My understanding was that it had not been posted.
> **Warby:** So what would you say as to the accuracy of your statement at page 16.4 that it had been posted?
> **Asquith:** It depends...
> **Warby:** (Slowly) Did you believe at the time you swore this affidavit, on 3rd August 1988, that the Delegates' Note of 16th July 1985 had been posted?
> **Asquith:** No I did not.

It was little wonder that Asquith was in an agony to be released, and none at all that Lightman later adjudged his affidavits "calculated to mislead."

Richard Charkin was an aggressive, self-important bloke, large going on obese, and as blunt and direct as the very word 'oaf' (though in fact he affirmed). His braggadocio soon got his lawyers into trouble when he recalled seeing a note on *Making Names* from Angela Blackburn to Hardy which he remembered as: "Here is a load of rubbish. God this is awful but, Henry, you might like to see it before it is rejected." No such note was in evidence, and Charkin's casual revelation (or invention) of it at once plunged Oxford into yet another discovery-muddle. His replies on the matter of the missing editorial meeting minutes were equally revealing:

> **Malcolm:** These important decisions [book approvals, the establish-
> ment of print-runs, prices etc.] were presumably recorded somewhere
> in some way?
> **Charkin:** No, I tried not to. It was part of my view that we had far too
> much paper in the organisation, and that wherever possible we did not
> keep minutes... It was my general instruction that there should not be
> minutes... I did not like anything that resulted in the proliferation of
> paper... [a good joke uttered in a courtroom by then knee-deep in the
> stuff, mostly emanated from OUP] I was worried by the length of the
> [Hardy/Malcolm] letters... One way we keep our overheads down is to
> avoid longwinded authors.

In his witness statement Charkin had proclaimed: "On 17th July 1985 I rejected *Making Names* using three criteria that I use to decide on books: profitability, quality and author." Given that he had had seen only the PPF, that this indicated good (green) profitability, and that he knew nothing about me or my book, I asked him where this left his 'three criteria'. The great professional had obviously been looking forward to this moment and was ready with some more nice patter:

> "This will all sound terribly self-serving... I am in the business of
> publishing, and have been in the business of publishing for a very long
> time. I am not in the horse-racing business and I am not in the Stock
> Exchange. One of the things you learn — and you do not always get it
> right, you sometimes get it wrong — is you make judgments..."

"You tell 'em guv," I thought. Another fine moment came when Charkin, having assured Lightman that "as it happens, we care about authors at OUP, and I still care about authors," further taunted that he and Hardy had been worried (smirking at me) because after his rejection of *Making Names* I was threatening to commit suicide. He seemed to be trying to turn the courtroom into a bear-pit, but instinct restrained me from rising to his bait. The tapes of my undisclosed conversations with Hardy later demonstrated that the nearest we had ever come to morbidity was when Hardy raised the possibility of Charkin being run over by a bus.

Charkin's role in the affair was, however, by then largely transparent, so there weren't any very interesting historical questions for him to answer. He had begun his witness statement with the grammatically novel but important pronouncement "Editors commission a book." Obvious enough, but I had found this an odd assertion from someone who wanted to argue that Hardy had had no contractual authority at OUP. Charkin's statement had also been ambiguous (canny?) about the circulation of the Delegates' Note, so I goaded him to absolute certainty on the question, and then confronted him with his own "I don't know if this particular Note was forwarded, but I don't think that it was". "That's right... absolutely certain... that's a different point..." he spluttered. The detail of Charkin's account of his spat with Hardy was, as usual, implausible (he had not, he said, asked Hardy whether or not the predated Delegates' Note in the file had been sent), but obviously he was never going to admit that the Delegates had in fact approved the book. In conclusion I did my own bit of bear-baiting by quoting and applauding a statement he had made in *The Bookseller* magazine lamenting the inadequacy of publishers' negotiating techniques; he duly rose out of his seat to protest, but was restrained by Lightman.

Charkin's most devastating display came during the exchanges that followed. Once I had sat down, he relaxed, and Lightman gently invited him to elucidate a rather sinister remark his keen eyes had spotted in Charkin's internal correspondence with Hardy. After Hardy's successful disciplinary appeal, Charkin had formally notified him of the withdrawal of his Stage Three Warning, adding:

> "If we were to tighten up the procedure such that matters like this could be seen in terms of black and white, I feel we would lose more than we would gain."

Once again I felt that inner glow, as Charkin's chest almost audibly expanded and he seized another chance to pontificate:

> **Charkin:** It was to do with the timing. In general publishing, particularly where you are dealing with literary agents — as you sometimes do, not in this case but sometimes — you actually have to think on your feet to a greater extent. Obviously in those cases one would try to get the

Delegates on your side 100 percent before you went ahead. So one of
the arguments at the disciplinary appeal was, "Well, we were doing our
thinking on our feet". If that is totally illegal, then it should be made
clear that we should never encourage authors. I was complaining that
they were encouraging too much, and the argument was, "Well, you
have to encourage a certain amount", and I agree.
Lightman: Is there is distinction between encouraging an author and
giving him a commitment?
Charkin: I think there is a distinction, but it is a very fine distinction.

So much for the pretence of a gentlemanly world. Here was now revealed
an explicit, deliberate, legally acute policy of tricking authors into doing
fruitless work. I don't know if any of the Court of Appeal judges later
found their way to this telling exchange, buried deep within the long
transcripts of trial evidence, but if so, I guess it may have been what
provoked Lord Justice Leggatt later to write "To suggest that Mr Hardy
intended to induce Mr Malcolm to revise the book by giving him a valueless
assurance would be tantamount to an imputation of fraud." Hardy's careful,
deniable use of the telephone, his charade of not having re-read my
'commitment' letter, his 'difficulty' in how to express OUP's 'decision' to
me, Oxford's obsessive, and repeatedly fantastical misuses of the word
'encouragement', all were now at once explained. No wonder that when
his turn came, Hardy's memory failed. *Caveat auctor.*

By now, it was mid-afternoon and I was tiring and my head beginning to
spin, with what on paper looked the most important scene still to come,
my confrontation with Hardy. (I imagine it is a routine ploy to have one's
most vulnerable witness appear as late as possible, so that the opposition's
questioning will by then be blunted by fatigue.) I need not have worried;
the day's promised main attraction turned out to be a bathetic anti-climax.
Hardy had already been quite discredited by his several dithering attempts
to amend his witness statement on the opening morning, and since then he
had spent most of the trial chattering to Oxford's solicitors, presumably
trying to hatch new strategies for them. I assume that his bosses had told
him: you got us into this mess, so you'd better bloody well get us out of it!
Often during the submissions, he was to be heard giggling and snickering
with Mr Shaw's Australian female assistant at the back of the courtroom. I
imagine that long before he took the witness-box he had come to cut a
mighty feeble figure with Lightman. Hardy's opening examination by
Warby set the tone:

Warby: [on Hardy's latest amendment] Having heard Mr Malcolm,
have you changed your mind about what took place?

Hardy: No. (Pause) Perhaps I should gloss that slightly. That still remains my recollection, but perhaps I should add that I am aware that recollections can be false...

Warby: [on the Delegates' Note] Do you know who composed the text?

Hardy: I believe that I composed it.

Warby: Can you recall when you wrote the manuscript addition?

Hardy: No.

Warby: Can you comment on its significance? What was it there for?

Hardy: I can make a guess, which I am willing to share with you, if that is permissible. [This elicited laughter from the courtroom and some polite sarcasm from Lightman.]

Warby: Would it be possible for a Delegates' Note to be forwarded and considered if no PPF had been signed?

Hardy: No.

Warby: Why not?

Hardy: Because... [35 words]... (pause) I think I should amend that... In fact, the procedures provide... [40 more words]... (pause) I think I should amend my reply. I am sorry about this... [162 more words]... So strictly speaking, the answer to your question is... yes.

With Hardy providing such rich entertainment at the hands of his own Q.C., it was not likely to require any razor-sharp questioning on my part to dismantle what remained of his credibility or story. And so it was: with only the gentlest of prompting, Hardy's tortured Oxfordese droned weakly on through the dying afternoon:

"...that was my surmise... I said when I made that answer that it was only a guess... I could not remember why I had written those words, but that was the only reason I could think of why I might have wished to do so... I have no recollection of when I put them on... My guess may be erroneous; it was the best answer I could give to Mr Warby's question... as to the completeness and accuracy of the transcript, I have no belief one way or the other... I have no belief as to the transcript's completeness. I do have a belief as to its accuracy... When I say I have a clear recollection, the clarity refers to the existence of the exchange, not to its detail..." and so on and so forth.

Far from being any sort of tense, testing duel, the day's predicted highlight was turning into a quiet, rather sombre spectacle, again something like a man's public nervous breakdown. When it came to Hardy's clash with Charkin, he could remember nothing, *absolutely* nothing. The courtroom fell silent, and solicitously, Lightman leant toward to the witness-box:

Lightman: Can I just ask you, has the whole of this incident really had rather a traumatic effect upon you?

Hardy: (quaveringly) It is one of the most disturbing experiences that
I have ever been through, my Lord. Perhaps one might speculate that
that is why I cannot remember any particular element of it in detail.
Lightman: It may well be.

Now firmly inside the hall of fractured mirrors that constituted the
remains of Hardy's 'memory', the twists and turns became ever more
byzantine. His explanation of his disciplinary correspondence was quite
giddying. As recounted, to adapt his statement to Oxford's new defence, at
the opening of the trial he had been obliged to have a 'fresh recollection' of
a conversation with me (he did not remember when) in which he had
warned me that the Delegates (he could not clarify which, or at what
stage) would have to approve *Making Names* (he did not say which version,
or when I was to have been told). No-one, of course, including Hardy himself,
could make any sense of this, and what (and all) he had in fact said to me
about the Delegates was in any case already in evidence (see page 19), but
his amendment now meant that he also had to explain why he had not
mentioned this point at the time in his disciplinary defence to Charkin (see
page 64), for it would have provided a complete answer to all of the
charges laid against him. In his witness-statement Hardy had written "I
was so shocked with the disciplinary action that I forgot to indicate, in
that letter that..." I cross-examined him on this strange explanation:

> **Malcolm:** Do you stand by that sentence?
> **Hardy:** I do. It was very stupid of me, but I think it was the result of
> the great shock I suffered when Mr Charkin told me that he was going
> to discipline me.
> **Malcolm:** So, here you are, in the middle of what you have just
> described as one of the most traumatic scenes in your life. Your career
> is possibly about to be terminated. You are facing a hearing before a
> panel who are going to decide whether you keep your job or not. You
> have to write a long defence in answer to Mr Charkin's charge. And
> you omit to mention the one fact — had it been a fact — that would
> have saved you or helped you?
> **Hardy:** It is a very remarkable omission and I have been kicking myself
> about it ever since.

Hardy continued publicly kicking himself, and even ended up denying any
recollection of things that had been said to him earlier in the trial, that is,
just two days beforehand. For a brief moment I actually caught myself
feeling sorry for the man. By about four o'clock though, a curious sense of
stasis, or emptiness, seemed to settle over the proceedings; Hardy's personality
lay around the room in sad little ruins; Warby and his aides had gone
uncharacteristically quiet; Lightman had clearly heard enough; and my

own questioning, though still in plentiful supply, had begun, even to me, to sound redundant. The horse was dead. At 4.15 I wound up, throat dry and thoroughly exhausted.

As I stumbled from the courtroom with Liz and my parents and we headed for the nearest pub, the daze of exhaustion was gradually overtaken by a daze of euphoria. It had been, for me, a great day; perhaps that greatest, performance-wise I had ever had. Of course none of Oxford's witnesses had admitted, straight out, that *Making Names* had been approved by the Delegates — they were never going to do that — but I do believe that with a mixture of luck, adroitness, and help from Lightman I had gone as far as I possibly could in discrediting their whole knavish pack. It seemed to have fallen out like a perfect hand of bridge, with every card in the right order, every uncertainty finessed, every trick that could have been taken, taken. Elliott had been reduced to a gibbering fool, Goodall to a nervous heap, Bion to a fuming rage, Asquith to a blundering liar, Charkin to a blustering cheat, and Hardy to a broken wreck. Mum gave us some money for champagne and we went to celebrate at the Savoy, getting ever-so-beautifully rat-arsed to the accompaniment of a fine ragtime pianist.

The next day, Thursday, was scheduled for both sides' final submissions, but Warby unexpectedly asked if he might first re-examine Hardy on a couple of points. I imagine they must have realised how pitiful his previous day's effort had been and hoped that he could somehow salvage some credibility with the judge; it was a forlorn hope and an even feebler attempt. All it did was provide a chance for Lightman to elicit from him further treasures like "I am not sure that I can answer that question without further guidance as to what you mean by 'a specific recollection', my Lord", and "The difficulty, my Lord, with assenting straight-forwardly to that as a likelihood is that the recollection that I have does not match the exchange". By the end, Hardy had uttered the words "I have no clear recollection" no less than *thirty* times. To everyone's immense relief and spared embarrassment, he finally left the witness-box at about 10.50. The final submissions commenced.

Warby began by producing a surprise four-page document he referred to as his 'skeleton'. Whereas Oxford's defence pleading was 'a bare traverse', an unelaborated "there was no contract", Warby's eleventh-hour skeleton was a mass of tiny, feathery bones. Its most abrupt changes of tack were (a) that the contract, if any, was conditional upon the Delegates' approval, now putting that vexed question at the very heart of the case, and (b) that the contract was incomplete because there had been no expressed agreement between myself and Hardy as to the book's print-run, format (hardback or paperback) and retail price. It also referred to various entirely new legal authorities. For over two hours Warby slogged on trying to get his rickety skeleton upright, with Lightman gently and carefully picking at each presented bone, leaving none standing. It was pointed out that even if there had been a 'condition precedent' of Delegates' approval, Oxford had not exercised it *bona fide*, for according to its own testimony the Delegates had never been presented with the book: *touché*. At one juncture, as Warby tried to echo Charkin's 'encouragement' jibe, Lightman retorted sharply: "So commitment now means *comfort* does it?" When it came to the print-run point, Lightman said "the number *is* difficult, how many to be awarded" and on more than one occasion he murmured loudly that he was having trouble with the word 'publication'. It began to sound to me as though in Lightman's mind the contract issue had been settled and that the question was becoming whether or not he could order OUP to print a specified run of *Making Names*, the top prize. With hindsight this was foolish, presumptuous optimism, but from a reading of the notes, it is clear that at this stage Warby shared my view of the way things were going, for towards the end of the morning he remarked resignedly: "Specific performance is now the real question."

In the afternoon, it was my turn. As to the contract's completeness and the questions of print-run, format and price, I pointed out that Oxford's exhibited *Memoranda of Agreement* (its printed forms, which nowhere, by the way, mention the word 'contract') demonstrated in their Clause 5 that these decisions are left exclusively to the publisher:

> "...the Publisher shall print and publish the Work in such editions as he considers appropriate... and shall have the sole control of all details of production advertising price sale and terms of sale of the Work..."

Lightman expressly assented to this (he had, I had discovered, a couple of books in print himself, so must have known something of the kind first-hand). If it was not common sense or knowledge, it was in any case enshrined in law by Lord Justice Bankes in 1921 in *Abrahams v. Reiach*:

> "The contract only imposes one obligation on the appellants [the publisher], namely, to publish. The question is what will satisfy that obligation? The appellants have a wide discretion; the time of publication, the number of copies to be printed, the price at which they are to be offered, and the form the book is to take are all left to their judgment..."

In short, it was already well established that an agreement to publish a certain text for a stated consideration (a royalty, say) and no more (that is, with no other details agreed) was a complete contract enforceable at law. Furthermore, as it happened, Hardy and I had said a surprising amount about all of these other matters and had come to a pretty good consensus on them, probably far better than first-time authors usually reach.

Then Oxford's phantom "Delegates' approval" condition was quickly disposed of; Lightman made it clear that he had never accepted its existence anyway. He reiterated that in Hardy's words of 20th May he found a firm commitment to OUP's publication of *Making Names*, provided the revised version was not worse than the first draft, which it uncontestedly was not. Lightman had also said, however, that he needed help with the meaning of the word 'publication', and I saw his problem: what exactly was OUP committed to doing? (This general question is addressed by literary lawyer Nicola Solomon in *The Author* of Summer 1991.) I tried to persuade him on the 'that is certain which can be made certain' principle, that in any order for specific performance he should rely on Hardy's intended figures in the PPF and Delegates' Note, but he objected that these had not been communicated to me at the time of the contract's formation. I recited Oxford's own dictionary definition of the word 'publication', which includes placing a book, once printed, before the public, and suggested that to allay any worries about the court having to enforce this latter aspect, the order should specify that Oxford deliver the printed books to me and that all further relations between us then be terminated (I am still unsure what is wrong with such a 'clean-break' remedy). The only problem that the court would need to resolve, I suggested, was a timetable. Lightman replied "We can work out a timetable after the order." Seeing that Elliott had returned to the spectators' benches, presumably in the hope of hearing Lightman's judgment, I concluded with a fierce attack upon the integrity and honour of OUP's entire hierarchy, re-enacting the Chief Executive's hilarious claim that 'list' means 'bundle', proposing my latest DIM-squad translation, and winding up at about 4.20. I think I may be forgiven for briefly imagining that I had won the case. That night, I even had a euphoric dream connecting the judge's name, Oxford's 'illuminatio' and certain, er, light-motifs that feature in *Making Names*; as I should have known, the room to which it awoke me was pitch-black.

15

Judgment Day

G AVIN LIGHTMAN started orating his drafted judgment at 11.00 on
Friday 16th March. Together with the ensuing exchanges on costs, his
conclusions, like the witnesses' evidence, were tape-recorded by the court, with
a transcript later becoming available from a professional court-accredited
company; the official version therefore cost some money and took some
time to obtain. In the meanwhile, all I had to go on (for example in discussions
on the merits of an appeal), were my and Liz's transcripts of Lightman's
oration. As will be explained, this circumstance generated a peculiar
irregularity which I have never fully understood. For true enthusiasts, the
judgment is posted complete on the Internet (see page 223), but most readers
will probably suffice with the following summary.

Lightman began by identifying three core issues: (1) Did the University, on
20th May 1985 make a commitment to me that they would publish
Making Names? (2) If made, did that commitment give rise to a legally
enforceable contract? and (3) If so, ought specific performance of it be
ordered? The University, he said, applied at the beginning of the trial to
raise another defence (4) that only the Delegates could authorise contracts,
and he swiftly explained (as above) why he had refused this late and dubious
application. He then went into the "largely common ground" facts of the
case, quoting verbatim my key paragraph of 24th March 1985, the pivotal
passages of 20th May and Hardy's confirmatory letters of 21st May and
14th June. He quoted at length the disciplinary proceedings between
Charkin and Hardy and also summarised the story about the Delegates'
Note and meeting of 23rd July, concluding from the evidence of Oxford's
witnesses (obviously he had to accept their six-fold corroboration) that the
Note had not been circulated. Turning to the three core issues, he at once
found himself perfectly satisfied that Oxford had given a clear commitment
to the publication of *Making Names*. He flatly dismissed Hardy's last-
minute recollection of a "Delegates' approval" condition and declared his
memory fatally traumatised: "I certainly cannot accept his evidence". He
rubbished Warby's suggestion that Hardy and Ryan had been committed
only to supporting the book before the Delegates, and pointed out that
even if this had been so, no such commitment was honoured. He repeatedly
concluded that an absolute, clear commitment was made, subject only to
the "improvement" condition, which he confirmed I had fulfilled.

Turning to the second core issue, he decided "with great regret" that Oxford's clear, absolute commitment did not give rise to an enforceable contract, for two reasons. It is here however, at this vital nub, that his orated draft and the later official version radically differ. Apparently, after the tape of a judgment is transcribed, the transcription is sent back to the judge to be initialled and for the correction of any mistakes, usually trivial spelling errors and suchlike. In this instance however, Lightman actually *rewrote* some of his reasoning, significantly altering his grounds for not finding a contract. Why this should have happened I do not know, and at the very least it suggests that he was deeply troubled by this section of his analysis. Unsurprisingly, the chief changes he made came at exactly the points on which I was later to win in the Court of Appeal. I will quote verbatim from the final, accredited judgment, marking his unorated addenda in square brackets:

> The first (reason) is that, in the case of a contract to publish a book, there are fundamental terms to be agreed beyond the matter of publication alone. These include the matters of royalty, the numbers to be published [and the form of publication (e.g. whether hardback or paperback). The parties may expressly agree these terms or they may do so impliedly by reason of some trade custom or usage or established course of dealing between the parties]. The parties may [also] agree a formula to resolve these matters, for example that they should be left to the publisher alone to decide in exercise of his judgment or discretion. (See, for example, *Abrahams v. Reiach* [1922] 1 K.B. 477.) But for there to be a valid contract these matters must be agreed or there must be agreed some formula for their resolution. In this case there is no agreement of the terms or a formula and there is no plea, evidence or suggestion of any trade custom or usage or any previous dealing between the parties. The internal documents of the university, setting out their proposals on these matters, since they were both tentative and never communicated to, let alone agreed by, Mr Malcolm, cannot furnish any comfort in this regard. The second reason is that the conversations of 26th April and 20th May both proceeded on the basis that there were matters to be agreed between the parties and incorporated in a contract... I reach this decision with great regret. I think that Mr Malcolm has been harshly and unfairly treated. I think he had a strong moral, though not a legal commitment. After reviewing these matters, it may be that the university will have second thoughts, or at least be minded to make some kind of amends, but I cannot in this court of law grant Mr Malcolm any relief.

Roughly speaking (though at the time I did not fully understand this part), Lightman found no contract because (a) Hardy and I had not expressly agreed the book's print-run or format, matters which (surely everyone knows) are rarely if ever stipulated in author-publisher agreements, and (b) our anticipated formal *Memorandum* had not been completed. Lightman's overlooking of Hardy's promised "fair royalty" seemed to be simply a mistake. I shall return to the implications of Lightman's analysis in due course, but for the moment will continue with the rest of his remarks. On the third core issue, the question of specific performance, he said:

> It is clear that in a proper case specific performance may be granted of a publishing contract. (See, for example, *Barrow v. Chappell & Co.* [1976] R.P.C. 355)... If the question had arisen, I would have declined to grant specific performance, for though I do not think that damages would be an adequate remedy and whilst I do think that it would be equitable to grant specific performance, I do not think it would be practicable to grant that remedy in this case... The enforcement of a continuing relationship [between Mr Malcolm and the university] is likely to be impossible... I would, however, have been minded to indicate that a substantial award of damages was called for to recompense Mr Malcolm for loss of the opportunity for him to enhance his reputation by securing the imprimatur of the Oxford University Press on his work. In all these circumstances and with great regret I must dismiss this action.

There followed an argument about the action's costs, which are normally awarded in full to the successful side. Warby at once half-conceded the time spent on Oxford's abortive new defence application, and admitted some of Oxford's irregularities over discovery of documents, including Asquith's and Hardy's false affidavits; there was an amusing moment when Lightman demonstrated to a visibly embarrassed Warby that even now, after all Oxford's lamentable failures, their very document *list* was still incorrect; Warby assured him that it was not, but was obliged to fumble amongst his papers, check it, and again concede. As he continued gamely to fight for the great University's money, Lightman at one point asked him, with a note of incredulity, "Your instructions are, notwithstanding the history of this matter or anything that I have said, that you are to press for an order for costs?" The body-language of Warby's reply that they were was touchingly apologetic.

Rather to my own surprise, I found that when it came to my turn to respond, I was still able to think and talk coherently. Somehow my disappointment at losing the trial stayed at bay, and did so for some days, perhaps in the way that accident-victims sometimes worry first about their spilt shopping, oblivious to their broken legs. I retrudged the well-worn discovery ground and also pointed out that if Alan Ryan had made a statement or sworn an affidavit early on, the whole course of the litigation, especially with respect to the Delegates' approval, might well have been different; his original intention to "gallop ahead" with *Making Names*, his presence at the relevant Delegates' meeting and his subsequent three-year silence, so far as I and my lawyers were concerned, all pointed the same way. "But you could have subpoenaed him to testify" Lightman replied. When I explained that Ryan had disappeared to America and that the difficulties of subpoenaing him from there had proved insurmountable, he held his head and groaned; simultaneously there was loud giggling from the back of the courtroom, where Hardy was once more ensconced with Mr Shaw's Australian assistant.

In addition to his particular remarks about Asquith and Hardy, Lightman castigated the University generally for its numerous failures of discovery:

> It seems to me that a matter that had figured very largely in Mr Malcolm's mind, and perfectly reasonably, and indeed permeated the whole way this case has been run, has been a concern that there has been a cover-up in regard to whether the Delegates did indeed approve publication of *Making Names*, and this was a perfectly fair inference to be drawn... It is fair to say that discovery has not been a signal success as far as Oxford is concerned... I have been concerned throughout this action by what appears to me to have been a failure by Oxford's solicitors to take sufficiently seriously their obligations in regard to discovery.

In the event, Lightman awarded Oxford seventy-five percent of its costs, but concluded: "I hope that the university will have in mind the merits of the case generally when it comes to any question of enforcement of this [costs] order." Dream on.

As I began packing my files and books, I was approached by a large, homely lady in a woolly cardigan who commiserated on the outcome and explained that she was from UPI, the press agency; I had a momentary flash of the women knitting by the guillotine, but thanked her for her sympathy. Mark Le Fanu had attended much of the trial and was agog at the judgment, which at an implicatory stroke apparently invalidated all existing authors' contracts. I shook hands with Warby, got a consolatory pat on the back from *Planchè v. Colburn* ("Horrid people Mr Malcolm, horrid people, I hear 'em talking, bunch of crooks, don't you worry about 'em") and made for the lift. As I crossed the foyer, where Shaw and co. were excitedly using the payphone, presumably to relay their good news back to Oxford, Hardy turned and gave me a sickly grin. From what he wrote years later, this moment apparently had a lasting effect upon him.

16

Down and Up in Hampstead and Brighton

BACK IN HAMPSTEAD I tried to collect my thoughts and to piece together Lightman's judgment from our notes. I telephoned my barrister with the news and read him some key passages. He is by nature a cautious, prudent, thoughtful man, but on this occasion he was uncharacteristically gung-ho. Almost at once he said, in gist, "Lightman's reasoning is clearly faulty, he's telling you to appeal, he's giving you a springboard, he's warning Oxford they must sort it out." Back in Brighton, Richard White was at first more pessimistic, and a latent depression set in as I contemplated yet another horribly expensive, risky and difficult lap. Articles appeared on the case in *The Times*, *The Telegraph* and *The Brighton Evening Argus*, all quoting at length Lightman's strong criticisms of Oxford and its solicitors, and all noting Oxford's strong moral commitment to publish *Making Names* and harsh and unfair treatment of me. *The Times* went in detail into Lightman's odd "no agreed print-run" reasoning. Some of this was, yes, encouraging.

One early move I made was to send all the current Delegates a copy of Lightman's judgment and costs remarks (in our version), with a covering letter inviting them to comment on Elliott's sworn testimony that in 1985 no records were kept of General Book approvals. Since 1988, Barr and Boardman had been replaced by: Professor F. G. B. Miller, Brasenose, a Professor of ancient history; Professor B. L. Trowell, Wadham, a musicologist, conductor and former head of BBC radio opera; Professor J. M. Brady, Keble, a mathematician and computing and information technologist; Mr P. J. Waller, Merton, a lecturer in modern history; Doctor C. J. Crouch, Trinity, a Professor of comparative social institutions; and Miss Joanna Innes, Somerville, a lecturer in modern history. This time, however, my letter elicited not a single reply, nor even an acknowledgment. *The Garden Path* had long seemed far too genteel; *Under the Skin* became the new front-runner.

I believe that this total silence from the Delegates is worth remarking. Later, Oxford was to state publicly that "some aspects of Mr Malcolm's conduct of the case only served to harden the Press's attitude", and I take this to refer to my writing to, speaking with and recording of the Delegates, as though I had in some way been infringing their privacy. By

the time of the trial I had communicated with, I guess, thirty to forty
senior University people in the hope that someone might intercede, but not
one had taken the slightest interest in the affair. This was the reverse of the
"old gentlemen who meet once a year" coin. Whilst the publishing
professionals in Walton Street regarded the Delegates as a tiresome,
background irrelevance, the Delegates themselves preferred not to know
what was actually happening down in the inky trenches. They simply
stopped their ears, like the right-honourable directors of arms companies
pretending not to know that their wealth derives from the sales of
grenades to Somali street-gangs or of electric truncheons to South
American torture-squads. The only advice I got, like Pears', was that going
to law was a waste of my time and money; this was sound, cynical worldly-
wisdom no doubt, but hardly an adequate, or even a moral, response.
Mustill LJ was later to ask:

> "Could it also be that the Delegates whose interests are so directly in
> suit were out of touch with what was going on in the action? Could it
> be that they did not know what had been, what was being, said about
> the stance adopted by the Press?"

So it must have seemed to him, but in fact I had by now sent every
Delegate a copy of Lightman's judgment, complete with its full account of
the story, its castigation of the University, and its obviously faulty no-
contract reasoning. I had even alluded to the highly damaging testimony of
several of Oxford's witnesses, some of which has been quoted above. Still
nothing happened. Presumably no-one intervened because they did not,
individually or collectively, feel themselves responsible and were assured
that it was all being taken care of by the executives and their lawyers. Fine,
(well no, actually, not fine), but where does this leave the University's
alleged Delegatorial control over its increasingly disreputable Press?

Two weeks later, Lightman's official judgment arrived, now with its odd
telltale amendments, and my and my lawyers' spirits began to rise further:
he had given us a great deal of ammunition, had gone a long way down
the road, and his final balking logic was patently flawed. Everyone knows
that books' print-runs and formats aren't normally agreed in publishing
contracts. Was it perhaps all a sort of lawyers' code? Lightman was a
young Q.C., still only a deputy judge, and to have found for a lone
pipsqueak author against the grand university on a matter that would
undoubtedly have made publishing waves... tsk, tsk. Or maybe he just
wanted to pass the decision upstairs, where perhaps it in any case
belonged? Maybe he genuinely believed that Oxford would heed his moral
pleas to "reconsider", "make amends" and at least would not enforce his

costs order. So ran the trains of unthinkable thought as my optimism circuits slowly began to re-engage.

Another early research was to track down John Cordy, the retired OUP editor who had been identified for the first time in court by Margaret Goodall as the man who in 1985 took the Delegates' minutes. I telephoned him on record and asked him the relevant questions. He did not seem to have been forewarned and was perfectly frank and open, but sounded rather frail, perhaps explaining why Oxford had gone to such lengths to keep him from the firing-line. He categorically confirmed that in 1985 *lists* were drawn up of General Books and that on these lists he would mark the books approved, deferred or rejected; he could not, however, remember particular books from that long ago. When I wrote asking for an affidavit from him to this effect, he declined, but if as a result of an appeal a new trial were ordered, Cordy would probably become an important new witness. A first plank was in place.

I began to contemplate a Notice of Appeal, trading several drafts with my barrister. Our final version was lodged on 18th April, citing these chief grounds:

1. A book's print-run and format do not have to be (are not normally) agreed in a complete publishing contract.

2. My book's print-run and format would not have been agreed in any formal memorandum.

3. On 20th May 1985 Hardy and I reached agreement on OUP's payment of "a fair royalty."

4. The weight of evidence indicated that on 23rd July 1985 the Delegates approved *Making Names.*

5. Specific performance (my proposal of a court-ordered print-run) was not impracticable.

Also in April, Alan Ryan wrote a remarkable article in *The Times* defending the protestors who had participated in the bloody anti-poll-tax riots in Trafalgar Square, and proclaiming, from the tranquility of Princeton, that a citizen sometimes has a duty to ignore the law. This provoked a flurry of letters to the newspaper and one from me to Ryan. I enclosed Lightman's judgment, now in its official form, and invited him to ignore its recommendations that Oxford should reconsider its decision (that is, should publish *Making Names*), should make amends, and should not press for its costs. Ryan, like Oxford, of course ignored all of these, but he did reply to me, with a strange, detached, stream-of-consciousness apology.

Because it is one of those special Oxford exhibits which seem to unlock some of the peculiar mysteries of the affair and perhaps also to have wider significance, I shall briefly examine it. Ryan began:

> "I must say I am more surprised by the behaviour of the Press's solicitors than anything. It is quite clear that Henry Hardy did *not* have the authority to issue a contract single-handed, and so far as I can see the Press would have been wise to rely on that defence from the beginning. As to the merits of the case, my own sense is that we [that is, presumably, Ryan and Malcolm] were at cross purposes from the start, and that that was at the heart of the matter. I liked the book on first reading and thought it would make an interesting introduction to philosophy, but..."

Like his Trafalgar Square comments, this was rich coming from the man who had "got the *Making Names* ball rolling" at Oxford and "had planned to gallop ahead with it" but had then vanished to America for three mute years. It also redemonstrated this senior left-wing scholar's wonderfully hazy hold on morality and even hazier grasp of the law. If the Press's solicitors had followed his advice and from the outset pleaded Hardy's non-authority, firstly Ryan's testimony would have been central and he would have been compulsorily roasted by any half-competent Q.C., and secondly Oxford would almost certainly have lost the case early in its first year.

Ryan says that he and I "were at cross purposes", but in fact of course, we were at no purposes at all. This post-trial letter was the first communication I had ever received from him. Ryan had evidently been at cross purposes with his editorial underlings too, for his letter continued by directly opposing many of the points that Hardy had carefully relayed to me, and even by contradicting Bion's final rejection: she pronounced my revised version "undoubtedly an improvement", he thought it had "gone downhill", adding that "it would always have to have been pruned of the play at the end." On the other hand he also found himself at cross purposes with Lightman, who described him as having "rubbished" *Making Names* on second reading: "that's not really my style" he corrected. Apart from this, he made not a single reference to any of Lightman's points nor any mention of the Delegates' meeting. In his final paragraph, the man who had, more than any other, been responsible for the trashing of my book, my contract, my career and about £70,000 of my money, and yet who evidently had not even bothered to read Hardy's letters to me, wanly concluded: "I am sorry you have had such a miserable time over this. As you know, I think the Press was legally absolutely in the right."

Turning to the wider implications of Ryan's letter, it seems to me that it directly pinpoints the oddness of OUP's status and the "difficult and delicate" relationship between the University and its Press, between the Delegates and their executive and editorial staff. Ryan was thinking and writing *as though* he and the other Delegates were publishers. He had *imagined* a correspondence with me, just as he subsequently *imagined* the revised book and *imagined* conducting the lawsuit. In fact he was off in the sylvan, subsidised glades of academe, irresponsible, without a care in the world or a personal penny piece at stake. He had been *playing at* publishing. It struck me that if Ryan and co. had been proper publishers, themselves negotiating with authors, agents, printers and booksellers, even if, implausibly, they made successful editorial and commercial decisions, they would go out of business within months simply because everyone would soon find them impossible to deal with. I would certainly never have revised *Making Names* if I had found myself negotiating with a jelly-brain like Ryan. No wonder OUP's commercial competitors view it with cynicism; when OUP does financially badly, as from time to time it has done, it goes cap-in-hand to the University to bail it out, yet despite its tax-exemption, the Press often donates only a very small proportion of its profits back. Nor can one imagine that an ordinary commercial publisher would have so bunglingly lost the estimated half-million pounds the action eventually cost. My writ, remember, was against the University, its owners, not against the Press as such, and the unique settlement agreement with which it concluded in perpetuity binds to certain terms not just serving OUP officers, but also all members of the University. I fancy that Oxford may shortly realise that its Press's ambivalent, privileged status is now a far greater curse than a blessing.

17

The Bookseller Letters

RETURNING TO the chronology, on 6th April *The Bookseller* magazine carried a report on the outcome of the trial headlined "OUP 'author' loses fight for publication". The piece that followed was unexceptionable, but why did its headline carry those demeaning inverted commas? What had I done to deserve such a typographical sneer? Was this just editorial punctiliousness or did it herald an unpleasant, fluting breeze beginning to blow into London from the Cotswolds? Besides, what sort of punctiliousness would this have been? Had I written a book or 'written' a 'book'? Had Hardy made a commitment or 'made' a 'commitment'? Was this some version of the Society of Authors' Catch-22 embargo, and if so, who defines a publisher's publication, as opposed to a 'publisher's' 'publication'? Or was it just Oxford's subtle way, perhaps, of suggesting that none of this had ever really happened, of fictionalising the whole 'affair'? An eerie feeling crept over me as I wondered if this was after all the truth, that I was perhaps actually becoming *an inverted commas person*. I clung to my italics and reminded myself that at least I was a litigant, not 'a litigant', and that in that role the *Bookseller* piece gave me a chance to air some overlooked facts and to put them before 'people in the trade'. As my letter of 11th May was mentioned by the appeal judges and may have sparked some of the remarkable events that ensued, I will quote it in full:

> Sir, I am writing in response to your report of 6th April, "OUP 'author' loses fight for publication". Since I am the 'author' in question and my fight in the High Court is now the subject of an appeal, I feel I must correct one or two minor inaccuracies of fact in your otherwise fair and sympathetic report.
>
> Firstly, OUP's and their senior editor Henry Hardy's commitment to the publication of my revised philosophical work *Making Names* did not reside merely in certain telephone conversations, as you suggest, but also in a lengthy correspondence over the preceding nine months and in a number of subsequent confirmatory letters and other documents, which included statements such as "I am pleased that we are going to do your book and hope that it's a terrific success... Don't worry about delay in revising the book, it's much more important that you get it right than that we publish it a month or two earlier... Let me try to summarise the changes we require (followed by a long list)" and so on.
>
> Everyone accepted that after seven months' further work I had fulfilled all of OUP's revision requirements. A royalty had been

confirmed, a short initial print-run in hardback had been agreed and even a retail price (of £15 to £20) had been envisaged; but the judge held that the Press's "absolute commitment" did not amount to an enforceable contract because of the technicality that a *numerical* print-run had not formally been contracted.

The implications of this judgment, if it is taken as a precedent, will be far-reaching. Not the least important of these is that very few existing author-publisher contracts are enforceable at law, since, as far as I know, very few such contracts specify (minimum) print-runs. All authors presently labouring away under the illusory protection of a publishing contract may well wish to ponder this point.

In my case, even this technicality is moot, for two of OUP's documents that were in evidence *do* specify an initial hardback print-run, of 2,000. The judge ruled that I could not rely on these documents because, he concluded, the Delegates (the ruling committee of the Press) had not, as I believe, formally approved the book's publication at a meeting on 23rd July 1985.

This conclusion rested in turn upon the testimony of OUP's chief executive Sir Roger Elliott, who stated that the lists and records of General Books considered at that meeting had never existed or had been destroyed. Alan Ryan, the philosopher/Delegate who supported the book at the meeting, has refused to make a statement and is now in the United States, at Princeton.

Yours sincerely,
Andrew Malcolm
address

Here were the contract, the state of play in the action, Ryan's and Elliott's roles, and Oxford's shredded defence with its crazy implications all together in a nutshell. Surely some publishing eminences would intervene and talk some sense into the blundering OUnuchs? The case, after all, was now being reported in the newspapers. While I waited, Mark Le Fanu responded with a letter (18th May) which was supportive of my cause, but which simultaneously tried to allay the fears of authors with formal contracts, assuring them that their protection was not illusory. He quoted Lightman's remark about Oxford's "harsh and unfair treatment", in turn provoking what for me is another of the affair's most prized exhibits, a perfectly idiotic letter (1st June) from Sir Roger Elliott, who I presume was by then conducting their defence. My first instinct was to omit Elliott's effort to avoid aggrandising its idiocy, but on reflection I guess this might be interpreted as bias, so here it is, again complete:

Sir, May I please respond to some of the points made in two letters you have published about the dispute between Mr Malcolm and OUP?

The plaintiff in his letter of 11th May gives, as might be expected, a biased view of the affair. Nothing is said about his own obsessive behaviour which led him secretly to record all his telephone conversations, or his attempts to take personal suit against Richard Charkin and to subpoena three people who are irrelevant to the case which had to be dismissed by the Master of the Court with costs to those concerned.

It also led him to spend five years trying to persuade OUP to publish his book, rather than seek an alternative publisher. But we did not think that Mr Malcolm's book had either the intellectual quality or the commercial potential necessary to justify publication by OUP.

It is a pity that Mr le Fanu was not present in Court or aware of any of the background to the case before he opined in his letter of 18th May that Mr Malcolm was treated harshly and unfairly.

The judge, for example, did not say that he would expect a print run to be specified in a contract but that the contract should contain a formula to determine this (which is normally at the publisher's discretion). OUP deals with several hundred satisfied authors each year, some of whom may even be members of the Society of Authors. It is surely in the interests of authors, as much as publishers, that contracts should be clearly set out in writing. I doubt if many authors would wish to be bound to oral arrangements which are likely to be full of uncertainties and liable to misinterpretation.

The judge's obvious sympathies lay with the plaintiff, who conducted his own case, and this led him to make remarks about OUP which are themselves otiose and unfair. But the fact of the matter is that Mr Lightman found that there was no contract between Mr Malcolm and OUP. Although the matter is now subject to appeal, I am confident that his decision will be upheld.

Yours truly
Roger Elliott
Chief Executive, OUP, Walton Street, Oxford

Having noted Elliott's careful, well-argued responses to the points in my letter, alert readers will doubtless then enjoy making their own *lists* of his many grammatical, stylistic, factual and legal errors, so I will confine myself merely to some general observations. First, it was clear that I was now dealing with a man who did not seek or heed legal or editorial advice, but who just garbled out whatever thoughts entered his thickety head. With its arguably defamatory remarks about myself and *Making Names* (one lawsuit at a time, I was advised), its bracketed own-goal, and its veiled threats in Mark Le Fanu's direction, it was shockingly injudicious and clearly demonstrated an attitude which I had sensed all along: these people thought just by virtue of their status that they were above the law, or perhaps even *were* the law. Here was a physicist who apparently couldn't put one logical proposition in front of another pompously lecturing a well-respected High Court judge. I do not know whether their Lords Justices of the Court of Appeal ever saw this exhibit, but if they had I imagine it would not have helped Oxford's increasingly ramshackle cause one bit. In *Private Eye*, Elliott had come to be known as Sir Roger Rabbit; in Brighton he became Sir Roger Otiose.

However, whilst revelling in Sir Otiose's folly, I felt the fluting Cotswold breeze now swelling into a dank Oxford gale, and heard from deep underground the clanging shut of certain heavy, unmarked iron doors. In openly denigrating me as obsessive and *Making Names* as worthless, Elliott was making it horribly clear that this had become the University's only public (and presumably private) justification of all of its chicanery, and that it would thereby in future be obliged to use its undoubted academic might to perpetuate my and my book's general non-acceptance. What had begun as an innocent attempt at publication appeared to be turning into a concerted orchestration of the exact opposite. It was later revealed that the OUnuchs had not even bothered to keep a copy of the script of which Elliott had come to hold such a low opinion, but who was now going to notice such trivial details as this?

I did not want to dignify Elliott's contribution with a response, so my second letter (8th June) instead questioned Mark Le Fanu's reassurance of other authors, challenging him to produce an example of a reneging publisher ever having been obliged by a court to publish a book 'contracted' under a standard memorandum, and concluding that if Lightman's judgment were allowed to stand, authors would have no legal position at all. Le Fanu's second letter (22nd June) failed to cite such an example, reiterated (wrongly, in my view) the importance of formal memoranda, and corrected some of Elliott's factual errors. A third letter from me understandably went unpublished (I could hear Louis Baum saying "that's enough Malcolm — ed."), but I gather that this correspondence had already generated much discussion in the book world. Le Fanu kindly offered to act as my expert witness on the point that publishing contracts rarely specify books' print-runs or formats, but he also tried to dissuade me from pursuing my appeal, which he predicted would be a costly failure. I was still ineligible for support from the Society of Authors.

The *Bookseller* exchanges enlisted me another ally too. I had first contacted Giles Gordon, one of London's leading literary agents, when in 1988 he wrote an open letter to Paul Hamlyn published in *Punch* attacking the new conglomeratisation of Octopus, which Richard Charkin was by then busy vandalising. I came to find Gordon one of the nicest, straightest men in British publishing, and when he learned of the 'no print-run' reasoning of Lightman's judgment and OUP's defence, he was appalled and outraged at such nonsense, volunteering to act as my witness on the point. *The Bookseller* is the pre-eminent magazine for people in the trade, and I have always found it amazing that when this absurd lie, and potentially disastrous legal mistake about print-runs was publicly aired in its columns, not one single other person stepped forward willing, let alone anxious, to nail it. No-one else ever even wrote to me to confirm or correct my assumptions, and the only man of honour and action proved to be Gordon. If I, with Gordon's help, had not gone successfully to appeal, and Lightman's judgment had been allowed to stand as a precedent, hardly a single author's contract in the UK would now be enforceable. In any dispute, the publisher (or author) would be able to cite *Malcolm v. Oxford* and say: "Look, our agreement does not specify a print-run, in law it is therefore incomplete." Lord Justice Nourse himself later confirmed and amplified this point in the appeal.

Another surprising side-effect of the *Bookseller* correspondence was that I was telephoned by one of Richard Charkin's new editors at Octopus, Tom Weldon of Heinemann, who said that he had read the letters with interest and had obtained my telephone number from someone who worked with Ivon Asquith. Heinemann had previously rejected *Making Names* on the grounds that they did not publish philosophy, yet now Weldon offered to publish the book, again sight unseen, because of its controversy-value. Presumably this was another example of Charkin thinking on, or with, his feet, but I'm afraid I shared neither his cynicism nor his desire to re-establish our relationship. Publishing, I was constantly advised, is a joint venture requiring mutual co-operation and trust. In any case, I could do nothing with the book until after the appeal; to have started dealing with another publisher at that stage would have compromised and perhaps annulled my claim, and Weldon's approach might even have been a legal trap. I therefore asked if I might put him on hold, and after an amicable conversation he agreed to send a list of his Heinemann books to my address as given in *The Bookseller*. Curiously, he read back my correct postcode, which had not appeared in the magazine, but then never wrote to me. I gather that Charkin subsequently put it about that I had never wanted *Making Names* published in the first place.

By this time, I had become quite nifty at all the procedures and paperwork required by the Appeal Court Registry, which itself seemed much more efficient than the Chancery Division's. I had my own photocopier and had become familiar with the offices in the Strand labyrinth, and even with some of their inmates. I pressed ahead with the preparation of the huge bundles of paper for the three judges and made sure, despite Dallas Brett's many stalling attempts, that everything was filed on time. I selected the most useful bits of Oxford's witnesses' testimony and at considerable expense ordered their official transcription. When I had committed myself to this outlay, Oxford trumped me by simply ordering the lot, which must have cost them thousands; as already noted however, they did not order a single syllable of *my* testimony, a curious omission for a confident litigant.

Oxford's lawyers took a long while to react to my Notice of Appeal, not countering with their own 'Respondents' Notice' until 18th May. Its chief point was that if there was a contract, it was conditional upon the Delegates' approval of the book. It said nothing about any requirement to agree a print-run, format or price. Here, now, formally, Oxford was staking everything on the Delegates.

This is perhaps another good moment to pause for reflection. I am aware that, if ever disseminated, this history may provoke debate, not only on various aspects of author-publisher law, but also on the relationship between Oxford University and its Press, the uneasiness which I believe lies at the heart of the whole débàcle. One question is: what would have happened if I had fallen foul of a Charkin-n-Hardy-style power-struggle (or *bona fide* disagreement) in a normal commercial publishing house? Suppose I had spent six months revising a book that had been contracted by an editor, only to find it then binned by his manager; surely an ordinary firm would at the very least have offered to pay me for my abortive work, or if faced with litigation, would simply have printed the initial 2,000 copies, in any case probably their cheaper option. Again one is reminded of Rupert Murdoch's recent swift settlement with Chris Patten (see page 45). As recommended by the PA code, most publishing contracts, including OUP's own *Memoranda*, specify an arbitration procedure in the event of such problems, which are presumably common enough. But OUP's internal documents show that right from the start, rather than treating their *Making Names* mess as the result of an in-house disagreement, their employees were dodging this way and that behind the ambiguous role of the Delegates, whom I take to be firmly on the University side of the Walton Street fence. Hardy had relied upon the support of the tergiversating Ryan; Charkin had written to me that it was *the Delegates* who had rejected the book. Throughout the lawsuit, the Press had invoked the University one minute and denied it the next, whilst the University had alternately disowned and defended its imprint as the circumstances suited. When, as I believe it eventually must, the logic, and the law, of this relationship comes into question, I would like its scrutineers to note that by Warby's skeleton argument of March 1990 and Respondents' Notice of May, the University's lawyers decided formally to rest their entire Court of Appeal defence in what had obviously become an important publishing-law case, upon the Delegates' alleged non-approval of a book proposal which, according to their own evidence, they had never considered.

Another, related question is: would an ordinary commercial publisher have been so tricky with an unknown, uninitiated author in the first place?

Would they, on receipt of the complete draft of a book and repeated requests for a firm commitment, have then gone through Hardy's long wheedling and backsliding telephone exercise to tease out six months' unprotected work? Would they have bandied as Oxford did so brazenly all those wilful misuses of the word "encouragement"? Would they have played so hard-to-get? These questions are of course hypothetical, but I suspect that the likely answer to each of them is no. Something about the behaviour then and since of the OUnuchs puts me in mind of the socialist intellectuals of recent years who, biting the bullet, have been obliged to 'go private' and then pursued their market advancement far more disreputably, far more pseudo-aggressively, than most normal businessmen. "We're just playing them at their own game" is the frequent excuse, but of course such people have usually imagined only caricatures of devilish private enterprise, the vast everyday bulk of which is conducted in reasonable and fair ways. In the real world, routinely crooked firms do not generally last long.

18

Molopolis

TWO DAYS AFTER I received Oxford's Respondents' Notice, I also received something which blew it to pieces. There occurred the first of two events which in many quarters have since generated a mass of speculation, hypothesis, gossip and rumour. For safety's and for certainty's sakes, I will stick to the bald facts. A brown A4 envelope arrived at my flat postmarked Cambridge 18th May 1990 and addressed without my postcode (the address that had appeared in *The Bookseller*). It contained a handwritten covering letter which read: "DEAR MR MALCOLM, HERE ARE THE PAPERS FOR THE GENERAL BOOKS THAT WERE CONSIDERED BY THE DELEGATES ON 23/7/85. I HOPE THEY ARE OF USE TO YOU. A WELL-WISHER" This was enclosed with a 5-page list (yes, list) of books (about 45) headed EDUCATIONAL DIVISION, together with ten separate Delegates' Notes, each headed TO ALL DELEGATES. Their titles included: *Heritage of Music* edited by Michael Raeburn and Alan Kendall; *Concise Dictionaries of Physics, Chemistry and Biology* edited respectively by Alan Isaacs, John Daintith and Elizabeth Martin (all on one Note); *The Oxford Companion to Popular Music* by Peter Gamond; *The Works of John Henry Newman* edited by Ian Ker; *The Oxford Dictionary of Modern Quotations* compiled by A. J. Augarde; and then five Notes headed GENERAL BOOKS: *Evelyn Waugh — A Critical Biography* by Ann Pasternak Slater; *The Southern Review: Essays on T. S. Eliot* compiled by James Olney (2 pages); *The Annotated Innocence of Father Brown* by Martin Gardner; *The New Oxford Book of Modern Verse* edited by James Fenton; and, wait for it, D19 for *Making Names* (oddly enough, this time without Hardy's extra handwritten date). With the arrival of this anonymous 'Cambridge Package', the plot was becoming worthy of Inspector Morse.

At almost the same time I was notified of the date of the appeal hearing, 17th October, which must have been something of a speed record and which, I think, came as quite a surprise and worry to the opposition. On 22nd May I received Dallas Brett's bill for seventy-five percent of Oxford's trial costs, itemised as £15,461.09 plus £2,319.16 VAT and totalling £17,780.25. My response was demanded within seven days. In addition there were the subpoenaed witnesses' three-day costs of £8,624.67 and a claim from Richard Charkin for travelling expenses of £39.60. It turned out that since OUP is VAT-registered and therefore able to reclaim the tax, it was a serious breach of the solicitors' code of conduct, a sort of fraud, to demand it. Although I had lost the trial itself and seventy-five percent of Oxford's costs stood against me, some of the earlier costs orders (most notably Master Barratt's on discovery of documents) were in my favour, so my own solicitor's not inconsiderable charges for that work could be deducted from Dallas Brett's bill. When I had my solicitor's figures, with Lightman's recommendations in mind, I made the University a 'without prejudice' offer of £7,000. In August Oxford declined my offer and initiated a taxation, that is, a court-ordered costs assessment and enforcement procedure which can result in the seizure of one's house and other assets.

In June I submitted an application to adduce new evidence at the appeal, including anticipated expert testimony as to the usual contents of publishing contracts, and a whole mass of new material which apparently confirmed the Delegates' approval of *Making Names* (The Cambridge Package, the Cordy and Pears transcripts, and the subpoenaed witnesses' affidavits). The rules concerning the adducing of new evidence are complex and strict, so it was likely to prove a battle even to have these exhibits admitted. Mercifully, the Appeals Registrar decided that, as the matters were so inter-related, this sub-issue should be decided by the Court of Appeal itself, at the same hearing.

At the end of July, I got a 'without prejudice' letter direct from Ivon Asquith (my first from anyone at the Press since 1986) suggesting a parley to see if we could "minimize the costs of further litigation". I agreed, and we arranged to meet in Fortnum & Mason's 'Soda Fountain' for a four o'clock tea. I remember threading my way with some disbelief through the throngs of fashionable London shoppers and smart foreign tourists sniffing the speciality herbs and glacéd fruit up to the frilly blue-and-pink tea-room, where prim waitresses in tight black dresses and starched white aprons were ferrying around stands of cakes and steaming pots of Assam Pekoe or Kenyan Blend. I was unintentionally late, so I think Asquith was perhaps already irritable with me when I arrived, though he did his best not to show it. I was probably wearing my usual brown leather jacket, and as I approached his table I jokingly opened it to demonstrate that I was not 'wired'. He, chinless and grey-suited as ever, got up to shake my hand fishily and then solemnly placed a briefcase on the next chair with one of its corners aimed pointedly towards me. How exciting, I thought, just like in a Bond movie! I guessed his Finance Committee bosses wanted to make their own private assessment of my morale.

Asquith ordered a pot of tea ("What variety shall we have?" "I'm easy, just Indian") and there was much fussing about our choice of sandwiches.

Unfortunately, he opted for prawn mayonnaise, and from quite early I had
to digest his proposals whilst watching a large, sticky white blob bobbing
up and down on his upper lip. Disappointingly though, his proposals did
not require much digestion, for they were simply this: if you abandon your
appeal, we will not press for our costs. I thanked him, but explained that
my advisers now thought I was likely to win the appeal and perhaps even
specific performance, so such an offer by itself was not obviously attractive,
though I would consider it. We chatted inconsequentially for a while, and
then, as we shook hands again when I was about to leave, he turned to me
and said something as it were, off the record; it was one of those precious
Oxford remarks which suddenly throw the whole world and all the morals
in it aspin and ajangle, as if the planets were momentarily being jolted
from their orbits. In a tone of childish petulance he said: "Don't you think
it terribly *unfair* that you have tapes of all your conversations with Hardy
and that we don't?" What *is it* with these people? I wondered, as I dreamily
but unsuccessfully tried to imagine Asquith's world-view on my way back
down Piccadilly. Over the next day or two I did consider his settlement
offer, and wrote back to say that if it could include OUP's printing of their
originally-planned 2,000 copies of *Making Names* costing, in their own
estimates, less than half their costs of fighting an appeal, then I would
accept it. They never replied.

Obviously there are legal problems over the reliabilty and validation of
anonymously-received evidence like my Cambridge Package: without a
named witness to authenticate it, there is a possibility of its being bogus
and inconclusive. Although the genuineness of the package was never
challenged by Oxford or its lawyers (they never even asked to inspect it),
and it included a *list* of Educational Books, thereby rendering Elliott's
courtroom testimony false, the *list* of General Books for the meeting was
still missing. In case there were yet more papers that could be flushed out
with the help of my mysterious well-wisher, in July, following the
tradition, I placed another advertisement in *The Spectator.*

> MALCOLM vs OXFORD UNIVERSITY PRESS.
> Dear Cambridge Well-wisher, Many thanks for the
> Delegates' papers, which are indeed most useful. Was there
> also *a list* of General Books for the 23/7/85 meeting? It has
> been stated that such lists were not drawn up in 1985.
> My appeal, by the way, is due to be heard on 17th October.
> Yours, Andrew Malcolm [& address].

By September, all the preparation for the appeal was completed, and Mark
Le Fanu and Giles Gordon had filed their evidence on my behalf confirming

that terms about books' print-runs (both affidavits), formats (both) and prices (Gordon's, but not Le Fanu's) were rarely agreed in publishing contracts. Gordon also went in detail into his experiences with OUP contracts, editors, and the Delegates' involvement, which he regarded as in practice marginal:

> Without exception, in my experience, editors at OUP negotiate with agents on behalf of authors as if they were editors at any other publishing house. Clearly, were the outside world of professional authors and agents to regard OUP employees as mere cyphers for the Delegates of the Press, a Ruritanian condition would have been created.
>
> I would have thought it impossible for an editor at the Press to have any self-respect at all, or for any author to take him or her seriously, were he obliged to keep saying 'I think your manuscript is jolly good, and so does the specialist reader to whom I sent it, but all this is irrelevant because it is the Delegates who have the power to decide whether or not we publish it.' Frankly, the mind boggles...

Readers may like to compare Gordon's commonsense account with Hardy's early one to me (see page 19), and then to contemplate all the defence pleadings and sworn statements that Oxford spewed in the interim. Once again one is confounded by the profound illogic of OUP's peculiar constitution, and as its denizens would probably say, the mind bogles.

With the paperwork completed, Liz and I spent an excellent two weeks' holiday in north-western Turkey, travelling along the sea of Marmaris and down to the Troad, visiting Erdek, Bursa, Assos and Troy. Meanwhile, with time running out, Oxford had made two extremely late applications, the first of which was to seek security of their costs of the appeal. This is the ploy whereby one party seeks to prevent the other's appeal from coming to court by arguing that they won't be able to pay their costs if they lose. (In 1989 this move was famously used by Lord Aldington to stifle Nikolai Tolstoy's appeal against his record £1.5 million libel damages over a leaflet alleging that in 1945 Aldington was responsible for the fatal post-war betrayal to the Soviets of 70,000 Cossacks and Yugoslavs.) As well as its various outstanding bills, Oxford sought an additional £11,000 surety from me to allow the appeal to proceed. This matter was fought out in a memorable hearing on 28th September before Lord Justice Stuart-Smith, who resoundingly rubbished every single aspect of Oxford's application — its lateness, its gross overestimate of the University's likely costs, its lack of evidence of my impecuniosity, and its misinterpretation of my correspondence. I was awarded the costs of the hearing and of Oxford's applications, and the judge also firmly settled the VAT question in my favour. It was my most decisive courtroom victory so far, and coming just three weeks before the appeal, it could not have been more timely.

This, perhaps, is a good moment to report my true financial situation. In mid-1989 I owned outright a large Brighton house, of which I let the upper floors, and lived in the separate basement flat. When I began to act in person on the lawsuit, greatly minimising my costs, I decided to protect the remainder of my cash reserve by taking out a loan and buying a nearby attractive investment property which had come up for auction and which was tenanted by an elderly lady by the name of Lilian Lewin. I fancied that if I lost the case and Oxford pressed to the hilt for its costs (which after the trial is exactly what it did), I would be able to resell the house and pay them off, or better still, simply hand it over to them and leave the DIM-squad to evict Mrs Lewin. At the security hearing I truthfully and successfully argued that in the event of my losing the appeal I would be able to pay all of Oxford's costs "by selling my house", not explaining of course, which one I meant.

Oxford's second application was to seek leave yet again (the third or fourth time) to re-amend its Respondents' Notice, now just three weeks before the appeal. At this eleventh hour its lawyers had decided after all to *abandon* the claim that my contract with Hardy was dependent upon the Delegates' approval. This fundamental climbdown was great news: the Delegates defence had been bogus from the start and was almost certainly unsustainable at law (there was absolutely no evidence of the condition ever having been stipulated), but their formal approval of the book was the one remaining fact of which I had been unable to persuade Gavin Lightman. Now, just as I had become able to prove it, I was relieved of the requirement to do so. The University's retraction of the claimed condition also meant that most of the past two years' costs of the action (my cross-examination of the Oxford Six, my purchase of the costly official transcripts of their testimony, and a whole lot else besides), had been spent, as it were, under Oxford's false pretences; it might even have been a deliberate strategy to drain my funds. Technically, of course, this retraction automatically entitled me to the expenses of that long wild-goose-chase, but actually now recovering them was sure to prove difficult. From Oxford's point of view, apart from amputating the chief remaining leg of its defence and making its whole strategy look bungled, the effect of the retraction was to block my application to adduce the new evidence. The Cordy and Pears transcripts, the subpoenaed witnesses' affidavits and the Cambridge Package would now not, after all, enter the arena and further embarrass Oxford's witnesses. The Delegates' approval, however, might yet turn out to be relevant to an order for specific performance, so for the moment my application remained 'live'. Whichever way one looked at it, Oxford was at last in serious retreat.

Early in October, Warby and I exchanged skeleton arguments for the appeal. Mine was three pages long, Warby's sixteen; the tables had thus already turned before the blow came that finally sent their counters flying. I received another anonymous package of OUP papers, postmarked Oxford 10th October 1990. A small, typed covering letter read: "Dear Mr Malcolm, Here is the list you asked for in The Spectator, plus some others from about that time. Good luck with your appeal! [then, by hand] *ADRASTEIA*". The envelope contained five lists all headed TO ALL DELEGATES and GENERAL BOOKS. The first four comprised: one undated, uncredited sheet apparently from a set of two or more listing twenty-two Oxford Paperback titles; a list dated May 1985 of nine titles in Oxford's World's Classics series, credited to W.P. Sulkin/Judith Luna; a list dated 23 May 1985 of eight Oxford Paperbacks credited to Henry Hardy; and a list dated 5 June 1985 of seventeen Oxford Paperbacks credited to W. P. Sulkin. The fifth read:

> The following will be published as OUP hardbacks:
> Ann Pasternak Slater: <u>Evelyn Waugh — A Critical Biography</u>
> James Olney (ed): <u>The Southern Review: Essays on T. S. Eliot</u>
> Martin Gardner: <u>The Annotated Innocence of Father Brown</u>
> Andrew Malcolm: <u>Making Names</u> (General Philosophy)
> James Fenton (ed): <u>The New Oxford Book of Modern Verse</u>
> 19 July 1985   W. P. Sulkin

According to Lemprière's Classical Dictionary, Adrast(e)ia was mentioned by the ancient Greek geographer Strabo as being in mythology the daughter of Jupiter and Necessity, and known by some as Nemesis, the punisher of injustice. It was also a region near Troy named after Adrastus, king of Argos, who had built a temple there to Nemesis. In a genuinely spooky coincidence, it seemed that Liz and I had recently, unwittingly, travelled to or near the very site of this supposed ancient temple. Leaving nothing to the Fates, I hurriedly made this 'Adrasteia Package' the subject of a second application to adduce new evidence.

The name Sulkin had unexpectedly reappeared. When Oxford eventually discovered its first batch of documents in March 1988, we learned that in 1985 Will Sulkin had been the head of OUP's General Books department, was designated on the PPF for *Making Names* as Managing Editor, and had sat on the panel at Hardy's disciplinary hearing. Hardy had written that he had at all stages kept Sulkin informed about the book. Since then,

Sulkin had moved first to Fabers and then to Jonathan Cape, and in 1988 my solicitor had spoken and corresponded with him and asked a number of questions about the affair. Sulkin had been perfectly pleasant and open, and had remembered having acted as Hardy's witness in the disciplinary proceedings, but had otherwise forgotten all the facts of the case; he had declined to be interviewed. On receipt of the Adrasteia Package, I telephoned him at Jonathan Cape (Random Century) and explained the new mystery. I recited the book titles on the lists bearing his name, and he recognised almost every one. When I came to the 19th July list, he remembered Slater's, Gardner's, Fenton's and my books, but not Olney's. However, given his poor memory, he thought they were all genuine lists. He also talked at length about how OUP's General Books department had worked and how its lists were compiled. His previously blank memory of the "explosive" editorial meeting of July 1985 began to return to him, and he added that the whole Delegate business "used to drive him up the wall". When I told him of Elliott's 'no lists' affidavit, he was amazed and derisive ("I can't believe he's lying... he's simply *wrong!*") and made some pithy remarks about the chief executive's general suitability. He offered to swear an affidavit confirming the Adrasteia lists' authenticity if I faxed them to him, but by the time I did so (I had no fax machine of my own then, so had to use a Brighton bureau), he had been contacted by Dallas Brett and asked to do likewise, but oppositely, on their behalf. In the end he wrote them not an affidavit, but a letter, saying that the first four lists looked genuine and that the fifth did not. A letter, unlike an affidavit, does not lay its author open to appearance and cross-examination in court, and is therefore of little evidential value.

As explained, Oxford had in any case by this time abandoned its 'Delegates' approval' defence, so all the evidence relating to it had become of marginal significance. Nevertheless, the production of Adrasteia's lists did oblige Elliott to go on affidavit again, now for the third time. In perfect contradiction of his 1989 effort, he stated:

> "I have checked the records that are kept of papers submitted to the Delegates' meetings and can confirm that the first four lists are genuine, but I am convinced that this [19 July] document is a forgery."

He gave no explanation of his 'conviction', and never asked to inspect the lists. I, unfortunately, never got the chance to cross-examine him about his checking of "the records that are kept of the papers that..."

19

The Court of Appeal

ON 12TH OCTOBER I was notified that the Court of Appeal triumvirate was to be their Lords Justices Mustill, Nourse and Leggatt. All three were Cambridge men and immediately adjudged by my advisers to be first-rate lawyers. The omens were good. On Wednesday 17th at 11.45, in Court 14 of the main building, the judges entered and took their seats. Mustill LJ, their 'leader', was short, florid, expressive and charming. Nourse LJ was quieter, but very deft and helpful. Leggatt LJ was impassive, steely and forbidding. It rapidly became clear that they had all read all the paperwork thoroughly and had analysed it with almost alarming acuity; equally rapidly it became clear that they were inclined to take my side on the central questions still at issue. They conferred, and in a stage-whisper agreed that Lightman's judgment was technically a poor one. Before the main contract argument, however, there were to be heard both sides' applications to adduce new evidence.

The first question was whether I should be allowed to rely upon Gordon's and Le Fanu's affidavits of expert testimony that books' print-runs and formats are rarely, if ever, agreed in author-publisher contracts. Oxford was by affidavit vigorously opposing the introduction of this new material on all the grounds its lawyers could muster. I had to demonstrate that such evidence had not been necessary at the trial because the question had not then been raised; this was not strictly true, for it had been mentioned and apparently agreed by Lightman that these were matters to be left to the publisher's discretion, as per Bankes LJ in *Abrahams and* Clause 5 of Oxford's standard *Memorandum.* These trial exchanges, however, had not been recorded, and the point only appeared in writing for the first time on the trial's penultimate day, in Warby's 'skeleton'. Also, the evidence showed that my whole negotiation with Hardy had proceeded on the assumption, frequently explicit, that these were matters for OUP. I quoted *Bigsby v. Dickinson* (1875), an appeal case relevant to the late emergence in the trial below of a technical matter for which the plaintiff had not been prepared. Dickinson was a manufacturer of tar, sulphate of ammonia and anthracene, the unpleasant odours from which had caused a nuisance to his neighbour. The legalities too were not unparalleled.

The fact that in his final written judgment Lightman had added certain crucial passages, in particular importing the legal phrase 'custom and usage' into the version he orated in court, soon became the focus of attention, and the judges warned that if the new material were allowed, a new trial might be necessary to allow Oxford to adduce expert counter-evidence of its own (to the effect that print-runs and formats *are* normally agreed in publishing contracts; to these Warby added retail price). It was noted that, though opposing my application, and despite having had six months to do so, Oxford had so far produced no such counter-evidence. The judges then turned their attention to my other new evidence application — the material relating to the Delegates' approval — and asked me to go in detail into the point's history. Although Oxford had now dropped this alleged condition from their defence, and the judges expressly stated that in their view Hardy's commitment was certainly *not* conditional upon the Delegates' approval, they seemed keen to test my claim that the question and evidence could still be relevant in other ways. It may be, however, that they just wanted to have this aspect clarified because they simply could not understand or believe the devious lengths to which Oxford's witnesses had apparently gone. Perhaps they were expecting Mark Warby to correct or interrupt my setting out of the story, but if so they were disappointed, for he said nothing. Nourse LJ cleverly noted that I could here rely on Oxford's documents (the PPF and Delegates' Note) *as they stood* as evidence on the previous point that the publisher was exercising his discretion on print-run and format, and was not intending to agree any formula with me on them.

At about 3.30 it was Warby's turn, and though I heard and took detailed notes of what he said, I could not at the time and cannot now for the life of me understand what his line of reasoning was supposed to be. He had been sent into the middle, of course, with an illogical, rubber cricket-bat, which bent and wobbled this way and that in the breeze; and there was a brisk breeze blowing from the three judges. His upshot seemed to be that although, as he tacitly admitted, an agreed print-run was never normally a term in a complete, written publishing contract and such matters were usually at the publisher's discretion, and although in my case they had informally been agreed anyway, my contract was incomplete because *a formula stating that* they were at the publisher's discretion had not formally been signed by both parties. That this gobbledegook, first glimpsed in Elliott's *Bookseller* letter, constituted Oxford's serious final defence to my four-year claim astounded the three judges. Nourse LJ mentioned my *Bookseller* letter, agreeing that if taken as a precedent, Oxford's argument would invalidate virtually all existing publishing contracts. "Suppose," he asked, "eminent authors like Ernest Hemingway

or Graham Greene were to say to their publishers: Look, since we haven't
agreed a print-run, this contract is invalid, I'll take my book elsewhere!"
"This would surely appal members of the book trade," added Mustill LJ,
"This would horrify publishers. It doesn't contractually protect them. Do
OUP truly *want* this?" "At what level of seniority within the University,"
asked Leggatt LJ, "has it been supported that this should be argued?"
Malcolm A was beginning to enjoy life.

On the next morning, Warby renewed his assertion that my contract was
uncertain because Hardy and I had agreed no print-run or retail price,
relying, perversely, on our (recorded) informal consensus on the points on
26th April to show that we had *intended* to make them terms of the contract,
and on the fact that I had not had OUP's formal *Memorandum* to argue
that I might not have *realised* that they were at the publisher's discretion.
Oxford's defence was now in full loop-the-loop mode, and spinning rapidly
out of control. I reiterated that, since I had submitted a complete text, the
chief points to be agreed between myself and Hardy were OUP's revision
requirements, and that I would therefore not have agreed to their printed
Memorandum's unamended opening "subject to the approval of the finished
script" clause. Warby then referred to this clause himself, saying that "he
was instructed" that such a term is found in all publishing agreements, and
he even tried, without warning, to adduce some 'evidence' on the point.
This assertion was again totally untrue; as mentioned, few publishers
nowadays are allowed, for example by agents, to get away with let-out-
clause wording anything like as draconian as OUP's. Warby continued by
questioning the reliability of Le Fanu's and Gordon's affidavits, quoting
various precedents about universality and certainty required of such
evidence. He introduced an obscure case from the New Zealand courts,
*Australia and New Zealand Banking Group Ltd. v. Frost Holdings Pty.
Ltd.* [1988] VP 695 about an agreement between a calendar-printer and a
bank over the production and purchase of 50,000 calendars featuring the
works of twelve Australian artists; the deal, and on appeal by the bank,
the printer's claim for damages, both failed because the calendars'
specifications and price had not been agreed and the contract had therefore
been incomplete. I heard the drone of a distant didjeridoo.

As Warby's position became more and more absurd, the judges became
more and more impatient, and at noon they called a halt to the exchanges
and retired to consider their decisions on the various new-evidence
questions. They returned fairly quickly and announced that they would
admit the Gordon and Le Fanu affidavits, but not the material relating to
the Delegates' approval or to Oxford's alleged 'extra' transcription (see
page 53). This issue settled, the judges invited argument on the substantive

appeal, the central issue in which now was: had Lightman been correct to decide that my contract with Hardy was vitiated because we had not expressly agreed the book's print-run and format? After four years of litigation, this is what it had all come down to: a roomful of the country's most eminent and expensive lawyers arguing a matter of arguably universal common knowledge — that it is the publisher of a book who decides how many copies to print and in what bindings.

There were some humorous moments. Nourse LJ envisaged a man employing a team of decorators to paint his home: the number of buckets to be used was a matter for the painters, not for their employer. Mustill LJ, his wig by now well awry, began referring to me as Mr Matthew and was corrected by the other judges: "It doesn't help" he apologised. I went through the predictable points one by one, and turned Warby's obscure Australian calendar dispute back on him, observing that the equivalent of authors in the story, the original artists, were the *last* people in it to be concerned or consulted about the calendar's print-run or production costs. "So you are regarding OUP merely as printers?" asked Mustill LJ. "Yes, I think perhaps I am" I replied. I reiterated that the chief formula to be agreed between myself and Hardy had been OUP's revision requirements, and that these had been detailed, and accepted by me even down to Oxford's three-point ellipses convention ("Dot, dot, dot" went Leggatt LJ). "What more", I asked rhetorically, "remained to be agreed, and how more careful could I have been? And short of writing the book himself, how more detailed could Hardy have got?" I pointed out that, with many authors — most of OUP's own, for example — the prestige of publication was a more important contractual 'consideration' than the allegedly essential royalty term, but that in my case "a fair royalty" had anyway expressly been agreed. Nourse LJ kindly rehearsed for me all the relevant passages from *Abrahams*, and I was then invited to turn to the question of remedy, and, in particular, to the subject of specific performance.

OUP's discovered PPF and Delegates' Note gave the detailed figures of Oxford's intended first print-run of *Making Names*, and at the trial I had argued that the court could base upon these an order for the production and delivery to me of the initial 2,000 hardback copies. Lightman, however, had accepted Oxford's denial of the Delegates' approval and concluded that, if he had found an enforceable contract, he would not have regarded specific performance as appropriate or practicable. When I repeated my proposal, all three appeal judges seemed firmly to endorse Lightman's view. Again I recited OUP's dictionary definition of 'publication', with its mention of two distinct functions, the printing and production of a book, and its distribution and marketing, and when I explained that I wanted merely the former, Lord Justice Mustill retorted that I was seeking to pick and choose only the parts of the deal I liked, and that the original contract would thereby be castrated, gelded, emasculated. His logic, not to mention the court's clear mood, at the time seemed unanswerable, so I immediately bowed to it. There followed another grilling of Warby on the meaning of the word 'commitment', which he proceeded to characterise as "the offering of a situation where the parties can investigate matters such as print-run, format etcetera in more depth", and Mustill LJ ended the afternoon by issuing him a polite invitation: "Your clients may want to make some statement about the ethical background to the case, or we might feel minded to express ourselves in public."

On Friday morning, as well as the usual few regular spectators, the court-room was graced by the arrival of Sir Otiose, resplendent in a dazzlingly fashionable, bright electric blue jacket, as if just descended from the Starship Enterprise. I guess he thought his personal gravitas would urge the triumvirate of his co-magisters to the right decision. Again he was to be disappointed. They announced that they would be reserving their judgment, and apart from Oxford's invited statement, it seemed that there was little more for anyone to add. Warby, however, presumably under last-ditch orders, began by ploughing yet again into the *Abrahams* case, this time trying to extract from it some new element of uncertainty as to 'custom and usage', as though my contract with OUP was vitiated by the fact that I was a *first-time* author and therefore might have been ignorant of what did (and did not) need to be agreed, a new ethically-cleansed policy that seemed to regard uninitiates not as being especially vulnerable, but rather as double-suckers. Warby shook his increasingly rattly skeleton again in case any meat fell from it on which the judges might nibble, but nothing came, and by 11.15, all he had left was Oxford's statement, presumably drafted overnight. The courtroom exchanges deserve reproduction:

> **Warby** (reading): "Oxford University Press has defended itself in this action to defend the status of its imprint which Mr Malcolm has coveted."
> **LJJ Leggatt & Nourse** in chorus: *Coveted*!?
> **Warby:** Yes, my Lords, *coveted.*
> **LJ Mustill:** You mean he wanted their colophon on his book?
> **LJ Leggatt:** Are these words out of *your* mouth, Mr Warby?
> **Warby:** The status of the statement is that is has been prepared by my clients, my Lords. [I would lay money on Captain Azure and his amanuensis Asquith.]
> **LJ Leggatt:** Of course they are out of your *mouth*, Mr Warby, but... (the judges laugh.)
> **Warby:** I do not feel I should put any gloss on the statement. (Resumes reading) "Notwithstanding what has been said in evidence, at all relevant

times books published by OUP had to obtain the approval of the Delegates. They are particularly concerned to maintain the high academic standards of their scholarly and pedagogic works. All the evidence indicates that Mr Malcolm's work did not reach the appropriate standard. Many manuscripts of greater merit have to be rejected by OUP every year. It was not until after legal proceedings were initiated that the Delegates were aware that Mr Hardy had made a commitment beyond the scope of his authority. He assured us, and we accepted what he said, that to be binding his decision had to be approved by the Delegates. OUP accepts that the negotiations were not handled as they should have been, and apologises for any pain and inconvenience caused. However, some aspects of Mr Malcolm's conduct of the case have only served to harden the Press's attitude."

There were gasps in the courtroom after this statement was read. For a few seconds the three judges stared ahead open-mouthed and silent; for a moment I fancied I saw a vapour emanating from around Leggatt LJ. Quite apart from the deafening diplomatic clanger that Oxford had just dropped and its repeated public denigration of my unread book, I sensed that the fragile skeins of argument that Warby had for the past three days been painstakingly trying to weave together had at a stroke been totally unravelled before him, leaving him quite forlorn. He must have felt he had the silliest clients in Christendom. I had learned to mistrust premature feelings of triumph, but this moment sorely tested that resolve. When equilibrium returned, Lord Justice Mustill said, almost by way of exclamation, "But if they were worried about their imprint, they could have run the case on the basis that specific performance was a non-starter. They were not at risk of being forced to publish. Their handling of it was a mess. They should at the outset have offered damages." He then invited me to reply briefly to Warby's final points.

I showed that one crazy consequence of Warby's newly-proposed "interlinked terms mathematical formula" was that contracted authors might actually end up owing their would-be publishers money (for example if a publisher were to overestimate the demand for a book or to cost it incompetently). Echoing the judges' question about the meaning of the word 'commitment', I drew their attention to Oxford's earlier answers to Lightman's similar inquiries ("a breach of discipline", "encouragement" and "comfort"), speculating whether Warby's latest "offering a situation where..." rigmarole might henceforth feature in the defendants' dictionary. "A good forensic point" agreed Nourse LJ. When I at last recited Hardy's written "I'm pleased we are going to do your book, and hope that it's a terrific success. As said, do get in touch if you have any queries as you work through it", Leggatt LJ sighed loudly. At 11.45 the court rose to consider its decision and everyone went home crossing their fingers.

The grotesquery of Oxford's 'apology' did not end with its recitation. Warby had undertaken to circulate photocopies of it both to myself and to the judges, and on the following Tuesday mine arrived. It was markedly different, though hardly improved, from the version he had delivered in court. Scholars and pedagogues everywhere will be interested to evaluate the merits of the statements orated (above) and typed (below) to decide which best maintains the appropriately high academic standards and reputation of Oxford's coveted imprimatur:

> Oxford University Press has defended itself in this action to defend the status of its imprint which Mr Malcolm has coveted. Notwithstanding what has been said in the evidence, all new titles published from Oxford have to obtain the approval of the Delegates. They are particularly concerned to maintain the high academic reputation of the scholarly and pedagogical books published in the name of the University. All the evidence available on Mr Malcolm's final manuscript indicated that it did not reach the appropriate standard. Many manuscripts of greater merit have to be rejected by OUP every year.
>
> It was not until after court proceedings were instigated that the senior Officers of the Press were aware, through the tape recordings, that the editor had made statements which could be interpreted as a commitment to publish. This was completely beyond his authority but we accept, as he firmly believes, that he made clear that anything he offered was subject to Delegates' approval and a final written contract.
>
> Having taken legal advice OUP believed that there was no binding contract, and this was borne out by the judgement of the court of first instance. It is hoped that this will be confirmed in this court.
>
> OUP accept that Mr Malcolm's book was not handled as it should have been, and apologise for the pain and inconvenience this may have caused. But, because of their obligation to maintain the academic standing of the Press, the Delegates were bound to oppose an action for specific performance. It is also true that some aspects of Mr Malcolm's conduct of the litigation have only served to harden the Press's attitude.

Eight nailbiting weeks went by, with every day a test of my steadily increasing faith in the probity and scrupulousness of the Supreme Court Judiciary against those dark, unworthy fears of secret deals and masonic compacts. At last, on 13th December, I got a phonecall from the Appeals Registry that the Court had completed its judgment, which would be 'handed down' (delivered) on the following Tuesday in Crypt Court 2, and that a typed draft would be available beforehand from the 'kiosk' at the main entrance at 3.30 on Monday. Liz and I made the necessary arrangements and arrived at the Strand just as a light snow was beginning to fall through the sickly London fog. I collected the awaiting heavy brown manila envelope from the kiosk, tore it open, but could not bear to read the thick document inside, leaving its deciphering to Liz. This took some time, partly because we were anxious to get out of the snow and into my barrister's chambers nearby in Lincoln's Inn, and partly because the judgment was very long: a detailed explanation by Mustill LJ of the history and the litigation (45 pages) followed by two careful, dense legal analyses by Nourse and Leggatt LJJ (7 pages and 5 pages). The nub of Lord Justice Mustill's judgment, 'contract or no contract?' came at page 40, somewhere around the back of the law courts, and Liz's voice dropped gloomily, quickly to rise again as her eyes then fell on his final, beautiful paragraph: "I have felt drawn, for the reasons stated, to propose that the appeal should be dismissed. My Lords are of a different opinion. For once, it is satisfying to be in a minority." A quick race across Lincoln's Inn and through Nourse and Leggatt LJJ's legalese confirmed the news: by a two-to-one majority my appeal had been allowed, with costs.

My ever-accommodating barrister welcomed us into his chambers in New Square and immediately uncorked a bottle of excellent red wine. As we pored (and poured) over the judgment in his room, it gradually became clear that this was not merely a victory, but was likely to become a legally important, famous one. It also became clear that the judges had devoted an enormous amount of time, thought and care to their reasonings, which together made, I do impartially believe, a document of some beauty. Mustill LJ's presentation, especially, is a masterpiece of completeness, succinctness and elegance, while Nourse and Leggatt LJJ's are sharp gems of penetrating logic. For the benefit of law scholars, I have added Nourse and Leggatt LJJ's core analyses as an appendix (see page 225), and for true fanatics, the complete judgment is again posted on the Internet (see page 223). Oddly, although he found against me at the nub, and with no clear explanation why, it was to Lord Justice Mustill that I at first felt most gratitude, gratitude that he had grasped and set down the whole business so thoroughly and so cleverly. Whatever happened next, the wait (not just the past two months, but the whole preceding four years) had been worth it: at last someone had *listened*. Equally oddly, rather as on receipt of Hardy's good news of five-and-a-half years earlier, my first reaction to the victory was one of daze, almost worry, rather than of euphoria. As previously, I think I sensed there were still some major problems ahead; little did I know how major.

The hearing on the following morning was merely a formal, public confirmation of the draft judgment's status, but it did provide some sort of ceremonial occasion to which a few close friends and supporters could hurriedly be invited; this time, however, no-one appeared from Oxford. Nourse LJ's section had ended: "For my part, I would allow the appeal and order an enquiry as to damages", and Leggatt LJ had added:

> "I agree with Nourse LJ that the appeal should be allowed and an
> enquiry ordered as to damages. But a becoming magnanimity on the
> respondents' part, matched on the part of Mr Malcolm by a realistic
> moderation, will avoid the need for any enquiry."

Clearly, the court assumed that Oxford would now make an offer of
damages and at last honourably settle the whole disastrous business. I
however did not share their faith in such an outcome and was worried by
two important costs orders that still stood against me (Justice Morritt's
seventy-five percent on my contempt motion and Master Barratt's on the
three subpoenas), which it now appeared had been secured under false
pretences, and against which I had therefore been seeking leave to appeal.
Understandably, however, the three judges assumed that everything would
soon be settled and wanted to hear nothing of these tiresome side-issues.
They quickly departed, leaving me to bid goodbye to a very grumpy Mark
Warby, to stammer out a few clichés for the nice knitting lady ("justice at
last done... hope authors now get fair deals... so forth"), and to some
slightly troubled celebrations with friends. Back out in the cold London
air, my unclear, unvoiced, unshared fears about the future turned out to be
icily well-founded.

Besides its legal importance, the judgment also looked on dissection likely
to provoke an academic scandal, for it was peppered with severe criticisms
of the Press, the Delegates, and Oxford's handling of the litigation:

> "I find it disturbing that when the appellant attempted to meet it
> [the print-run and format point] with evidence from the trade the
> respondents stoutly resisted its introduction: and yet, when it was
> introduced they caved in and made no attempt to controvert it. The
> respondents had ample notice of the application and the fact that they
> had not come to the hearing of the appeal armed with evidence to the
> contrary must show that there was no such evidence to get. The Press is
> one of the longest-established publishing houses in the United
> Kingdom, and no doubt in the world. They must have been aware from
> the outset that the absence of agreement on the matters in question was
> not, in the trade, regarded as preventing a formal agreement from
> coming into existence. Candour would, I believe, have required that
> this should have been made clear to the judge and ourselves, rather
> than a determined refusal to let the true position come to light.
> This is not quite all. I do not know whether an outsider studying
> the history of this transaction and of this litigation would feel that, in
> his self-financed struggle with the assembled Chancellor, Masters and
> Scholars of the University of Oxford the appellant has had a fair crack
> of the whip. I certainly do not... If the evidence adduced by the Press is
> to be relied upon, the project was never the subject of grave deliberation
> by the Delegates on whether the intellectual merits of *Making Names*

would measure up to the high standards which the Press had always set for itself. The staff of the Press stopped the project before it ever reached the Delegates. Mr Charkin took the decision, not because he thought the book was no good — he had never seen it and the reports were favourable — but because he thought it would not sell. Let there be no mistake about it, the failure of this transaction was about money, not prestige. Nor does the course of the litigation give any reason to suppose that the Press had any interest but to resist the claim, no matter on what grounds, so long as they succeeded.

The history of the interlocutory proceedings suggested that there was a failure of communication between the respondents' legal advisers and those in charge at the Press. Could it also be that the Delegates whose interests are so directly in suit were out of touch with what was going on in the action? Could it be that they did not know what had been, what was being, said about the stance adopted by the Press?" (Mustill LJ)

"It is difficult to know what the Deputy Judge [Lightman] meant by a 'firm commitment' other than an intention to create legal relations. Nothing short of that would have had any value whatever for Mr Malcolm. He had made it clear that without a commitment he was not prepared to undertake the work of revision expected of him. To suggest that Mr Hardy intended to induce Mr Malcolm to revise the book by giving him a valueless assurance would be tantamount to an imputation of fraud... It follows that in my judgment when Mr Hardy used the expressions 'commitment' and 'a fair royalty' he did in fact mean what he said; and I venture to think that it would take a lawyer to arrive at any other conclusion. There was therefore an enforceable contract for the publication of Mr Malcolm's book." (Leggatt LJ)

The judges found Oxford's final statement "unworthy of them", and after reproducing its typed version in full, Mustill LJ simply added the words "Who runs may read", a reference to the Old Testament book of Habbakuk:

"And the Lord answered me, and said, Write the vision, and make it plain upon tables, that he may run that readeth it... Woe to him that coveteth an evil covetousness to his house, that he may set his nest on high, that he may be delivered from the power of evil! Thou hast consulted shame to thy house by cutting off many people, and hast sinned against thy soul." (Chapter 2, verses 2, 9 and 10.)

The Guardian, The Telegraph, The Times, and *The Brighton Argus* all reported my victory ("Appeal court backs author", "Appeal judges bring publishers to book", "Writer wins legal battle"). Now I had become "The author Andrew Malcolm...", and even "The philosopher Andrew Malcolm..." with no ifs, buts, or inverted commas, and despite the fact that no-one from any of these papers had contacted me or knew anything about the book. The reports, however, omitted quotation of the judges' numerous anti-Oxford comments and the newspapers generally showed no further interest in the story. The only exception was Laurence Marks, an *Observer* correspondent to whom I had recently been introduced by Mark Le Fanu. Marks did take an interest, seemed an excellent journalist and a delightful man, and shared a keen disrespect for academe. He was thrilled by my victory, promised a large article, and travelled down to Brighton for an interview (I declined a session entreated by the paper's photo-desk). For me 1990 had been, besides everything else, a heavy building-work year: I had moved up the road from my basement to another, larger flat which I had previously been letting and was now renovating, and there had been a spectacular police-chase-cum-stolen-truck-crash into the front of my original house, which was extensively damaged. I think Marks was impressed as much by the resulting practical chaos he witnessed as by my legal success: his article of 23rd December was headlined "A builder's dialogue that silenced OUP" and began with a Jimmy Durante joke: *'They said Mozart was mad. They said Puccini was mad. They said Louie was mad.' Who's Louie? 'My uncle. He <u>was</u> mad!'* Marks quoted the annual turnover of Oxford's 'charitable' Press as £133 million and hailed my result as historic: "It is the first time in living memory that Grub Street has won such a victory over its oppressors." He went on to spare Oxford none of the appeal judges' brickbats and his was the only report, then or since, to mention any of the numerous disreputable aspects of Oxford's conduct of the litigation. In lieu of a photograph of me, as an illustration for the piece *The Observer* used OUP's DIM colophon. Marks concluded by suggesting for this his own translation of Oxford's "new rib-busting ethos": "Never give a sucker an even break".

Another practical problem arose with the freezing- and then seizing-up of my car, leaving myself and Liz without transport over Xmas. To keep us going I bought an MOT-legal but very wrecked old Vauxhall VX4/90 for £50 from a nearby team of salvagers. Its bodywork (silver with black PVC roof) was so shot through with rust-holes that we sickly christened it *the Basra*. Its exhaust blew throatily like a souped motorbike; and every time it revved hard, a broken mounting threw the rear of the gear-box and the prop-shaft upwards into the floor of the car, giving passengers the impression that it was rocket-powered. However, its unsilenced two-litre engine was superb, it out-accelerated any other motor we encountered, and its faded leopard-skin seats, chrome radio and wide-boy trim still gave it a certain raffish style. Distributing cases of Australian fizz round the Inns of Court in fake fur and this loud, fast, unlikely heap, we for a few days felt as though we had at last won something.

20

Making Law

In his peculiar preface to *Publishing Agreements* (1993), Charles Clark states that as a result of *Malcolm v. Oxford University*, the question of what are the essential terms of author-publisher contracts "is currently being hotly debated in international copyright circles", and proposes seven minimum requirements, each one of which could doubtless generate a fresh law-library of ambiguities, loopholes and disputes. Fortunately though, in the real world, law is not made by jet-setting potentates cell-telephoning one another, tut-tutting and dreaming up fancy rules, it is made, and only made, by individuals taking disputes to Court and by judges making reasoned decisions upon their particular facts. Clark concedes that in my case the right decision was made on the ground of individual justice, but of course the point is that in practice *there is no other kind of ground*. As Laurence Marks wrote, I now had the doubtful honour of joining the ranks of "that great army of bloody-minded upon whose intransigence English common law has been built throughout the centuries." And as Mustill LJ had snapped at some untimely interruption during the Appeal, "Shush, we are making law here!"

The few serious reports on the case all concentrated on the fact that my contract with Hardy was consummated by telephone. In July 1986 Hugh Jones himself wrote a two-page analysis for *The Bookseller* actually headed "Publishing Contracts by Telephone". The story was sometimes even presented as though Hardy's commitment had been made *casually*, when of course in fact it had been made in the context of a very careful, year-long negotiation with copious correspondence, both before and after our 20th May conversation, and as I have suggested, I might well have had a case *without* any recording tapes. Of the four most recent publishing contract precedents in the books (*Warne v. Routledge* [1873] L.R.18 497, *Abrahams v. Reiach* [1922] 1 K.B. 477, *Joseph v. National Magazine Co.* [1959] 1 Ch 14 and *Barrow v. Chappell* (1951) [1976] R.P.C. 355), three of the contracts pleaded were oral (not even recorded) and their existence was uncontested, while in the fourth it was unclear; the issues were all to do with the contracts' consequences and effects in law. Obviously my telephone point was noteworthy, but it was by far the least interesting or legally important aspect, and would have had no significance at all if, for example, Hardy had simply told the truth. I believe that to this day most commentators have missed the case's main implications, which in roughly ascending order of importance I take to be:

1. That a publisher's agreement to publish (a certain text) for a stated consideration and no more (with no agreed specification as to print-run, format, retail price etc.) is sufficiently complete to be enforceable. It may be said that this merely reaffirms the view accepted in *Abrahams*, but firstly it is always important to have such points reiterated, and secondly, that case, unlike mine, did not concern a previously-unpublished book: the athletes' material had already appeared in a magazine.

2. As noted in *Chitty* (2-082), that the absence of a formal signed *Memorandum of Agreement* or other such document does not vitiate a contract. There is much other familiar case-law on the point, but again it is good to have it reaffirmed, and in a publishing context.

3. Again as noted in *Chitty* (2-102), that an editor's phrase "a fair royalty" can constitute a sufficiently certain term as to 'stated consideration'. Although similar usages have been established in other areas of law, this is the first time in a publishing contract.

4. That an author's contract to revise according to agreed criteria A, B, C... a submitted but (to the author and/or publisher) unsatisfactory text can be legally binding on the publisher. One might add provisos that, to be sustainable, the criteria must be reasonable and their fulfilment within reason; no publisher, not even OUP, could reject a script on the grounds of a mistyped comma. Put this another way: *Malcolm* is effectively the first instance of an enforceable contract being found where, at the time of the contract's formation, the text to be published was yet to be finally written. I say 'effectively' because in *Abrahams*, the material had been published prior to the breach as a series of magazine articles, so there was by then no uncertainty as to the text. I believe that this is the first time that such a 'revision conditional' contract claim has been won in court, and that it is a major and so far unremarked gain for authors, demonstrating that a publisher's draconian 'subject to our approval of the finished script' clause can be avoided. In short, working on a contracted script at a publisher's behest (cf. *Planchè v. Colburn* [1831] Binghams C.P. 8 14) has at last gained the status of 'ordinary' work like plumbing or printing.

5. That in the event of a breach of contract, a publisher may be liable to pay an author damages under at least two heads: loss of opportunity to establish or enhance reputation and loss of estimated royalties. This may

be thought taken as legally read, but it has never before been so clearly tested in court over an unpublished book. For publishers this is potentially the costliest point of all. In practice, it has been the custom that when a publisher 'routinely' reneges on a contract, they forfeit the author's advance. Post-*Malcolm*, it is now open to such authors, if they (can prove that they) met all the conditions incumbent upon them, and do not sell their scripts elsewhere, to claim damages perhaps far in excess of their usually niggardly advances. Further, my subsequent damages enquiry has provided a model, albeit a flawed one, for such calculations. (See pages 230 and 239 for appendices on authors' damages and on the *Malcolm*-derived case of *Myers v. Macmillan*.)

As far as I know, none of these interesting legal implications has ever properly, publicly been aired and examined, and most authors (and publishers) are probably still unaware of them.

On the question of remedy, all three of the Court of Appeal judges agreed with Lightman that specific performance was not practicable, and at the time I yielded to Mustill LJ's logic about the 'gelding' of the contract. Now I am not so sure. Lightman's reasoning on this point was that relations between myself and the University had (admittedly and obviously) broken down and that our co-operation would be required for any publication to be completed. But by the court-order stage *any* such relationship must be assumed defunct, yet specific performance is not uncommon. Obviously a court will not want to enforce continuing co-operation between parties who have fallen out, but why should an ordered one-off printing of a certain text necessarily be impracticable? My subsequent two years of very hit-and-miss (and hugely expensive) damages proceedings, and their consequences, appear to me to indicate that a compulsory printing might sometimes be both a simpler clean-break settlement and a more equitable remedy. Could not a court reasonably 'geld' such a contract if justice seemed to require it? Hugh Jones' remarks on the question imply that, even in normal circumstances (where a contracted author does not seek or reach agreement as to his book's initial print-run and format, or obtain his publisher's internal documents about them), 'ungelded' specific performance might now be granted. Maybe in a case where a book's print-run and format are not agreed but can be inferred because it had been planned to appear in an established series, it might be held appropriate. But whether, given that this might also entail the assignment of the author's rights to a now-hostile publisher, and the printed copies remaining that publisher's property, such 'full' specific performance could ever be a desirable outcome is another question.

It has been suggested that although *Malcolm v. Oxford* did not itself achieve the elusive remedy of specific performance (a court-ordered book-publication), it may have brought such a possibility closer. In a case deemed appropriate, what might a court enforce? There is a legal principle that no defendant should be obliged to fulfill more than their minimum or least costly obligations under the terms of the breached contract. In the case of an author-publisher agreement, the publisher's obligations are normally notoriously vague (see again Nicola Solomon's article in *The Author* of Summer 1991), and in *Abrahams*, Mr Jowitt had argued for the publisher that "he need not publish more than one edition [copy]". The courts rejected this submission, seeking instead to establish what constituted "a reasonable publication" of the book in order to assess Abrahams' and Liddell's entitlement to damages (they were seeking only their lost royalties). The first judge estimated 30,000 copies yielding £500, and on appeal by the publisher the higher Court reduced this to 6,000 copies yielding £100. In his judgment, Bankes LJ mentions a principle extracted from *Reade v. Bentley* (1858) 4 K&J 656 that a publisher who has agreed to publish a work must publish it, but is not bound to continue publishing it. *Barrow v. Chappell* (1951) [1976] R.P.C. 355 concerned a piece of already-performed music, the score of which was to have appeared in a magazine with an established circulation, so questions about print-run and distribution did not arise. Here, Justice Danckwerts held that, notwithstanding uncertainties about the written score, damages would be difficult to assess and not provide an adequate remedy, though he did not elaborate why. He ordered specific performance and £75 damages for loss through delay.

In May 1995 I was informed by Mark Le Fanu that the Society of Authors was backing an action on behalf of a group of twelve or so poets whose contracts, entered into by Christopher Sinclair-Stevenson, had recently been breached by Charkin's Reed International (Reed had bought out Sinclair-Stevenson's imprint and then sacked him, casually consigning his contracted poetry to the shredder). My case was being cited on the poets' behalf and specific performance (their publication by Reed) was being sought. This set me thinking. The purpose of the law is to restore the successful plaintiff to the position they would have enjoyed had their contract been fulfilled as contemplated by both parties at its inception. But of course the law's only currency is money, not that elusive commodity literary reputation, which was probably higher in the poets' minds than lucrative royalties. I could therefore imagine a court here repeating the line adopted by Danckwerts J. Again, one is reminded that for many (would-be) authors, such as Oxford's own stable of scholars, publication, and thereby reputation, may in itself be sufficient contractual consideration;

not everyone is in it for the cash, even the less immediate cash. I imagine too that for poets, the 'hostile publisher' problem may not arise because the distribution and promotion of new poetry is notoriously poor anyway, and most sales occur through readings and private circulation. Surely an order entitling the poets to buy a proportion of their enforced reasonable print-runs at cost-price would not constitute an unwarranted 'gelding' of their contracts? Curiously, the Society of Authors' *Quick Guide to Contracts* backtracks here: "Even when the the contract contains a firm undertaking to publish, the publishers probably cannot be compelled to publish the book." I wonder if this use of the word 'probably' may not just signal a general reluctance to think clearly and bravely.

The poets' situation however, also highlights the peculiarity of author-publisher contracts where the literary work submitted is already finished and accepted as such. In such a case there is no uncertainty as to the text to be published, but also no more work to be done by the author, so there arises the question: what does the author lose if the publisher later, for whatever reason, changes their mind and reneges on their agreement? Some precious hopes are dashed, obviously, and some valuable time may have been wasted, but whatever the book's projected sales, it might be hard for its author to prove any serious financial disentitlement. With some of the poets, the time between "Yes we will publish you" and "No sorry, we won't" was only a month or two. Further, contract law requires that in the event of a breach, both parties try to minimise any losses in which it results, and no doubt a court would ask the poets if they had then tried taking their work elsewhere, as Reed presumably invited them to do. When a work is submitted as complete, envisaged royalties and a chance of enhanced reputation may be lost by a its non-publication, but little or nothing may have been done or lost by the author *as a result of being given a contract*. As Hugh Jones points out, my case was very different, for I was contracted to spend an envisaged six months revising a book to OUP's specific requirements. No doubt too, if Oxford had made any serious attempt to recompense me for my wasted work or to help me get *Making Names* published elsewhere, I and the court might have taken different lines, but by, for example, Elliott's public defamation of it, the University instead appeared to want to *sabotage* any constructive alternatives.

One corollary of all this is to ask why any publisher which has landed itself with a contract to publish some work about which it subsequently (genuinely) changes its mind, and which then finds itself in dispute with an aggrieved author, doesn't simply print their damned book and have done with it. Reasonable-quality, short-run printing is getting increasingly inexpensive (see Appendix 4, page 243), and the publisher would not have to spend or do much to fulfill its obligations. A lady recently won a case (*Steans v. West*, 1997) against a crooked vanity publisher when her few supplied copies fell to bits, but surely even OUP should by now have mastered the art of book-binding? (Mind you, when returning my two typescripts of *Making Names* in 1989, they did manage to wrap them both — over 1,000 A4 sheets weighing more than five kilograms — in a single thin sheet of manila paper, ensuring their destruction in the post.) *Malcolm v. Oxford* may, I suppose, have helped to make such out-of-court, properly-bound 'remedies' more common, in which case, well, hallelujah! I gather that of the Reed Twelve, the three who had Reed's printed *Memoranda* (Alice Kavounas, Herbert Lomas and Michael Glover) persuaded Reed to publish them, but that all but one of the rest, who had less formal agreements, settled out of court for cash payments ranging from £500—1,000. In June 1997 the last outstanding claim was won in the Whitehaven County Court by Christopher Pilling, who was awarded damages of £1,250 (his intended advance of £1,000 plus £250 for lost reputation) and costs. Pilling had no formal memorandum and only the sparsest of correspondence, but was in the interesting position of having Sinclair-Stevenson himself testifying on his behalf as to the validity of their contract. However, as Pilling's claim was for damages only, the question of what might constitute 'a proper case' for a court-ordered book-publication remains unelucidated.

21

The Unforgiving

RETURNING TO my narrative, around Xmas 1990 the generally bad publicity for Oxford continued to swell, and it was assumed that surely the University would now heed the Court's judgment, this time the *Appeal* Court's judgment, and at last settle the awful business decently. *The Guardian* and *The Telegraph* quoted Nourse LJ's hope that "Mr Malcolm would be spared the anxiety of further litigation and that, with goodwill on both sides, it would be possible to agree the amount of damages. If not, the damages issue would be referred to a senior High Court official for determination." Everyone — the lawyers, the newspapers, various disinterested academic spectators — everyone now expected Oxford to show some sign of Lord Justice Leggatt's "becoming magnanimity"; everyone that is, except my increasingly pessimistic self. Christmas went by, but no sign came, until 4th January 1991, when I received another of Ivon Asquith's invitations to talk over tea. His suggested date was the afternoon of the 23rd, and this time his chosen venue was Brown's, the exclusive Mayfair hotel.

Early on in the action, I picked up from Richard White a good lawyer's habit which I strongly recommend to authors, or indeed to anyone, involved in any sort of putative negotiation: always make a note as soon and as comprehensively as possible after any unrecorded exchange, meeting or other incident, however apparently trivial. Try to write down everything that happened and all that was said, if possible verbatim, whilst the impressions are still fresh. If my memory is anything to go by, the wax melts and distorts with alarming rapidity, and if events are not noted quickly others soon erase them or render them mythological, even to oneself. Fortunately, my Brown's meeting with Asquith was one of the incidents I managed to note thoroughly, on the train back to Brighton, and the resulting script now provides one of the affair's most precious cameos. I will try to condense its five pages into as many paragraphs.

This time it was I who arrived first, to be advised at the door by the hotel staff that leather jackets were not allowed and that ties were obligatory (a metaphor, perhaps, for my whole Oxford encounter?) The staff were helpful, however, offering to lend me a tweed and producing a box of assorted ties they kept for this very emergency. We compromised on just the latter, and as I sank into one of the lounge's deep armchairs I wondered whether I was the first person ever to have taken tea at Brown's (*"a reminder of the finer things of life"*) wearing a blouson. Asquith entered soon after and pressed his face up against the dimpled brown glass of the lobby to see if I had already arrived; the only result of this was to make him look first doubly fishlike, and then when I waved at him, dumbly embarrassed. We shook hands, but he offered no congratulations, or even comment, on my result, clucking on instead about the horrid London traffic, the state of the tube system, the advantages of living in the provinces, so forth. When a handsome tea was at length presented, Asquith said "I must watch my figure, I put on weight so easily." This at once rang an alarm bell, for Asquith was at best a beanpole and at worst undernourished; there was certainly a serious lack of weight in the chin area. His ensuing eating pattern did nothing to reassure: slow, tentative nibbles at mini-teacakes lightly dusted with cream and jam followed, very late on, by a surprising, hearty lunge for the cheese rolls. Prattle continued about the cucumber sandwiches (of course), about Brown's being the perfect set for *Earnest*, "Wilde used to stay here you know...", "...and Kipling I believe", before Asquith felt ready to announce "I am only here to discuss damages." Phew, I was beginning to wonder.

What Asquith really meant was that he was *not* here to discuss costs, which he anticipated going through a long taxation palaver. I explained that I had been advised to expect, and to request, a 'global' settlement of the whole claim, damages, costs and the lot, so that we could quickly put it all behind us, and so that I, as Nourse LJ had said, would be spared the anxiety of further litigation. I reminded him that there were several large costs orders still in dispute between us, so if lawyers were going to have to continue working on these and on a complex taxation, then they might as well draw up a damages claim too. I also warned him of a lesson I had already learnt that any costs saved *by* a taxation would, as likely as not, be spent *on* it. This provoked a surprisingly intimate and prescient response: "Ah yes, something like that happened to me in litigation with my *ghastly* ex-wife... she was demanding that I pay our boy's private school fees, which are unnecessary anyway in the Oxford area; I offered two-thirds into court, the court awarded half-and-half, and she then had to pay the costs of the hearing. Mind you, my solicitor in that case was a lot more competent than ours have been in this..." I further reminded him that in any event Oxford would have to pay *both* sides' costs of an assessment, and that if the University did not start to settle things soon, I would reinstruct Richard White rather than continue to act in person. "Why?" he asked, chuckling feebly, "you seem to be rather good at it." "I've had enough," I replied, "and besides, I think these arguments about money are, are..." "...distasteful, yes" he completed, between mouthfuls. But none of it seemed to be going in: with no figures mentioned by either side, we were already, as Ryan would say, at cross purposes, and I was already contemplating the anxiety of further litigation.

When it did come to figures, things got even less promising. Asquith suggested that Oxford might concede damages based on the PPF print-run, that is, about £2,000. I reminded him of Ryan's comparisons with *The Outsider* and *Gödel, Escher, Bach* and produced two extracts from my privileged conversations with Hardy in which he had talked of his plan to put *Making Names* straight into paperback. I watched Asquith's eyes skate sightlessly over the pages, only *as if* reading them. Amazingly, he warned that Oxford would be calling Charkin ("a friend of mine") as a witness against the unread book's prospects, exclaiming "Surely you do not doubt that he is an *extremely* successful publisher?" "But that's just business isn't it? Haggling with agents, stitching up reversion rights, sacking people, accountancy?" I suggested that a court would presumably prefer to rely upon the opinions expressed at the time by Ryan, Strawson and Hardy, the men who had read the book, together contracted it, and who had intended to "gallop ahead" with its publication. "But these are only a couple of academics and a not-very-successful editor!" he snorted back. I conceded that my *Outsider*-based claim was obviously exaggerated, and I relayed Richard White's accurate calculation that, counting his and my barrister's three years' fees and my own two years' work (litigants-in-person are allowed about one-third of solicitors' going rates), plus mark-up and disbursements, a taxation would probably allow me between fifty-five and sixty thousand pounds costs, and that a global sum of about double this would therefore settle it. Asquith appeared to be writing down the figures, but from where I sat I could not see if there was any ink in his pen; he certainly made it clear that he did not believe I could possibly have spent anything like that kind of money. Maybe I should have borrowed Brown's tweed after all.

Asquith revealed that he had been 'handling' their end of the case since 1988 [I imagine he had taken it over from Charkin], and in his head still seemed to be fighting it: "In the end you won, but the judges were two-all", he whined, revealing his total lack of grasp or reasoning, as though he had just been playing the odds. Then, as we drifted into a more general discussion of authors' and publishers' legal rights, to which I will return later, he repeated Fortnum's famous dislocatory "Don't you think it quite *unfair* that you have the tapes and we don't?" Suddenly, again, that all-pervading sense of unreality, truthlessness, moral vacuum. He was obviously burning to know what had passed in my privileged conversations with Hardy, so I gave him a flavour of them, and when I mentioned

Hardy's dictation of a letter he had asked me to write, Asquith sat up in surprise: "What? He dictated you a letter?" "Yes, haven't you read my witness statement?" "No." (In fact I had also told Asquith about Hardy's letter-dictation at our Soda Fountain frolic, yet because I had told him, I guess he had not heard; similarly, he was fixated on the privileged tapes he could not have, yet for three years had been uninterested to hear the contractual exchange.) This was all extraordinary, but worse was to come: "Have you read *Abrahams v. Reiach* (eight pages), the main authority in the case, especially on damages?" "No." "Have you read my Further and Better Particulars, the pleading on damages you specifically requested in October 1989?" "No." I felt I might as well have been talking to the cakestand.

Again, *what is it* with these people? Ethics apart, their life is the printed word, their every business is papers, articles, books, writing, yet nothing, nothing, even now after a five-year blizzard of litigation, was ever being *read* by anyone. OUP holds Britain's record for most prolific publisher: in 1995 it launched over 2,400 new titles and editions. Yet here was Charkin allergic to paper, forbidding the taking of minutes, there was Hardy in court with his umpteen different versions of history swimming before him like tabloids in a torrent, everywhere ran a whole river of Oxford affidavits and testimonies hardly a single one of which was true, and now came Asquith to a meeting he had specially called to discuss damages, without having bothered to read my two little sides on the subject. Perhaps these people's consumption by printed matter engenders some sort of intellectual dyslexia or semantic breakdown, I don't know; all I can say is that *I* was lost for words when Asquith gaped back at me so dreamily, so vacantly. Tea at Brown's was all very nice, but I had travelled from Brighton for this meeting and he seemed to be just wasting my time. I quickly wrapped things up with a handshake and bade him a pessimistic goodbye. In two-and-a-half hours Asquith had made no offer and mentioned not a single figure of his own, save for the PPF's £2,000; as he said, he felt we were "poles apart". He was right there, I thought, as I handed my tie back to the receptionist.

The Court of Appeal had warned me against making an excessive claim. Lord Justice Leggatt urged "a realistic moderation", while Lord Justice Mustill, marvelling at the lengths to which the University had gone in defending the action, said:

> As to the financial side, although the trial judge said that if he had found a breach of contract the damages would have been 'substantial', too much should not be built on this. *Making Names* might have been

one of the rarities in the field of mathematics, logic and metaphysics which captured the attention of the non-specialist purchaser. Equally, it might like its distinguished predecessor have 'fallen dead-born from the press'. Contingencies of this nature must have entailed that even if the appellant's action were to succeed, the financial recovery could not be on an extravagant scale. This being so, a settlement fair to both sides should not be beyond reach.

I took Mustill LJ's oblique confusion of my loss of reputation (OUP's imprimatur) with my lost royalties as a deliberate non-sequitur, and his "distinguished predecessor" to be David Hume's classic *Treatise of Human Nature*, which happens to be much-quoted in *Making Names*. In fact, perhaps tellingly, Hume's *Treatise* was only taken up by OUP later, its original abortive publication in 1739 having been by one "JOHN NOON, at the *White-Hart*, near *Mercer's-Chapel*, in *Cheapſide*, LONDON". Mustill LJ could also, of course, have been offering an even obliquer reminder that people can easily be proved wrong about books, one way and the other. But just as the Court of Appeal had not been privy to the transcripts which revealed the Charkin-n-Hardy feud, so it had not read of the latter's ambitious plans to put *Making Names* straightaway into paperback. I realise that it is unusual for philosophers, or indeed for many authors, to make much money from their work, but here, on all the evidence, was surely a most unusual publication: a controversial, general readers' text, published under the OUP imprint, by an editor hoping for a terrific success, to be launched in the mass-market, and with two key Sunday newspaper reviewers apparently already onside. Even leaving aside 'the merits' of the case, the seven years it had now taken, and its ruination of my writing career, surely I had some realistic legal grounds for anticipating a *moderately* good settlement?

Over the next few weeks Oxford still made no offer of any kind, so in February I reinstructed Richard White, thinking that the prospect of fresh, professional proceedings might coax a little magnanimity from the rudely wealthy press. Damages was an entirely new area of law of which I was ignorant, and whatever happened the opposition would now be paying my costs. However, far from making any offer, Oxford sacked Dallas Brett and in their stead instructed Clifford Chance, one of London's most expensive and heaviest-duty commercial lawyers, to continue the fight against me, and appointed Harvey McGregor Q.C. their leading Counsel. McGregor was an occasionally-practising barrister, Warden since 1985 of New College, and editor since 1961 of English law's 'Bible' on the subject of damages. Mark Warby was also retained in an advisory capacity, presumably because of his knowledge of the background. Chancers' solicitor entrusted with the case was another oily man, this time of the Scottish variety, by the name of Michael Smyth who, according to *Private Eye's* 'Bookworm', charged Oxford £275 an hour plus VAT for his damage-limitation services. McGregor's book, as I had already discovered for myself, is a lucid and refreshingly unstuffy work, but my lawyers were scathing of its author's practical abilities, as far as they knew of them (though I had earlier witnessed the practising professionals' scorn for those who choose a quiet life amongst the dreaming spires). There was no doubting, however, the likely size of McGregor's fees. This was some magnanimity; the 'David and Goliath' tag was proving way too puny.

Besides Oxford's evident lack of contrition and its disdain for the Court's findings, Asquith's remark had confirmed that the OUnuchs laid the main blame for their defeat at the door of their local solicitors Dallas Brett. I believe this is an injustice. Undoubtedly Dallas Brett made a few mistakes, some of which baffled Richard White, but a solicitor can only take his client's instructions on any decision and only take his client's word for the truth. Oxford's various witnesses had a documented history of disagreeing and deceiving one another (never mind me, or themselves), so it was hardly likely that their lawyers would ever get a straight or consistent story. Nourse and Leggatt LJJ expressly confirmed that they had found a complete contract in Hardy's original words to me, and had not needed to infer any terms. Their analysis has to stand up, does and will stand up, to the scrutiny of future generations of lawmen. Whomever Oxford had instructed, and however much money it had thrown at the problem, I believe its rotten ship would always have been wrecked on these implacable factual rocks, to which I imagine it still remains resolutely blind. Bizarrely, after four years of litigation, the case had in the end been decided entirely on analysis of one comparatively simple exchange, evidence which was offered (but declined) long before I had consulted a lawyer, let alone served a writ. Brett's most obvious mistake was not to request this central evidence immediately upon their instruction (at the appeal Warby admitted that he had *never* heard the 20th May recording). But as said, shouldn't Oxford already (in July 1986) have asked for it themselves? I, of course, am not privy to their original advice from Counsel; if everyone was persevering under the "no contract without a memorandum" assumption, then maybe the University did have a right to feel badly advised, but can one seriously imagine that such a grand a legal institution, so bristling with senior lawyers, could for so long have been fooled into such an elementary mistake? Still, for people who "hate paying lawyers' fees" (R. Charkin, October 1986), they had proved good enough suckers already, so maybe.

Oxford's deadline for appealing to the House of Lords passed nervously but without incident. Way back at the start of the action Charkin had threatened that the University would take the case that far, and I guess they may have considered doing so, but the Court of Appeal judgment was extremely thorough and left them little or no forward room. Although Lord Justice Mustill had found no contract, his full account of the history was irreparably damaging of Oxford's integrity, and, unlike the other judges' acute dissections, his reasoning at the nub was pointedly thin. It was hard to imagine any argument that the University could still run. Although at the appeal I had jokingly suggested that in May 1985 there was evidence of some residual uncertainty about the book's agreed *subtitle* and that Oxford might now wish to re-plead its defence along these lines, my invitation was declined.

Lord Justice Nourse's hope that I be spared the anxiety of further litigation was, however, soon dashed. The blizzard restarted in March with a demand from Clifford Chance that I hand over all the correspondence (including any tape-recordings or notes thereof) I had ever had with any other publishers relating to any earlier versions of *Making Names* ("including, but not limited to Penguin, Blackwell's, Allen & Unwin, *et cetera.*"). They also demanded to see my entire income tax file, continued to pursue the fiction that the University had nothing to do with the subpoenaed witnesses, requested that Richard White draw up his provisional bill, served a summons on me to appear before Master Barratt to obtain his (their) directions, and set out an extended timetable for a damages enquiry which they obviously expected to take at least another year. Victory provides no refuge in *Bleak Hut*, or, risking an unsporting allusion to the former Mrs Asquith, Hell has no fury like an élite rumbled.

In a twist that neither Dickens, Shakespeare nor even Congreve would have devised, the taxation of Sir Michael Atiyah's costs coincided with my sister's death from cancer, while outside, the legal wind-chill factor intensified. Dallas Brett had never been remiss in seizing a fee-charging opportunity — writing two or three letters where two or three lines would do — but Clifford Chance, we quickly realised, were serious clockers. Judging from our file's rapid thickening, their cash tachometer must have been way up at full torque from the off, with procedural issues multiplying exponentially. As demanded, I provided my file of correspondence with pre-OUP publishers, including Routledge, Allen & Unwin, Macmillan, Blackwell, Collins, Abacus, Paladin, Chatto & Windus, Harvester, Dent, Gollancz, Harrap, Duckworth, Weidenfeld, Secker & Warburg, Sidgwick & Jackson, Deutsch, Sage, Scolar, Constable, Hamish Hamilton, Edinburgh U.P. and

Americans McGraw-Hill, Basic Books, Pantheon and Braziller. Though none of these except Granada had ever looked at *Making Names,* the bulky file no doubt did wonders for Chancers' account. Ironically, the whole purpose of Oxford's ensuing lavish expense of its 'trading surplus' was to try to prove that publishing books, especially philosophical books, never makes any money. I, on the other hand, had by this time discovered that *The Outsider* (1956) and *Gödel, Escher, Bach* (1979) had each sold between two and three hundred thousand copies (still large underestimates, as it turned out) in their first five years of publication.

Another twist came when OUP was obliged to reveal that, after all, it held no copy of *Making Names.* We had assumed that they would have kept a photocopy, if only for legal reasons, but apparently they did not think that the book itself — its content, for example — was relevant to any aspect of the case. Now that I had established a contract and the issue was one of damages, they needed a script for 'independent expert evaluation'. This meant that Elliott's *Bookseller* letter, if not Oxford's public statement, advisedly now gave me solid grounds for a libel action. I resisted this temptation, but did succumb to the immense pleasure of selling my first copy of the book, in A4 format and under the very strictest terms of protection, to none other than Oxford University, at a price of £101.86, this figure being arrived at on the basis of Chancers' own bargain copying charges. I had scored my own personal sale of the century.

Readers who, like good lawyers, have been attending to the fine detail in the case, will remember that in the Adrasteia package, there was one undated, uncredited Delegates' paper apparently from a set of two or more pages listing twenty-two OUP General Books paperback titles. In his third affidavit, Sir Otiose had asserted that this document was genuine, but had not volunteered its date. We now questioned Chancers, and they gave it as 20th July 1984, exactly one year earlier than the meeting at which *Making Names* had apparently been approved. This confirmed that, especially at these extra-large summer vacation meetings, the Delegates habitually approved long lists of General Books paperbacks. So where, now, was the equivalent list for 1985? Yet another important document was demonstrably still missing. The only plausible conclusion was that, in line with Hardy's plan confided to me on the telephone at the time, *Making Names* had formally been approved by the Delegates as both a hardback *and* a paperback, a revelation which now further supported a more ambitious damages claim. This conclusion was, of course, denied by Oxford's lawyers, but to this day the paperbacks list for that 23rd July meeting remains undiscovered.

Under pressure from Chancers' increasingly complex demands, the 8th
May assessment date we had obtained was postponed until 10th July. Still
they tried every procedural move and objection they could to stall any
progress, but at a hearing on 19th April, Master Barratt set out a timetable
for the proceedings up to July, specifying clear time limits and restricting
the number of witnesses to three per side; he added that he did not want to
hear from anyone who had not read the book. The hearing was scheduled
for two days, and was be be in camera, in Barratt's camera, on the sixth
floor of the Thomas More building. Chancers' day-to-day donkey-work on
the case was now being done by one Karen Anderson, a bright, neat young
woman originally from South Africa, I think, who somehow seemed
unsuited to her dull grey work clothes. She was very sharp and efficient at
her job, but from time to time I got the impression that she felt miserable
in it. On one occasion when we were chatting in some corridor, she told
me that she had had ambitions to be an actress and had been involved
with the Cambridge Footlights Club, where she had come to much admire
Hugh Laurie. I had had some Footlights experiences too, so we traded
stories; I said nothing about her day-job.

At the directions hearing, I had notified Anderson that Richard White was
going on holiday and that while he was away I would again be acting in
person. On hearing this news, Oxford at last made me an offer of
settlement, over four months since the Court of Appeal's ruling and after
three months of highly intense new litigation, which had already cost me
over £5,000. Trickier still, Oxford's offer was made in the form of a
payment into court, with respect to the damages only, not to the costs,
which the University still disputed. Oddly, Oxford estimated its own costs
of the four-plus years of litigation to appeal at about £40,000 but valued
mine at less than £10,000. As White was away, it was some time before
the significance of this move was fully explained to me. Payment into court
is an established legal technique whereby a party defending a damages suit
can protect themselves against an over-ambitious claimant. According to
the rules, when a payment-in is made of £x, the claimant is allowed three
weeks to decide whether or not to withdraw (accept) the money, and the
defendant's costs are thereafter at the claimant's risk. If the eventual
assessment arrives at a figure of less than £x, the claimant may have to pay
all costs incurred by the defendant after the three-week deadline.

Although Oxford's payment-in was very belated and not a global
settlement of the kind I had anticipated, still entailing complex costs
arguments and arduous taxation proceedings, I was advised that as far as
it went the offer was a reasonably good one. (Because of its relation to the

ultimate confidential settlement, I cannot reveal its size.) If an offer like this had been made back in January, with the disputed costs conceded, I might have haggled a bit but would almost certainly have accepted. However, coming so late, with the legal battle well-and-truly rejoined, and my damages claim by now assembled and in full swing, I was faced with a genuine dilemma. Furthermore, Chancers' tone on the disputed costs — most importantly those of the Morritt hearing and of the subpoenaed witnesses, totalling perhaps £15,000 — was getting more and more belligerent, so the overall value of the deal was worryingly unclear. Whatever I chose to do, litigation of one sort and another still stretched way ahead.

22

Between Nought and Ten Million

IT WAS ACCEPTED by McGregor that I was entitled to damages under two heads: (1) loss of opportunity to enhance my reputation by securing OUP's imprimatur on my work; and (2) royalties estimated to have been lost due to Oxford's non-publication of the book. To these I added: (3) the loss of my ability to have any further dealings with publishers; and (4) pain and suffering. I knew full well that (3) and (4) were not heads of damages which the law normally recognises as recoverable, as they were not matters "in contemplation between the parties" at the time of the contract, but I mentioned them nonetheless, for they were real and depressing enough. Nor does the law recognise what is probably the most serious loss of all in such experiences: one's general disillusionment and demoralisation, a theft, a violation for which there is no remedy at all, in or out of court. (*Making Names* had been intended as a positive, helpful, optimistic book; I certainly could not, I am unhappy to confess, intend such a thing now.) Back with the kinds of loss that the law *does* recognise as recoverable and quantifiable, head (1), loss of reputation, invoked various precedents listed in the law-books: *Chaplin v. Hicks* [1911] 2 K. B. 786, *Marbé v. Edwardes* [1928] 1 K. B. 269, *Clayton v. Oliver* [1930] A.C. 209, *Tolnay v. Criterion Films* [1936] 2 All ER 1626 and *Joseph v. National Magazine Co.* [1959] Ch 14. Quantifying loss of reputation, however, or the value of OUP's imprimatur, is obviously a highly subjective matter, and not one admitting of much argument or reasoning; all a claimant can do is to mention the awards made in the earlier cases, none of which was in truth very comparable with mine, and plead.

On both sides therefore, most attention was focussed on head (2), *Making Names'* lost royalties. As Master Barratt was later to concede in his findings, the calculation of these could be decided by little more than a guess, but by May 1991, certain ground-rules had been accepted in the pleadings, rules which I guess could form the starting-point for any future such awards. McGregor eschewed argument on the *Reade v. Bentley* principle (see page 148), and agreed with me that the calculation should be based on the estimated sales during the book's first five years (the period from its planned launch to the court's assessment, a limitation which is perhaps questionable – see *Myers v. Macmillan*, page 239), using the figures for comparable books. He also agreed that *Making Names* would have been published, as per the PPF, first for a year as a hardback, and then if successful as a paperback, and that seventy-five percent of the total five years' sales would probably have occurred in the first two years (this factor was important with respect to interest). There were small differences between our various suggested retail prices, royalty rates and production timetables, but obviously, the chief question in issue was the book's estimated sales figure; as everyone knows, some books sell in millions, some in only hundreds, with the reasons why often being unclear. Oxford, naturally, withdrew its former optimistic comparisons with *The Outsider* and *Gödel, Escher, Bach* and now suggested that Hardy's "terrific success" would after all have been pushed to achieve sales of zero. (Ryan eventually estimated down to 400 copies.) Why on earth, we wondered, had a publisher as sensible as OUP contracted to publish a general book which they thought would sell just a few copies, or none at all? What a mysterious business publishing is.

At the directions hearing, Master Barratt had pressed Oxford to present him with a realistic minimum figure from which he could arrive, I presumed, at some sort of compromise with my more ambitious ones. Anderson had agreed to offer such a figure, but Oxford's formal 'Points of Defence' of 15th May still bore no bottom-line number of either copies or pounds. When the payment-out deadline approached, Oxford was two weeks behind schedule with its remaining defence pleading and still had not offered any estimate of the lost royalties. It had, however, given the approximate sales of four 'model' philosophy books: Jonathan Glover's *Causing Death and Saving Lives* (Penguin, 1977, selling 4,500 copies per year), and Derek Parfit's *Reasons and Persons*, R. M. Hare's *Moral Thinking* and D. D. Raphael's *Moral Philosophy* (all OUP, 1984, 1981 and 1981, selling, reportedly, 12,000, 10,000 and 8,000 copies in five years). Although these were rather more specialist books than mine, the comparisons were flattering and the calculations they generated not unencouraging. I wrote to Jonathan Glover and he very kindly sent me copies of his royalty statements, which in fact totalled over 30,000 copies in five years; using *Causing Death and Saving Lives* as a model put my lost royalties and interest at around £37,000. Also, at about this time, the student son of a senior man at my barrister's chambers, who had heard about the case and was interested in *Making Names,* told us of an OUP book which Oxford had curiously omitted to mention but which in many respects could almost have been drafted from mine's synopsis. Thomas Nagel's *What Does It All Mean?* was billed as a general reader's introduction, cast in ten chapters with headings and topics very similar to mine, was published in 1987, was endorsed by Alan Ryan, was adopted by the Open University and so on; by coincidence, even its introductory example of the 'other minds' problem, like mine, invoked two people tasting ice-cream. To my lawyers this book looked like the obvious compromise model that might recommend itself to an impartial court. Its sales figure at once explained Oxford's reticence — already over 60,000 copies. I was beginning to feel, and was being advised, that here were some reasonable grounds for expecting my damages to be higher than Oxford's payment-in.

On the other hand, Chancers' hysterical conduct of the proceedings had amply demonstrated their ability to stack up gratuitous costs thick and fast, so the risks of continuing with the litigation were increasing too. I asked for extra time so that I might discuss Oxford's payment-in with Richard White when he returned from holiday, but this was refused. In the end I, via White, replied that if Oxford would roughly double their offer, thereby protecting me against the disputed costs claims, I would agree to settle, but Smyth simply broke off the negotiation before reporting my counter-offer to Oxford. I reckon that Oxford's failure to settle at this point may eventually have cost it a further £300,000. Towards the end of May, simply to get shot of the whole business, I reduced my asking-price to £65,000, but this was again declined. Instead, on *the day after* the deadline passed, Chancers issued a summons applying for the discovery of all my remaining (four-plus hours' worth) of original, five-years-old, privileged telephone conversations with Hardy: thousands of lawyer-hours were now to be spent analysing the scandalous but entirely spurious historical detail of the Charkin-n-Hardy power-feud. Oxford's negotiators were not behaving like people trying to bring an end to litigation; rather, it was as though they were now using the litigation to exact various kinds of revenge. I admit that by this stage perhaps I too was was becoming subject to a perverse motivation: a desire to see just how mad Oxford would get. In this regard at least, I was not to be disappointed.

On 31st May, in Barratt's absence, Chancery Master Dyson ordered the privilged tapes' production. With Oxford's 'offer' withdrawn, my only way forward was to fight on through the assessment and to try to beat the payment-in figure. Dyson's decision was undoubtedly correct in law; I had begun using various extracts from Hardy's post-contract conversations to demonstrate his original sales ambitions for *Making Names* — his paper-back plans, his price estimates and so on — so legal practice required the conversations' full disclosure. Chancers' motives for obtaining the material were obvious, simply to multiply their costs as fast as possible (they later copied back the transcripts to me with numerous illegible annotations which were of no relevance to anything). But what could have been the reasons of whoever was issuing Oxford's instructions? They may, of course, have simply, maliciously, wanted to pile up costs which they hoped would later be deducted from my damages award, and doubtless this was a powerful instinct, but there was also an echo of Elliott's trial-displayed obsession with OUP's discipline and security, and of Asquith's creepy tape remarks at Fortnum's and Brown's. Was this perhaps the loser's craving to expose the winner's poker-hand, just to discover how thoroughly they'd been bluffed? (Of course, there is no bluffing in litigation, there is only the choice as to how to plead one's case.) Or had they perhaps become fascinated to learn exactly what Hardy had said to me about Charkin, about his bosses, and about OUP's internal affairs — a sort of disciplinary navel-gazing? As with their ordering of their witnesses' trial evidence, fixation with their own skulduggery appeared to be a far more powerful motive than any hope of legal relevance or advantage, and of course money, so long as it was not for me, was no object. With Oxford Chance's intent now clear, the prospect of any settlement nil, and the complexity of the proceedings resuming loony level, I decided from the beginning of June to act in person again, retaining Richard White as my adviser: if the OUnuchs wanted to play the costs-frightening game, I might as well give them a good, free run around.

Hardy, by this time, had gently been relieved of his OUP job and given a Wolfson College grant to edit Isaiah Berlin's papers (he had already edited a number of collections of Berlin's essays). I telephoned his home to warn him of the privileged recordings' impending release. He did not seem too worried, but of course he had no clear recollection of what he had said in them, and in any case I guess for him it was by then all Lethe-water under some ancient Oxford bridge. I gather that he is now *persona non grata* at the Press. With the contract question irrevocably settled by the Court of Appeal, apart from any eventual costs implications, the discovery of these recordings now held no great risks for me, and indeed their inclusion at last allowed me to quote in court Hardy's numerous scandalous admissions, including the one which I took to be the theme-tune for the whole absurd legal dance in which we were presently engaged, and which will perhaps make my epitaph: "*Making Names* isn't going to get a fair hearing here now that it has been treated in this way." In the July assessment, this was to become my closing reminder to Master Barratt.

In the absence of any offer from Oxford, and with a hearing looming, from February 1991 onwards I had pondered who might be willing and suitable candidates to endorse *Making Names* in court. An attractive first, fleeting thought suggested Hardy and Strawson, both of whom had indicated their continuing faith in the book; in theory, as the law says, "there is no property in a witness". In practice however, Hardy's long Oxford "instruction" obviously ruled him out, and in a telephone call made early in the lawsuit, though approachable and sympathetic, Strawson wisely preferred to distance himself from the affair. Also, in 1989, OUP had published his own, second philosophical text *The Secret Connexion*, on Hume's theory of causation, coincidentally adopting, as proposed in my third chapter, Hume's original spelling. And of course the only other person who had read *Making Names*, Alan Ryan, had already disobliged Richard White with the word "excrescence". As so often in this saga, I found myself back at square one, forced again into the increasingly distasteful role of hustler for my own book.

Giles Gordon had kindly agreed to testify for me a second time on general matters like domestic and foreign royalty rates, the frequency of royalty accounts, production timetables, the general prospects for OUP trade books and so forth, and he liked *Making Names'* general style, but not being a philosopher himself, felt unqualified to pass judgment on its academic merits. Oxford had suggested a limit of two witnesses per side, and Master Barratt had raised this to three, so what I ideally needed was a professional philosopher to vouch for the book's intellectual value and a professional book-trader to volunteer an estimate of its likely sales. However, finding anyone willing to read the book now proved even harder than it had in 1984. Some obvious early targets were my former teachers at Cambridge, but none was willing to help. Years before, I had shown arch-R.C. Anscombe an early draft of the book and she had homed like a search-engine onto its one anti-Catholic remark and detonated ("I find the tone of this work foul..."), rendering her unapproachable. I remember visiting her in Cambridge and being struck by the large, grim, hardwood crucifixes darkening her living room; I immediately realised my mistake, but by then it was too late. Renford Bambrough, who at Cambridge I had always found impressive, and into whom I had later rather spookily bumped at the 1988 World Congress of Philosophy in Brighton, liked *Making Names* but regretted that he was too busy to get involved on its behalf. Bernard Williams was kind and concerned as always, but seemed unimpressed by the book, and was perhaps embarrassed by his recent appointment to a senior Oxford chair. I was once more reduced to cold-mailing total strangers.

Eminent people, of course, are busy people, and are unlikely to want to read the work of a complete unknown. They are even less likely to risk entanglement in the sordid business of someone else's lawsuit, and are virtually certain not to if the unknown's opponents are Oxford University and its powerful Press. A session with OUP's General Catalogue (its Big List), will quickly reveal that there is hardly a reputable academic in the land who does not have or hope to have some book, or some interest in some book, in print with them. Certainly anyone with aspirations to an academic career is ill-advised to make an enemy of the great University. By this time too Sir Roger Elliott had become Treasurer, and then Vice-president, of the Publishers' Association. I pestered numerous independent scholars to read *Making Names*, but all politely declined. Alan Ryan's reference to A-Level and Open University courses naturally made these especially useful targets, so I decided to write to Rosalind Hursthouse, the Open University's head of Philosophy and someone who I thought might be sympathetic to both my book and plight. It turned out that she too lived in Oxford, but her first reply was enthusiastic:

> I was delighted to get your letter and would love to read your book — it sounds very intriguing. I have been following your case with great interest in the papers, because Henry Hardy is not only an ex-pupil but an old friend of mine, and I have much respect for both his philosophical judgment and his integrity... We are at the moment compiling a very short list of introductory textbooks we might recommend to O.U. students interested in philosophy, and haven't got much beyond Nagel's *The View From Nowhere*: yours sounds very promising, and I should like to read it.

Then, in an odd about-turn and with a curious non-sequitur letter, she returned the book unread. All was explained in July, when I found myself in court facing an Open University drone. A similar fate befell my approach to the A-Level Board, whose administrator eventually replied on the very day the evidence deadline expired. Again, an A-Level official later appeared in court to trash a book he had never seen.

In June I had a breakthrough. Ben Gibbs of Sussex University introduced me to Roy Edgley, a retired, senior left-wing philosophy lecturer, ex-Bristol and ex-Sussex, who had written and edited a number of philosophical books and journals. He was a delightful, open-minded man who was uncowed by the idea of opposing Oxford and its lawyers and who, most preciously, had the inclination and time to read *Making Names*. He liked the book, the more so the more he read it, and invited me to have a face-to-face discussion of its arguments. He was the very first person, it seemed to me, who came to a clear understanding of what I was trying to say, and to see the philosophy in the way I saw it. He agreed to swear an affidavit on my and the book's behalf and quite unprompted, drafted a beauty:

> I think *Making Names* an exceptional piece of work. Malcolm's use of the dialogue form is in certain ways more fully dramatic than Plato's or Berkeley's. Interspersed in the dialogue are brief passages of narrative that set the scene for the discussion... The effect of all this is to keep our feet on the ground while the philosophical content reaches the

highest levels of abstraction, to remind us of what philosophy tempts us to forget — ordinary everyday life and its inescapable reality.

But it's not until the final chapter that Malcolm's fusion of philosophy and drama takes its most audacious step, Here, at what can only be called the climax of the book, Malcolm presents us with his own version of the tragedy of Electra.

This brings me to the content of the book. Malcolm has many interesting things to say, more or less new or unusual, about the philosophical problems he tackles, and though he mentions other philosophers rather little, his arguments continually bear, usually in a critical way, on their views. In this regard, I found chapters 5, 6, 7 and 8 all very fruitful, in particular for their relations to Wittgenstein on the theory of language and Feyerabend on the philosophy of science. Like Wittgenstein he is fascinated by and knowledgeable about language, and like Feyerabend (and unlike many philosophers of science) he clearly knows a good deal of modern physics, which I guess he must have had some training in.

I conclude that the book would be of great interest to professional philosophers, and I imagine that physicists and other scientists would also find it worth studying. But its appeal would go well beyond that rather select readership. Malcolm's writing is fluent and, given the difficulty of the topics, wonderfully easy to read. This, together with its dramatic style, its humour and its total lack of academic formality and fustiness, would extend its accessibility to students. I mean students in general: university, open university, and polytechnic students in fields other than just philosophy, and also students still at school, especially now that philosophy is making its way onto the school curriculum. It has been said that Bertrand Russell had the rare ability to write books that were both original contributions to philosophy and at the same time introductions for beginners. It seems to me that Malcolm has something of that kind of talent. It's even possible, I suppose, that his book might gain some degree of 'popular' readership. I certainly found it a good read, and I think others would too.

Edgley's estimation of *Making Names* was, I suppose, the only intellectually gratifying thing that had happened to me for six years, and whatever its effect was to be on the outcome of the assessment, I found it a mighty morale-booster.

Under Master Barratt's schedule, Oxford and I were directed to exchange witness statements on 21st June, three weeks before the hearing. This was to occasion one of those hilarious sketches in terms of which I now try to remember the whole affair. The idea of such exchanges is that the two sides should swap their statements simultaneously so that neither steals a march on the other by learning beforehand the identity of its witnesses. As is the normal practice, I had simply posted my two affidavits

(Giles Gordon's and Roy Edgley's, together making five pages) by recorded delivery. Since Oxford Chance had originally requested two witnesses, I was expecting their two affidavits to arrive in exchange, probably by motorcycle courier; with the costs-cock now fully open, Chancers had taken to sending trivial one-page letters down to Brighton by bike. On this occasion even I had underestimated their extravagance: when summoned by the doorbell I was amazed to find at the step not as usual a leather-clad biker, but the driver of a thirty-five-foot articulated T.N.T. truck, the kind used to deliver *The Sun* nationwide, which had evidently had to manoeuvre its way through the narrow, hilly back-streets of Brighton's Hanover area to my flat. Having ascertained that he was in the right place, the driver clambered up onto his trailer, drew back the PVC shuttering and revealed... one small A4-sized package.

23

The Oxford Circus

H AVING SOLEMNLY SIGNED for the package, I soon discovered that it too was the legal equivalent of a pantechnicon delivering a postcard. When I had pieced it all together (much of the material was randomised and at least eight pages were missing), it appeared that Oxford had filed no less than *thirteen* affidavits comprising some 264 pages of new 'independent expert' witnesses, only one of whom claimed to have read *Making Names*. In no particular order, I *list* them below:

1. Ivon Asquith, despite his two earlier mendacious efforts, had been wheeled out for a third time to testify as to the nuts and bolts of OUP authors' contracts, of which he exhibited "a random sample" of eleven, including those of A.J. Ayer, R. M. Hare, Richard Norman, Robert Solomon, Felipe Fernandez-Armesto, S. P. Uglow, Miriam Allott, John Sutherland, Laurence Cohen and Chin Liew Ten. One curious feature of these contracts, given OUP's insistence upon the importance of its formal *Memorandum*, was that only two were properly signed. Another oddity was that included amongst them was one agent's contract (David Higham Associates, on behalf of Kenneth Morgan for a book on Labour Party leaders since 1900), which demonstrated just how diametrically the two types of contract were opposed, and which Oxford had not signed at all (a general policy, I wondered?). Asquith denied my proposed straightforward ten percent royalty of the hardback's published price and averaged the notional paperback rate down to 9.5 percent of net receipts while denying Hardy's paperback plan (the published-price versus net-receipts technicality will be explained in due course). He reduced Hardy's price estimates, set the average production time as one year, and stated that OUP royalties are paid annually. To support his claims (although they did not in fact all do so), Asquith also presented some more detailed sales figures for *Reasons and Persons*, *Moral Thinking* and *Moral Philosophy*, OUP's three in-house models, but he vouchsafed no opinion whatever about *Making Names*.

2. Jonathan Riley, the Executive Editor of Penguin, confirmed Glover's royalties from *Causing Death and Saving Lives* and stated that Penguin's standard UK hardback rate was ten percent of published price. But he made no comment on *Making Names*.

3. David Croom, the Managing Director of the Routledge conglomerate, provided recent sales figures for Wittgenstein's *Tractatus* (1921), Popper's *The Open Society and its Enemies* (1945) and Peter Winch's *The Idea of a Social Science* (1958). Again he addressed royalty rates but passed no comment on *Making Names*.

4. Stephan Chambers, a philosophy editor at Blackwell, provided the sales and royalty figures for two more philosophy books, Hollis's *Invitation to Philosophy*, and Dancy's *Introduction to Contemporary Epistemology* (both 1985). He did not mention *Making Names*.

5. Tim Farmiloe, the publishing director of Macmillan, and one of my 1984 duplicated-slip-wise synopsis-rejecters, confirmed that he had not read or published *Making Names* and could not remember it.

6. Ian Paten, now the Editorial Director of HarperCollins, confirmed that in 1984, as the paperback non-fiction editor of Granada, he had found *Making Names* "extremely impressive" but had not published it.

7. Peter Wright, an arts editor for the Open University, stated that from being shown *Making Names'* 1984 synopsis (by now so photocopied it was barely legible), he personally concluded that it could not have become a set text for any Open University course, and that in any case Open University students were not expected to read its recommended books.

8. Colin Mitchell of the Associated Examining (A-Level) Board confirmed that *Making Names* was being considered for inclusion on the AEB's recommended reading list but that as yet no decision had been taken.

9. Kim Pickin, the former Blackwell philosophy editor (she had left in 1986) who in 1984 had apologised for keeping *Making Names* unread for five months on her filing cabinet, stated that she was now a Corporate Identity Advertising Consultant with the PR firm Wolff Olins.

10. Galen Strawson reaffirmed his 1985, 2-day, "bits of", favourable report on *Making Names'* first draft.

11. Richard Charkin, now the Chief Executive of Reed International, passed no opinion on *Making Names,* but did repeat his trial version of OUP's internal procedures, his 'three criteria' mantra, and his spiel about Angela Blackburn's undiscovered note. This meant that Blackburn herself then had to swear an affidavit in which she said she could remember using an elastic band to secure to my synopsis a pink transmittal slip, but could not recall what she had written on it.

12. Alan Ryan, already discredited and still safe from cross-examination in the USA, at last filed an affidavit, whose contents readers may wish to compare with his earlier reports (see pages 61 and 62). Five years later, he now found *Making Names'* style and argument "eccentric, quirky, boorish, alienating, very unclear, unfathomable and overlong, a thoroughly unacademic essay on the meaning of life." Of its sales prospects, he added:

> "I did not think then and do not believe now, that it could have been a textbook for any academic course whatsoever... In my opinion, *Making Names* was not a plausible commercial proposition... it seemed to me very likely to sell only four or five hundred copies and vanish from sight... I certainly had no thought in my mind [that word again] that it might have anything like the kind of success of *The Outsider* or *Gödel, Escher, Bach*... I believe it would have sunk without trace."

Incidentally, the chameleon reviewer had by now changed his opinion of Hofstadter's magnum opus too: the book which privately "he hadn't liked at all, to tell you the truth", now publicly became "infinitely better constructed, and calculated to reassure professional philosophers." In 'not my style' Ryan's book on Russell, by this time itself published and remaindered, he praises Russell's "deep moral revulsion at any philosophy which could play fast and loose with the truth." Sick-bag city.

Having dispassionately rubbished *Making Names*, the gibbering commissar then volunteered this amazing incidental paragraph:

> "General [as opposed to Academic] books were submitted to the Editorial Committee for approval, and if approved, then reported on to the Delegates. The Delegates did not have the same role in their approval, because the intellectual name of the Press was not at risk: such books were aimed at the general reader rather than the scholar, and do not carry the academic imprint of the Press."

Here again, five years' of litigation, by now costing hundreds of thousands of pounds, is tossed into the air as if just so much confetti. The switchback of Press-University blame-denial is once more in nosedive, with Oxford's four-year defence, or pretence, abandoned as a whim, its Court of Appeal statement shredded, and even Hardy's original Stage Three travestied. Don't these people care that whilst they are contradicting themselves so dimly, so dreamily, so *academically*, that others' lives, jobs, and very industries are being convulsed? Do they ever.

13. It was left to one Jeremy Mynott, the Editorial Director of OUP's 'independent sister', Cambridge University Press, to provide Oxford's

single evaluation of *Making Names*. I read his report with some trepidation, assuming that it would offer a competent critical analysis of my arguments and presentations, but in fact, as Master Barratt later recorded in his findings, Mynott was quite complimentary about the book itself, and I myself could hardly have improved on his synopsis of it:

> "Mr Malcolm's work is unusual in some ways. It is a wide-ranging discussion of various traditional philosophical problems in metaphysics, epistemology and the philosophy of science, but it is set in the form of a dialogue between two men and concludes with an allegorical drama based on the *Electra* story in Greek tragedy. The first eight dialectical chapters introduce and explore many of the standard philosophical problems which figure in most introductions to the subject: minds and bodies, other minds, induction, cause and effect, freedom and determinism, universals and particulars, consciousness, language and the world, the definition of good, and the nature of explanation in scientific theory. This last topic emerges as one of the central themes of the work, and the progress of the dialogue challenges, both directly and by implication, what are taken to be the guiding principles of modern physics and cosmology, particularly in respect of particle theory. The general tendency is highly critical of positivism and the scientistic attitudes it is associated with; and this in turn is connected with attitudes to modern technology, nuclear weaponry and other socio-political issues of that kind. The purpose of the final chapter is to express and dramatise some of the central conclusions of the work in a different, more purely literary, medium... The author is evidently well informed about these issues and debates... The dialogue is not badly done... Malcolm presents us with a sort of voyage of discovery which, because it was *his* voyage, was of great interest to him. This is in a way admirable, and is one sort of justification for a work of philosophy or literature."

But despite offering this flattering characterisation of the book, Mynott was then bafflingly pessimistic about its sales prospects:

> "My overall assessment is that this work is not publishable in its present or in anything like its present form. This is not at all to say that the work is without merit or is 'wrong' in some technically demonstrable or qualifying way. But the work in the end is unpublishable because it would not find a real readership and is not addressed to a real readership. It is aimed at everyone and no-one... The famous general readers, alas, are never there when you need them... My guess is that OUP would have managed well under 1,000 sales."

It transpired that when Oxford Chance received the script of *Making Names* in May, they passed it straight to Mynott without making a copy;

they were remarkably confident of their only independent evaluator's sales pessimism.

In summary, although alarming in terms of weight and bulk, Oxford's T.N.T. truckparcel-bomb thus turned out to be a damp squib. Given that an officeful of lawyers on bottomless expense accounts had evidently been scouring my 1984 rejection-file and half the UK publishing industry besides, they had come up with very little that was unobvious. There was no philosopher, heavyweight or otherwise, dissecting the book's thesis or disputing its validity, Ryan's degradation was now complete and manifest, and several of Oxford's model sales figures were quite promising. The only certain bad news was that Chancers' greaser Smyth was laughing tin hats, and his firm all the way to the bank.

From a legal standpoint, the ineffectuality of Oxford's squib was good news, but in other ways it was something of a disappointment. In my imagination of Oxford's imagination, *Making Names* had become an evil monstrosity, a seditious blasphemy to be suppressed at all costs, yet here was Mynott passing nice, mild, laudatory comments upon it; he didn't even seem to find it controversial, and his worst epithet for my writing style was the unsurprising "dated". Oxford's 'apology' had pontificated about "the obligation to maintain the University's high academic reputation for scholarly and pedagogical works", yet here was its chief witness going out of his way to say that I was well informed about my subject-matter and that my arguments were not demonstrably wrong, claims which I myself might have hesitated to make. The book, after all, was not *that* bad. So what on earth had the whole five-year farce been about? If not money or prestige, it couldn't, again, have been about *power* could it — at first the power of a manager over an editor, but later the general power of publishers over authors and the particular power of Oxford over Academia UK? I tried hard not to entertain such thoughts, but the disappointment persisted. My unfulfilled Charkin-n-Hardy dream-showdown had, I guess, been supplanted by a fantasy Athenian-style courtroom debate over the philosophical merits of *Making Names*, and now I was to be denied even that. In the event, the emptiness of Oxford's juggernaut proved a fitting harbinger of the dismal, venal little dispute that in reality materialised.

Ryan's odd use of the perfectly empty, comic phrase "the meaning of life" sparked my imagination in several ways. It had only ever crossed my mind, or my path, twice: first as the title of Monty Python's wonderful film (I faintly saw Ryan in John Cleese's American restaurant discussing Salena Jones — "Strawson's got *two* 's's in it, so he must be a really *serious* philosopher!"); and second as the title of the last chapter of Thomas Nagel's *What Does It All Mean?*: "Perhaps you have had the thought that nothing really matters, because in two hundred years we'll all be dead... Life may be not only meaningless but absurd." Whatever life was up to, some of its absurd Oxford sub-plots were certainly coming full-circle. In mid-June I telephoned Nagel in Paris and asked him about the sales of his increasingly interesting book. His answer was about 20,000 copies in its first year and 15,000 annually since, and I used these for a moderate, compromise calculation in my 'Points of Reply' submission to the court, requesting OUP's documented figures. Oxford at first promised to include these with its witnesses' statements but then failed to do so. Instead, the OUnuchs claimed that OUP (USA) — the book was first published in America — was "a separate Delaware corporation" whose papers they were unable to obtain.

During the days leading up to the hearing, Oxford Chance objected to almost every bit of evidence I tried to adduce: they objected to my production of a page on royalties from the 1984 *Writers' & Artists' Yearbook (W.A.Y.)*; they objected to a *Bookseller* article by Tim Hely Hutchinson about general publishing economics; they objected to a letter from Douglas Hofstadter quoting the sales figures for his *Gödel, Escher, Bach* (now, incidentally, over a million); they objected to a published essay by Colin Wilson about his earnings from *The Outsider* (now, incidentally, up to £20,000 in its first year, 1956); they objected to statements made by Jonathan Glover and Derek Parfit about their books (the latter now up to about 14,000 copies); they even objected to the casefile of primary documents, including Ryan's and Strawson's original reports on *Making Names*, material which had already been in evidence for over five years. They did, however, obtain by fax from New York some unsupported sales figures for *What Does It All Mean?*

These various Oxford Chancery moves in turn necessitated an extra, preliminary hearing on 2nd July, at which Master Barratt overruled their numerous objections, restricted their witnesses to five plus an absent Ryan, allowed me another three (I was given a generous three working days in which to find them), and ordered the discovery of Nagel's actual royalty sheets. When these at last arrived they showed that OUP's New York fax had reduced the true figures by about one-third, so Oxford was then ordered to produce its internal accounts for the book. I was beginning to feel quite glad that I wasn't a 'successful' author. Prior to the formal acrimonies of the hearing, Karen Anderson had confided to me casually "Congratulations on the book, by the way, I'm really enjoying it." I guess she meant well, but it was hard not to hear this as a taunt, nor to find it deeply unencouraging.

I could not, of course, whistle up three more useful witnesses to read *Making Names* in three days, but the extra time did give me a chance to plug one hole in my armoury: testimony from a professional, experienced book-marketeer. I had been introduced to Fred Nolan, a likeable former executive of Corgi, Penguin, Collins, Granada and Ballantine (US) who was now a professional author with over sixty books published. He seemed to know everything there was to know about the business, was something of a maverick, and at once took to *Making Names*, which he described as "readable, provocative, and most importantly, accessible." In a few short sentences, his breezy affidavit cut through the fatuous mountain of paper steadily being assembled by the lawyers (and myself):

> Its success thereafter would be based on (a) the amount of effort the publisher put into publishing and marketing it and (b) its acceptance by readers... If a book is timely, literate, stimulating and well published, it will find a market. Were the eight million people worldwide who bought Stephen Hawking's *A Brief History of Time* all academics? Did the publisher *have any idea when he commissioned it* how successful that book would be? [A point Barratt later echoed in his judgment] It is my experience that publishers operate on a mixture of past experience, 'hunch' and 'feel'. Market research of any kind is practically non-existent.

Nolan went on to explain in detail the disadvantages to an author of a 'net receipts' (as opposed to a 'published price') royalty deal, for which Oxford, with the help of Asquith's affidavit, was now apparently beginning to argue. As will be explained later, one is usually assured that the two different methods of calculation balance out mathematically, and that it therefore does not matter for authors that the general trend is towards 'net receipts' agreements. Nolan, however, viewed things rather differently:

> In the US — and increasingly in the UK — retail chain booksellers call the tune. Mainstream publishers have little choice but to accede to their demands for ever-increasing discounts. It makes sense for the publisher to pay the author on the basis of what he receives, but it by no means makes it a good deal for the author. Example: 10,000 copies of a $20 book with a 10 percent published-price royalty earn the author $20,000. The same number sold but discounted at 55 percent with a (say) 12.5 percent net-receipts royalty [the differential cited in Oxford's evidence as equivalent] will earn him only $11,250. Among the many advantages to the publisher of such contracts is the fact that they make possible what is called a 'sheet deal'. In this, a multinational publisher of that same 10,000 print-run can substantially reduce his printing costs by 'running on' a further 10,000 copies (that is to say, printing but not binding them), and then further profit by selling on these 'sheets' at cost-price or lower to overseas subsidiaries or branches. The

author will get 12.5 percent 'net receipts' of this artificially-deflated sheet deal, while the overseas subsidiary then binds up the sheets and sells the book at full price and a nice profit, of which the author gets zero.

The morals of all this for authors like Nagel, the sheets of whose UK edition of *What Does It All Mean?* use American spelling, are obvious when applied to a multinational like OUP, with its "separate Delaware corporation" subsidiary. The more you think about it, the more you realise that such sheet-dealing can come pretty close to legalised piracy, and its respectable practitioners pretty close to the back-street copyright-infringers of Bombay and Shanghai. Who would be an author now? Nolan's affidavit was sworn at the eleventh hour — or rather on 11th July — just in time to be admissible in court.

24

The Assessment

ON WEDNESDAY 10TH JULY I arrived at Master Barratt's Room 605 with a friend Jayne who had agreed to transcribe the hearing for me. The Chancers were already bustling around as we took our seats: Anderson, Smyth (with mobile phone on the go, of course), Asquith (ditto), clerks, and then a flurry of more clerks and much paper-shuffling heralded the sighting of the great McGregor. The diminutive grandee entered imperiously, and a path cleared before him. He spoke and moved rapidly, as if embarrassed to be found in such humble surroundings on such a sordid mission, but he was perfectly fine and formal with myself and with Master Barratt, greeting us most politely. He was, however, perfectly beastly to his numerous minions, snapping instructions at them like a petulant poodle, and soon getting poor Karen into a bit of a flap. To my surprise, the word that I found to best describe his manner was 'camp' and the nickname that immediately stuck was 'McMouse'.

The weather was steamy-hot and windless, and there was much tie-loosening and fiddling with ventilation. When all had settled and the procedural preliminaries were being discussed, I tried to put it from my mind that, along with Ryan and Elliott, Barratt and McGregor were both Oxford, even both New College men, and that the latter was a senior legal authority and the former only a Chancery Master. I refused to believe that any element of professional intimidation would be allowed, or that any deference would be tolerated. Oxford had requested cross-examination of all my witnesses, and I had reciprocated, although I was unsure as to what was to be gained by this. As far as I was concerned, most of the technical questions of publication were by now clarified or could quickly be agreed, but when I suggested this to McGregor, he firmly dissented, indicating much nit-picking ahead. I assumed that by now the chief issues were (a) is *Making Names* any good? and (b) how many copies would it, on the evidence, have sold, and in particular, which of the various suggested books offered its most likely sales model? I took my task to be to steer Barratt as hard as possible towards Nagel (the models were labelled by author). McGregor wanted to have all the witnesses examined on the first day, leaving the second free for argument, but for me, Giles Gordon and Fred Nolan had both preferred to come on the Thursday. Roy Edgley was due to arrive at about 11.00 that morning, but somehow, inexplicably, it

was decided that all of Oxford's witnesses should go first, leaving poor
Edgley sitting the whole day at the back of the room listening to a dreary
litany about overseas royalty rates, production timetables and trade
publishing practices; he told me afterwards that he had found watching
Oxford's suited menagerie unutterably depressing. I suppose that, as at the
trial, it was the good old 'tire the opposition' ploy.

Master Barratt had by formal order limited Oxford to five of its thirteen
witnesses plus Ryan's American affidavit undefended, and Oxford had
chosen to axe Charkin, Strawson, Chambers, Farmiloe and Paten, leaving,
in order: Asquith (OUP), Riley (Penguin), Wright (Open University),
Mitchell (AEB A-Level Board), Pickin (ex-Blackwell), Croom (Routledge)
and Mynott (CUP). This in fact made seven, not five, but again this was
certainly just a mathematical mistake on Barratt's part, not a result of any
deference. The law, I had long since discovered, moved in many mysterious
ways. Goofball Asquith's long, long, opening performance was all geared
to arguing for a net-receipts rather than a published-price royalty calculation,
to shaving down the percentage rates and estimated prices, to lengthening
the timetables, and perhaps simply to bamboozling and boring poor
Barratt with jargon about general versus philosophy publishing, trade
versus academic paperbacks, storage and warehousing costs, bulk paper
prices and so forth. One of the first nits Mighty McMouse wanted to pick
was the book's publication schedule, a factor which affected the interest
component payable on the lost royalties. The Society of Authors Quick
Guide maximum is one year from the author's presentation of the script,
and, given Hardy's "no editing needed" remarks and already completed
cast-off and PPF preparations, I had suggested nine months from February
1986, in line with the Delegates' Note specification. The affidavit evidence
too varied from nine months (Gordon, Croom), to twelve (Asquith, Riley,
Mynott). McGregor, however, at once began insisting upon *fifteen*
months. By so advancing the publication date, arguing for yearly (as
opposed to the usual half-yearly) royalty statements, and insisting that
OUP's first payment to me would not have been made until four months
after that, on 31st July 1988, he wanted to set the whole process an
additional ten months forward so as to deny me the interest accruing on
the book's imagined first year's sales.

At the start of his examination, Asquith had presented two pages of
unsupported royalty statistics, including those for Parfit's *Reasons and
Persons*. He pooh-poohed my comparison with Nagel on the grounds that
(a) it was only 100 pages long and (b) he was a well-known author, so I
decided to take him up on Parfit, which had also sold reasonably well. He
was obliged to admit that Parfit was 550 fine-print pages, at least forty

percent longer than mine, that, like mine, it had been its author's first book, and that Parfit had had a published-price royalty deal. A memorable moment amidst the drear came when he explained "But his reputation preceded him!" "What, his reputation preceded his book's publication?" "Yes, yes," piped Asquith, "in Oxford his work was already known to be one of *genius!*" I held up the copy on my desk and displayed its back-cover quote: "Something close to a work of genius" — Alan Ryan, *Sunday Times*, and I noted that the book's acknowledgments mentioned no less than *ninety* names, at least ten of which had featured in my lawsuit. Another small joy came when Master Barratt asked him if *Reasons and Persons* was in any way comparable with *Making Names*. "Not remotely, Master," he shuddered, "not *remotely!*" I took this to be an own goal, for it expressly crossed from the list one of the less ambitious models on offer. (The utterance "not remotely Master", with a suitably Asquithian, overly-rounded, oh-so-Oxonian 'o' in the 'remotely', was to become yet another of the case's hit-refrains.) Asquith was then obliged to admit that he had never actually opened *Making Names*.

Even after lunch, McGregor persevered with the ever-lanternless Asquith, and I felt the whole day draining away in an endless burble about published-price versus net-receipts royalties and what constituted 'a general book'. But at last, at 2.15, it was Riley's turn. I was puzzled that Oxford had called him, for his arithmetic apparently supported mine against Asquith's and confirmed that Glover's *Causing Death and Saving Lives* had sold over 30,000 copies in its first five years, though his own figures differed slightly from those in Glover's royalty statements. Penguin, he confirmed, paid royalties *half*-yearly, at ten percent published-price (UK) and the equivalent of seven-and-a-half percent published-price (export). These were exactly the figures I had proposed. Riley, however, also kindly volunteered the details of Glover's less lucrative books, and at the end of his testimony further departed from his script to mention a Penguin dialogue which had sold only 5,000 copies. However, because his afterthoughts were impromptu and came with no supporting evidence, he was not invited to elaborate upon them.

Peter Wright of the Open University was to have come next, but for no specified reason was unable to attend, and with impeccable rigour his place was 'taken' and his affidavit 'spoken to' by one Giles Clarke, who was introduced as the Deputy Managing Editor of the O.U.'s Book Trade Department. Clarke had not seen *Making Names* or the O.U.'s recommended reading (as opposed to set text) lists, which, oddly, were unexhibited, and he had no idea what books were on them. His only point seemed to be that it took at least five years for any new publication to get onto any O.U. list, a claim which was immediately trumped by noting the appearance of Nagel's book as an O.U. set text in its first year. The most interesting moment came when Clarke tried to explain an odd assertion in his proxy-affidavit, which I quoted back to him and pursued:

> **Malcolm** (reading): "The Open University recommended reading lists are optional, and it is not expected that any student would read all of the recommended books. Course Teams do not expect the majority of students to draw on the recommended reading list, and it is expected that those who do would not purchase such books, but would turn to libraries. Only a very small number of students would be likely to purchase a recommended text." What do you mean by recommending a book to a student? Surely when you recommend a book to a student, it is a recommendation that he goes and at least reads it, if not buys it?
> **Clarke:** No it is not.
> **Malcolm:** So you prefer them not to read the recommended books? So you're not actually suggesting with the recommended list that people should go out and read these books?
> **Clarke:** Certainly not.

This exchange occurred in 1991, so perhaps by now Open University students are actually *prohibited* from reading the books on their recommended lists. If not, I assume that they should at once be circulated with this imaginative new policy.

Mitchell of the A-Level Board was little more help. His main points were that *Making Names* could not go on the A-Level reading list because (a) it was still only in script form and had not been printed and (b) their appointed referee had not yet had time to read it. (In the event he did like it and did recommend its inclusion on the reading list; when eventually it was printed, his school purchased six copies.) Mitchell got into an amusing muddle over Descartes' *Meditations* and Hume's *Treatise*, citing them as works of recent philosophy, and he did not even remember having seen *Making Names'* synopsis, but none of this was really helping to move the proceedings along. It struck me that so far the assessment had demonstrated nothing at all about *Making Names*, but a very great deal about the workings of the UK's academic publishing industry; perhaps, it occurred to me, it was the latter that was now on trial.

Kim Pickin, the corporate identity advertising consultant, was cheerful, good-looking and did provide some welcome surreal relief, though she was apparently unaware that years earlier she had admitted returning *Making Names* unopened. When asked what she could remember about the book, she paused and then hesitantly tried, as I remember, something like

"Schopenhauer's waterbed of life...?" (Jayne's laughter got the better of her note-taking at this point). There was a wry pause while I, Barratt and McGregor looked askance at one another, before the latter changed the subject and asked Kim to elaborate her affidavit comments on *Causing Death and Saving Lives*. "Erm... I think there's not much more I can add..." she smiled prettily. An imperious hand waved her away, and I could feel its owner beginning to squirm with impatience at the shower of witnesses with which he had been landed.

Croom was grim and businesslike, and his affidavit confined to the same sort of dull, mathematical stuff as Asquith's and Riley's. There was, however, one oddity: his original statement had been withdrawn and amended in respect of the paragraph which addressed the published-price-versus-net-receipts question. His three examples, Wittgenstein, Popper and Winch, each gave two rates, with a published-price rate on sales with a discount of *up to* fifty percent and a net-receipts rate on sales with a discount *above* fifty percent, but then in their totals the different rates and discounts were not distinguished. His first draft had gone:

> I have provided details of the rates of royalties and the price of the book in respect of the period shown and have calculated the maximum royalty payable, assuming that all copies sold in the UK are at the highest applicable published price. Royalties may be paid as a percentage of published price or of publisher's net receipts (that is, published price less discount). Discounts range from a minimum trade discount of 25 percent to a maximum of 80 percent in the case of bulk overseas sales; the standard discount used by Routledge in costing a new book is 37 percent on home sales and 40 percent on export sales.

In his amended, working version, the first sentence of this paragraph had been shortened to "I have provided details of the rates of royalties and the price of the book in respect of the period shown and the royalties paid." I could not quite understand, Nagel-style, what it all meant, and some of the figures in the tables did not seem to tally anyway, but as this paragraph had evidently been a worry to him, I asked for an explanation of his amendment. I must have hit a raw nerve, for Croom and McGregor at once both rounded on me irritably, insisting that there had been no change. I recited the two versions carefully and Croom then mumbled something about having been given mistaken information by his royalties department. I gather that Routledge's sales to its own American sister company involve the huge 80 percent discount he mentions, so perhaps I was straying dangerously close to the sensitive subject of Nolan's sheet-dealing. Whatever the raw nerve was, from then on, our trivial exchanges became inexplicably acrimonious.

As Croom's testimony ground heavily on about book-trade recessions and corporate mergers, and I absently groped for useful questions to ask, I began to wonder what on earth all of this was about. What were all these people doing here? What was *I* doing here? What did any of it have to do with anything? It was four o'clock in the afternoon, and no-one had yet uttered a single syllable about *Making Names*, or even about the contents of books, let alone about writing or reading or ideas or philosophy. The point, of course, was that these people were experts in *publishing*. Bulk overseas discount percentages, trade sales fluctuations, the standardisation of escalation-clauses, these were their specialisms, their margins of success or failure, the matters on their minds, and so they had become the subjects they most wanted to discuss. McGregor and Croom's recurring insistence on the trade's switch over recent years from published-price to net-receipts royalty agreements began, however, to signal a warning, like the burglar whose house is being searched compulsively glancing where he's stashed the booty.

At four-fifteen it was time for Jeremy Mynott, whom I had been told was a friend of Charkin's. I was therefore surprised to find him a very gentle, elderly, soft-spoken man who answered all my questions carefully and calmly and was not at all confrontational. His affidavit too had been careful and considered and actually rather kind about *Making Names* (see page 172), so I eschewed an adversarial approach. He for his gentlemanly part apparently wanted to avoid derogating my book's style or content, and just kept insisting that it nevertheless lacked 'publishability', as though this were an attribute logically independent of anything else one might be able say about it. We flirted ritually with this mysterious concept and at one point when I inquired if it might have anything to do with a work's merits or lack of them, Master Barratt interrupted sharply with the Charkinesque reminder "My job is to award money, not to decide how well written the book is. It is only saleable value I am interested in." I asked Mynott whether in his time at CUP he had ever, as Ryan had put it, "taken a chance and won", that is, whether he had ever attempted to publish a potential mass-market, ideas book like *The Outsider*, or, arguably, *Making Names*. To my, and I think Barratt's bemusement, Mynott smilingly replied "The Bible?"

Long-suffering Roy Edgley finally got to say his piece at about five o'clock, hours after most of the other courtrooms in the building had become as empty as my now exhausted brain; the opposition-tiring strategy had certainly worked this time. I had no clear idea what was required of Edgley and had rehearsed nothing with him, so I simply invited him to amplify the remarks in his affidavit. Fortunately, the dreariness of the proceedings had failed to dull his own lucidity one syllable, and quietly, uninterruptedly, he eulogised *Making Names* in a way that I had never dared to imagine. It was a subjective impression and I was drifting into an cripplingly emotional state, but as I gazed out of the window at the sea of grey court rooves, I fancied that for the first time all day, the courtroom was actually falling silent; that Barratt, McGregor and Anderson were for the first time truly *listening* as Edgley, obviously from his heart, politely told them what he thought. No doubt they were in fact wondering what trains they would be catching or what they were missing on TV, but to me it felt as though in ten beautiful minutes Edgley was blowing all of OUP's testimony away, was bringing home the true criminality of this mighty Oxford folly, and was perhaps even vindicating my whole twenty-year effort. When he finished I could hardly speak.

McGregor too was visibly and audibly taken aback. He made a gentle attempt to discredit Edgley's competence to predict books' sales, but Edgley at once agreed that this was not his area of expertise. McGregor then quickly informed Barratt that he would not after all be needing to cross-examine my two remaining witnesses, Giles Gordon and Fred Nolan, who were due to appear on the following morning. This meant that their affidavits would stand unchallenged and that they would be spared the bother of attending the court. McGregor obviously felt that one Edgley-style performance was enough, and witness-wise had hoisted the white flag. Dizzy with emotion I bade Edgley goodbye and headed with Jayne for the pub.

25

The Squeaking Pips

T HE FOLLOWING DAY, for which Liz returned as my transcriber, was now clear for the legal argument, and at his request, I began by taking Master Barratt carefully through the most important parts of Gordon's and Nolan's affidavits. McGregor then introduced Ryan's, and I reminded them that however much Ryan's 'mind' had changed since 1985, the purpose of the assessment was to decide how well the book would have sold if it had been published by OUP back when he was intending to "gallop ahead" with a new *Outsider*. I also reminded them of the importance of the publisher's status and power, and that he and Oxford could turn a book like Parfit's into "a work of genius" even before it had come off the press. I pointed out too that all three of the 'blockbusters' mentioned in the evidence, *The Outsider, Gödel, Escher, Bach* and *A Brief History of Time* had, at one time or another and by several imprints and experts, been expressly described as 'unpublishable'.

After lunch, the argument moved back to the miserable mathematical disputes about royalties, prices and timetables, which I assumed had already been settled. I think my morning's presentation had gone fairly well, and that the Chancers were beginning to worry that Barratt was not necessarily going to tow their line. Again I proposed reasonable compromises on all the points, but again McGregor kept arguing and arguing whilst his minions fiddled with calculators, until, by about three o'clock, we arrived at the nub: which model book (sales multiplier) should the court apply? Step by logical step I steered Barratt towards the Nagel or Glover models, either of which would have done me handsomely and both of which seemed reasonable on the evidence. Finally, when he asked me to put a quantum on the reputation-value of OUP's lost imprimatur, I suggested with what I thought was realistic moderation a figure of fifteen thousand pounds, pointing out that this was less than an Oxford lecturer's yearly salary. I also noted that according to Oxford's Appeal Court 'apology' and its lawyers' fees, the University itself had valued its coveted imprimatur at over *fifty* thousand. "Let's stick with the fifteen shall we" chorused Barratt and McGregor.

Then it was McGregor's turn. He repeated all of Oxford's well-worn litanies, and as he yet again went over the published-price versus net-receipts argument, I began, I think for the first time, properly to understand what all this arcane stuff was about. My agreement with Hardy, remember, had been for the payment of "no advance, but a fair royalty, so that if the book does well, you will do well out of it." Citing this, the Court of Appeal had found that Oxford had contracted to pay me a fair royalty, while Master Barratt, with equal justification, had made it clear that he was assuming that I would have been remunerated at OUP's usual going rates. I had not dreamed that Oxford would be arguing otherwise, that their going rates were less than the trade norms, or other than 'fair', but it now appeared that that was exactly what McGregor had all along deliberately and unashamedly been proposing.

I had always taken as my standard text on the question of royalties the opening paragraphs on the subject in the *Writers' & Artists' Yearbook* (A&C Black). Although their wording has changed slightly over the years, their upshot has not, asserting that an author's royalty for a general book normally starts at ten percent of its UK published price. Mention is also made of the recent introduction of an alternative system based on higher percentages of the publisher's net receipts (published price less booksellers' discount), which are said to be easier for publishers to computerise, but in the 1984 edition there was an assurance that "this arrangement is of no disadvantage to the author." By 1991 the worrying word "intrinsic" had come to qualify "disadvantage", but in principle the assurance still stood. The Society of Authors' *Quick Guide* is more cautious on the subject; in gist it says:

> "Hardback royalties in the UK market should generally be calculated on the UK published price (example given: 10% on first 2,500 copies sold, 12.5% on next 2,500 and 15% thereafter). If calculated for a particular reason on the publisher's receipts, the author should be careful to see that the rates are correspondingly higher... In the case of hardback export royalties, some contracts provide for an overseas royalty lower than the home royalty, calculated on the UK published price, but most are calculated on the publisher's receipts... Paperback royalties should start at not less than 7.5% (home) and 6% (export) of the retail price, rising to 10% (home) after, say, 30,000 copies..."

This trend from published-price to net-receipts royalty agreements was evidently a sensitive subject, and Giles Gordon and Fred Nolan were in no doubt that the former are preferable from the author's point of view, but the official story has always been that it makes no difference, provided the correct equivalences are maintained between the percentage rates. On the opening morning, this had been agreed by Master Barratt, who made it clear that for the ease of his calculation, he wanted to establish simple, unstepped rates based on *Making Names'* estimated hardback and paperback published prices. I had proposed the fair, straightforward, realistically moderate published-price rates of ten percent (UK hardback), seven-and-a-half percent (export hardback and UK paperback) and five percent (export paperback), and understood that these had been accepted. They were in line with all the evidence (for example my friend's exhibited OUP *Memorandum*), and even seemed to be confirmed by Hardy's unsigned, unagreed PPF, which, heavy with correcting fluid, specified hardback net-receipts rates of twelve percent (UK) and ten percent (export); Jonathan Riley had deposed that a ten percent net-receipts rate was equivalent to a seven-and-a-half percent published-price rate. All ways round, the rates issue, at least, seemed to have been settled, and for some while Barratt had been urging McGregor that the key figure he now needed was the multiplier, Oxford's suggested or 'offered' sales figure. Barratt was repeatedly disappointed, and late on the second afternoon, McGregor launched into yet another attempt to realign the basis of the calculation, and at last I understood why Oxford had been so keen to keep my *W.A.Y.* page and Hely-Hutchinson's article out of the evidence. His explanation of the two royalty systems is perhaps the first recorded official statement by a publisher of the modern author's true position:

> **McGregor:** First of all we've got to get to the royalty rate...
> **Barratt:** I was assuming that you were going to agree 10 percent of the published price of the UK hardback, 7.5 percent for the export hard-back, 7.5 percent for the UK paperback and 5 percent for the export paperback. That, I think, is what Mr Malcolm said he would agree.
> **McGregor:** These figures are far too high in my submission... you did say that it is OUP's practice we are looking at here, not the world's generally, and it's true that the Court may have said this is a contract for fair royalties... but unless it can be shown that OUP are acting unconscionably in the way they fix their royalties, then I think it's what you would anticipate you would get from OUP that matters. Now the first thing is that the evidence is clear that you are moving from the early 1980s from the published-price-based royalty to the net-receipts-based royalty. Now it may be that it doesn't make all that much difference, but it depends on how you do your calculations. If you do your calculations so that the discount equals the difference, then of course it doesn't, but quite often the discount may be quite high and will therefore give the publisher a better deal and the author not such a good deal, which is one of the reasons why publishers are moving over to net-receipts royalties... The other question is that of the discount... Mr Asquith's affidavit tells you that OUP's average discount on UK sales is 40 percent and on foreign sales is higher, generally around 60 percent...
> **Barratt:** I'm trying to work out the figures: supposing you've got £100 worth of published-price books and you get 10 percent on the published-

price royalty, that's £10. If they are all sold in the UK, you knock it down
by 40 percent, which is £60 for the receipts... am I not doing it right?
McGregor: Well look, first of all, you get 12 percent of the £100,
because that's what the document [the PPF] says, you get £12... erm...
No, no, do it the other way... Alright, you come down to... you get
£7.20, you get 12 percent of £6...
Barratt: £60... Yes, that is where the difference lies: under your system,
on £100 worth of published-price books, you get £7.20.
McGregor: That's right, yes.
Malcolm: But I thought the point of the two systems was that they
worked out the same, roughly speaking.
McGregor: Well they don't work out precisely the same.
Barratt: On these figures, as far as I can make out, you in practice
would be getting 7.2 percent of published price.
Malcolm: Well that would manifestly be an unfair royalty wouldn't it?
McGregor: Well, no, it's not an unfair royalty.
Barratt: This, we are told by Mr McGregor is the reasonable, standard
amount that OUP pays, and I'm just seeing what that amounts to in
percentages of the published price.
Malcolm: But I thought, Master, we had agreed yesterday that it didn't
matter which system you choose as long as the percentages are correct.
McGregor: You may have agreed, but I hadn't agreed.
Malcolm: Oh, I thought the courtroom had agreed.
Barratt: And so did I (laughing). I had put forward the proposition that
as long as the percentage figures came to the same eventually, it did not
matter by which route... But these two examples do not come to the
same result.
McGregor: I think one of the reasons is *because you don't know what
the net receipts are*, and therefore sometimes you might do better, and
sometimes you might do worse. But on the standard practice of OUP,
the discounts are 40 percent UK and 60 percent export. Well, now I
don't want to, er, um, to belabour this, and what I would propose is it
would come down to 7.2 percent.
Barratt: Yes.

Turning to the royalty rates for the paperback, McGregor went on to
plumb even deeper depths:

"Now, Mr Asquith has assumed rates of ten percent UK and eight
percent export, both on net-receipts, er, so converted to percentages of
cover price, these come out at roughly six-and-a-half percent home and
five percent export... [Barratt and Malcolm: six-and-a-half percent?!?
McGregor turns graciously to Malcolm]... No, I'll be generous, I'll say
six-and-*two-thirds* percent, six-and-*two-thirds* percent... [Barratt
exhales frustratedly]... for simplicity Master, you can put that up to
seven percent, seven percent... I am happy with that... The... the
export... the export figure of five percent is the same as Mr

Malcolm's... foreign, yes... I would, er, [anxious squeaking and fiddling with calculators]... er, I would be happier if, if, er, if we could have, um... you've, you've put seven percent have you, for the first one?... I'm trying to get easy figures... if you'd accept that putting it up to seven percent is, is favourable to Mr Malcolm, I'm, I'm happy at seven percent... Er... [more fiddling, more squeaking] ... May I just support my ten percent and eight percent figures... the exhibit to Mr, Mr, um, Asquith's affidavit I, I, I ...if you look at the paperback, you'll find that there are quite a lot of ten percent and eight percent, which is what Mr Asquith said in his affidavit it ought to be... all net-receipts... [whispering, whiskering]... if I knock, if I knock, er, the ten percent down by, um by forty percent, I would be down to six percent, er, and I've said, I have in fact said seven percent, um... and I think I really should, erm... I think I'm being slightly unfair to myself... Um, I think I ought to knock the seven percent down to six-and-a-half percent... [Malcolm, joking: Or to six-and-*two-thirds* percent?] ... Well, six-and-two-thirds percent. I don't mind six-and-two-thirds percent... I, I, but what I was going to say is that I think that the other perhaps should be below five percent, but let's leave it at that... [Barratt reminds him that the number of copies sold is the important figure; further calculating] ... That is, that is true, um, but, but, nev... nevertheless, I am eager just to finalise this... Um, the, er, if, if, if, if, you see, if, if there's a sixty percent reduction on, er, eight percent, it really would only be *three-point-two* percent and therefore I think that I should... I'm sorry, but I think I should go a little *below* five percent... [Barratt (amazed): *Below five percent*?!? Well, so what? The new offer is?] ... Well, let's say... four-and-a-half percent... I mean, that's how it would work out... Now we come to the question of the, erm, erm, erm, ermounts..."

Strangely, McGregor failed to divulge the royalties he earns from his own masterwork, currently retailing at a moderate £195, but he did then go through Oxford's offered Parfit, Hare and Raphael models, rounding down their sales figures. He contemptuously dismissed the Nagel, focussing instead upon the Glover as the most appropriate. At about five-thirty, he seemed ready to offer its 30,000 sales ("It could be a possible parallel." Barratt: "Yes"), but almost as soon as it slipped out, he bit it back, veering off into an analysis of some mistake he thought he had found in Glover's own arithmetic. By this time, the chatter of calculators was continuous, and even McGregor himself started angrily poking at one, apparently with little luck. Smyth was pacing about with his phone jammed permanently to his ear, and Anderson was spewing notes like a tickertape machine, but every time His Great Eminence seemed at last ready to spit out a figure, there would be another flurry and he would dive back into the royalty-rate waffle, obviously stalling while the flunkeys did the necessary maths. At five-forty-five, already way over time, Barratt yet again reminded him that the multiplier was the important factor and that still none had been offered. McGregor's final virtuoso performance I will quote in full and unvarnished (readers are here invited to sketch their own Michael Heath cartoon):

"You may think that's the last of my submissions, er, on this, but it isn't... now it may be thought that £2,100 [the PPF figure] after all this is a little too little, er, on royalties to propose, erm, and, going on to Lord Justice Leggatt's, erm, er, judgment, um, I am proposing to indulge in an exercise in magnanimity in my coming submissions... er, one... we have tried to, to see if we can avoid the need for an inquiry, er... it hasn't been... proved possible... I will do what I will, and I, I, I, I stress this on, on, the, on the basis that, um, the, the, the figures I'm proposing may be a little over what, er, speculation might lead you to... but I'm content to accept, um... the, the, the figures that you have... (frantic calculating and whispering)... um, can I, can I come to the question of rate?... um, if you take the, the, the hardback... if you... take the price of £15, which is agreed... now, I'm going to assume for the moment, if I may... and this is the most complicated part of the calculation, er, and I think this is entirely fair, that we assume for the purpose of calculation that there is a hardback and a paperback throughout the five-year period, er, and that we then assume that 75 percent of those sales comes in the first two years, er... and that the sales are going to be one-fifth hardback, four-fifths paperback... er, now, to that extent I don't think it is necessary to consider, er, I mean, even if the paperback had come in the second year, er, to consider the rise, the rise in the price to £23 because that would have happened at a time after the hardback had fallen away, er, and the, the... without trying to trouble you, although I may, er, have to look at the one, um... er, one set of figures again (shuffling of notes), er, is that I think it therefore is reasonable to multiply by 15 and not by an increased figure... if we then take, er, my, um, er, er, my, um, um, erm... (long pause, whispering) ... figure of eight percent of the published price for UK and six percent for, um, er, for, for abroad, you'd come down to £1.05 a copy... hardback... um, if you were to... even, even if you were to, to, to take, er, Mr... and Mr Malcolm's of course would be, um, er, is, is... if you're going on the £1.50 price, erm, his wouldn't be all that much higher because he's got ten percent for the hardback, er, in, in, in the UK and he's got seven-and-a-half percent for export, so it would probably come out at, um, er, if you take it in between the two, eight-and-three-quarters percent, er, it's going to come out at that model... it's going to come out about £1.25... (pause) at £1.30... about £1.31... so there's not a great deal between us, but I mean those... that's the range there in my submission... when it comes to... and then we have to multiply by a figure... (urgent whispering) um, when it comes to the paperback, er, we are pretty well agreed, er, that it's going to be moving from, um, £7 in February 1987 to £8 in 1988, to £9 in 1989, to £10 in 1992... um, I would be prepared to, er, take an overall... I mean what if... if one was to take... if... one starts at £8... let us take a, a, an overall figure of £9... I think that's generous... rather than multiply different years... you then have to multiply £9, er, um, by... the, um, er, the net receipts, and now we're down from twelve percent and ten percent to ten percent and eight percent, er, no, so... of the net receipts... and we came to my six-and-two-thirds percent and my four-and-a-half percent or something like that... um, in an attempt to be generous, um, I would be happy to multiply by something like, er, six percent, er, or five-and-a-half percent... this is the percentage you're multiplying the published price by... the percentage is six-and-two-thirds for home and four-and-a-half for... so it's got to be somewhere in between the two to cover both... and the reason that I say, um, five-and-a-half percent is that if you multiply that by £9, £9, £9, you come out at about 50p a copy... so that my figure would be to multiply by 50p. Now Mr Malcolm's is not going to be all that different because he's got... he's got, um, seven-and-a-half percent for UK and five percent for export... er, if you were to bring that down... take it halfway between that six-and-three-quarters percent and multiply... again he can't be multiplying by more than £9, er, you're still only, er, at, um, um, you're still only at, um... (long pause, passing of notes)... six-and-three-quarters times nine... at 60p, 60p and 75p, so it's somewhere between 50p and 60p on, on his figures and mine... so we're not all that far apart, but of course if you immediately start multiplying that by 100,000 copies, it's going to make a lot of difference... um, now, Jonathan's Glover book... and that's going to the top of the range, er, has sold 30,000... (urgent whispering)... now you cannot, Master, er, if you assume that that is an appropriate book, er, and it's true that Mem Nagel has done 60,000 in a slightly shorter period... I think that's an inappropriate book, it's an American book, it's cheaper, it's not in context, so I'd rather concentrate on, on Glover... but if you take Glover at 30,000, you cannot, er, assume the same a number of sales... this is a gamble; it might have worked and it might not have worked... *Chaplin & Hicks* and other cases talk about loss of a chance... you may get five percent because you didn't enter the beauty competition in time... er, I am prepared to say, let's take *half of* the Glover sales... (Barratt heaves sigh of relief, sinks back in chair, makes note... more frantic whispering stage right)... well, at 15,000... I mean... it's not my submission of what I think would have sold... I don't believe they'd be sold... I think this is magna, magnanimity running, running away... now, could, could we take... could we take... er... could, could we start with 10,000, just because it's an easier calculation... if we take 10,000 sales... Perhaps, Master, you'd like to write this down..."

And so it was that at ten minutes past six on the second day of a two-day hearing held seven months after the Court of Appeal had delivered its judgment, Oxford finally, fleetingly proposed an estimate of *Making Names'* lost sales. And so it was too that this "offer" was immediately accepted by the court. McGregor then turned to loss of reputation and laughingly enunciated an interesting new damages principle that, as far as I know, has yet to feature in his book: "If we are going to award money on publicity, I shall have to retract my money on earnings." He went on to cite *Joseph v. National Magazine Co.* (a dispute in 1956 over the mis-editing of an article about jade carvings), equating the status of Oxford University Press with that of *The Connoisseur* antiques magazine, and valuing OUP's imprimatur at £2,000. Barratt, for his part, asserted that this head of damages could not yield more than half the royalties figure, or about £5,000. I've no idea where his own, spontaneous "not more than half" rule came from, but he seemed adamant, so I did not challenge it. In conclusion McGregor declared: "I'm talking on my figures of an award of £15,000", and I repeated my plea for the Nagel model, observing how odd it was that one moment Oxford had found Glover's book appropriate and the next had halved its sales; but that, I guessed, was the publishing business. Barratt then announced that his judgment would be reserved until mid-August, and Chancers' greaser Smyth improperly and unsuccessfully tried to arrange a costs showdown before Barratt was to deliver it. The hearing finished at ten past seven and everyone bade Master Barratt goodnight. I proffered my hand to McGregor, who seemed slightly embarrassed, I am not sure whether by his afternoon's miserable work or because it was I who had done the proffering. Whichever it was, we shook and he scuttled off down the corridor as fast as his mousey legs could carry him.

26

Magnanimity Running Away

ANOTHER SUB-ACTION in the case had in the meantime been grinding on. Because Oxford was still contesting the costs of the Morritt hearing and of the subpoenas, which it now appeared were based upon false evidence or misleading affidavits (the date obscured from the Delegates' Note, Hardy's 'forgetfulness' over his telephone script, the existence of Delegates' book-lists and so forth), I had applied to have these rulings overturned. After an adjournment, a hearing of my appeal against the first of them had, it happened, been scheduled for 19th July, just eight days after the assessment. I will not try the reader with its wearisome detail, save to record that I won and had a further thirty percent of Oxford's seventy-five percent costs standing against me disallowed, together with the costs of the hearing itself. Afterwards, Karen Anderson, now back with Mark Warby again, laughingly reminded me that in a single hour Chancers could clock up far more costs than I could in a whole week (month? year?) of acting in person. I said I fully understood the fact, but why, I wondered, as I was packing up their latest six-inch-thick file of abortive affidavits, was she telling *me* this?

In mid-August Master Barratt's assessment findings duly arrived and duly confirmed that he had simply accepted Oxford's last-minute figure of 15,000 copies. He applied averaged home-and-export published-price royalties of eight percent (hardback) and five-and-a-half percent (paperback) at prices of £15-£23 and £8-£10. He worked out that I would not have received my first royalties until the end of July 1988 (two years and five months after the delivery of the script), and assumed that payments would then have been made annually. He accepted our agreed 50/50 home/export assumption and 1/4 hardback/paperback split, but then made the glaring, and very costly mistake of spreading the latter evenly over the whole five-year period. As McGregor had said, virtually all of the hardback sales would have come in the first year and then dropped off when the paperback was published in the second. Barratt computed the lost royalties as £9,937.50, the interest as £2,009.63 and the loss of reputation as £6,000, giving a total of £17,947.13, some way short of Oxford's payment-in. Oxford at once issued a summons to attend a hearing on 19th November to argue for a deduction of notional tax from the interest component and for the apportionment of their costs. In September Chancers wrote that though their costs draftsman had, inexplicably, doubled their estimate of my own likely taxed costs of the case, because of the expense of McGregor and co., I would probably end up owing the University money. As I had imagined, this prospect must have rather worried them, for they nevertheless generously offered me £13,500 in full and final global settlement. Unfortunately, their new offer had lapsed by the time I replied.

Dickens was now superseded by Kafka. At the November hearing, Oxford's tax-exempt press, argued that in accordance with the provisions of Section 349(2) of the Income and Corporation Taxes Act of 1988, as a Case III of Schedule D, the sum of £502.28 should be deducted from the interest component of my damages total. Oxford Chancers also sought exemption from paying the imagined royalties' interest component from the date of the payment-in (£232.49) and an order that, following the Practice Note (1988) 3 All ER 896, and the ruling in *Polish Steamship Co. v. Atlantic Maritime Co., The Garden City* (1985) QB 41 (1984) 3 All ER 59, CA, any interest accruing on the payment-in between the date of the payment-in and the date of the judgment should be paid to the charitable University. I imagine that Anderson's research and supporting affidavits (perhaps even just her letter to me), never mind her attendance at the hearing, must have cost more than these amounts, but, having absolutely no thoughts at all about any of these fascinating matters, I made no attempt to argue their tosses.

As was expected, Chancers sought an order that I pay all their costs from the date of Oxford's payment-in. What was not expected was that Master Barratt granted them an order that I pay their costs from the date of Oxford's *instruction of Harvey McGregor*. This at once appeared to be an absurd mistake arising from the Chancers' deception. At the assessment hearing, McGregor had explained to Barratt that his great authority and wisdom (and fees) had been justified on this trivial zero-sales trifle due to the inflation of my claim by Ryan's comparison of *Making Names* with *The Outsider* and *Gödel, Escher, Bach*. At the costs hearing Anderson explained that McGregor had been instructed from mid-April, so naturally Barratt assumed that my claim had formally been lodged *after* Oxford's payment-in and McGregor then been instructed then. In fact, McGregor was consulted much earlier and was on hire from 15th March, my claim was served on 30th March and Oxford's offer was not made until 2nd May — precisely the reverse of Barratt's assumed order. (He confirmed that he had been misled in a subsequent phonecall.) This meant that there had been an obvious and hugely expensive misapplication of the costs/payment-in rules. What with Barratt's other obvious (deliberate?) mathematical mistakes in calculating the lost royalties, there was only one way forward: "Grounds for appeal!" chorused my lawyers.

I lodged my appeal against both Master Barratt's damages assessment and his costs orders on 18th December 1991, citing as my chief grounds (1) that he had been wrong simply to accept without argument Oxford's 15,000 copies estimate, and (2) that even accepting the 15,000 figure, he had made clear and large mathematical errors by (a) spreading the hardback sales over five years, (b) postulating a 29-month delay, and (c) applying insupportably low royalty rates. I also ordered the transcription of Roy Edgley's testimony (curiously, Oxford decided to counter this with transcriptions of Mynott, Pickin and Croom). It seemed fairly certain to my lawyers that I would succeed to some extent with this appeal: the Court would be unlikely to reduce Oxford's offered multiplier of 15,000, some of Barratt's mathematical mistakes were glaring and even contradicted agreed points, and his costs order was a clear misapplication of the rules. What was not so certain, however, was how high any increase on appeal might go, and whether it would exceed Oxford's payment-in target. It was not even clear what would happen to Oxford's costs if an intermediate figure were awarded; I asked this of several senior lawyers but none could give a confident answer. The only certainties were that Chancers would go into cash-hyperdrive and that my financial risk would get uncomfortable.

Sure enough, the first things Oxford did were to freeze the money paid into court, to demand £25,000 for security of costs (an application later aborted) and to lodge its own (very weak) cross-appeal to reduce the damages, now standing at £17,444.73. Over the Festive Season Chancers then made various moves to stall the handover of any of the money. At the end of January 1992 Barratt ordered a payment-out of £3,000, but even this token was delayed until mid-March. Meanwhile, I was pressing ahead with the paperwork and preparations, and Oxford had seriously to start contemplating the possibility of another public fiasco at the hands of the Court of Appeal, this time on the touchy subject of authors' royalties and damages. At the end of March Oxford proposed a new version of their preceding May deal. This time the offer was distinctly tempting and the risks of continuing distinctly alarming. Although my lawyers were confident that the damages quantum would be substantially increased, any gain might well be dwarfed by the appeal's uncertain costs. Besides, the prospect of having to repeat before their Lordships days of miserable argument about royalty-rates and interest-dates was not, dare I say, very appealing. This time, Chancers' tone was different too: no more take-it-or-leave-it deadlines, no more pompous jibes or ambiguities; this time the Morritt costs had been settled; this time the subpoenaed witnesses were prevailed upon. This time everyone had had enough.

I soon learnt that even when both parties to litigation have decided to extricate themselves from it, the very extrication process can easily become as tricky and acrimonious as the worst stages of their dispute. Our settlement negotiation began in April 1992, though was delayed for a while by Richard White's undergoing a hospital operation. By early May the terms of the deal had been agreed, but not the method by which it was to be executed. I was being strongly advised to insist upon a court-sealed 'consent' or 'Tomlin' order (an order ratified by Master Barratt to which the terms could be attached in the form of a schedule and placed on the court's archive file). Then there occurred two surprises that threw Chancers' dealings into an uncharacteristic fluster. First, Oxford suddenly realised, very late in the day, that it had omitted to mention its foremost worry, confidentiality. Second, I was notified that the damages appeal was to be heard comparatively quickly, on 20th July; Oxford's solicitors had assumed that it could not come on before the autumn, and once again my listing-speed had taken them by surprise. Furthermore, I learned that the court was to be their Lords Justices Scott (later Sir Richard of Iraq), Stuart-Smith (the hero of my earlier security hearing) and Lloyd (of East Sussex) — another very eminent, all-Cambridge team.

An agreement to end litigation is, like any other agreement, and perhaps especially so, governed by the law of contract, one of whose principles is that once a complete bargain has been struck, it cannot then by either party be unstruck, or without mutual consent then be renegotiated to include new conditions or terms (see *Malcolm v. the Chancellor Masters and Scholars of the University of Oxford* [1990] C.A.). It therefore followed as night day that if Oxford belatedly wanted our settlement to include various new confidentiality clauses, it would itself have to offer some *quids pro quo*. And so it was. Because our eventual agreement's terms are confidential, I had better not reveal the nature of the University's *quids*, even though they are arguably not themselves covered by the clauses, but I do not believe that I am taking any risk or liberty to disclose (a) that, as may be assumed, they were not of the cash variety and (b) that every time I think of them I laugh and thank the stars. Chancers also had to bite the bullet and consent to a consent order, the form of agreement upon which my lawyers were insisting. Oxford's growing anxiety over the confidentiality of our settlement, presumably fuelled by the fear that its public knowledge might set a precedent for other aggrieved authors and make OUP a laughing-stock and a liability for the rest of the trade, was finally satisfied by a further agreement that its schedule of terms be placed on the court file in an envelope sealed from journalists' prying eyes with a seal that can only be broken by further order of the court, amen. Its signing ceremony before Master Barratt took place on the 1st of July 1992.

According to Clause 6 of the schedule, when questioned concerning the settlement, the parties shall reply with the following words: "The parties have agreed to settle their outstanding claims but are bound by mutual undertakings of confidentiality and accordingly are not at liberty to discuss or comment upon the terms of the settlement." There, I've uttered them at last. Even so, I did not receive any cheque until 24th July, but when it came it certainly smelt sweet. It was now over a year since Barratt's assessment, a year-and-a-half since the Court of Appeal's public prayer that I be spared the worry of further litigation, nearly two-and-a-half years since Sir Otiose's courtroom assertion that "it would depend how long it was before the matter was put straight", and *seven* years since Hardy had declared "I have made a commitment to you which I think we should honour collectively."

The whole damages exercise had, of course, been a great folly. The very idea of dozens of suited law-people in courtrooms fiddling with calculators trying to work out how many copies would have been sold five years beforehand of an imaginary book which none had read is, of course, preposterous, even more preposterous than the idea of similar suited persons in great publishing combines presently trying to guess what the public wants to read. The last year had also been a personal folly for me: in strict financial terms I was probably worse off than if I had accepted Oxford's payment-in in May 1991, although there would have been many uncertainties and disputes in its acceptance and I would still have faced some complex taxations. To boot, Mrs Lewin's home insurance policy had proved a folly too: Brighton Council had spontaneously decided to re-house the old lady and then pronounced her former home structurally dangerous, at a stroke more than wiping out any financial gain I had made from the lawsuit. On the other hand, I did now have the priceless settlement, I had had the differing but equally unforgettable honours of meeting Roy Edgley and Harvey McGregor, I had completed my exploration through to Academia's dark heart, and I was at least still solvent. For Oxford, by contrast, the folly had been in scale with its enormous self-opinion. Despite its obsession with secrecy, soon after our settlement had been signed, *Private Eye's* 'Bookworm' columnist learned, via an apparently reliable source within Chancers, that the University had spent over £400,000 on the lawyers, suggesting that its total payout, to Dallas Brett and all, was almost half a million. I have no idea how accurate Bookworm's figure is, but it would not surprise me a bit: in one letter, Chancers boasted to me that they had notched up £45,000 in just eight weeks. As in the best tradition of divorce proceedings, one side will happily spend a thousand pounds to deny the other a hundred, or ten.

27

Book, What Book?

IT WAS TIME to put all the dreadful lawyering behind and return to *Making Names*. I had long since resolved, for reasons that will by now need no explanation, to have nothing further to do with UK publishers, most of whom in any case would presumably have nothing further to do with me. The offer from Tom Weldon had already demonstrated that a straightforward, honest publication of *Making Names*, for example one inspired by a genuine belief in it, was now an impossibility, at least in the UK. Hard-bitten realists may wonder at such idealism, but realists can have little idea of the revulsion generated by such an unrealistic lawsuit, especially in its assessment phase. Self-publication now appeared the only incorrupt and trustworthy option. Self-publication presented some financial attractions too. By this time I had learned enough of publishing economics to know that I would earn a lot more per copy self-sold than I would from any McGregor-style royalties, and I assumed, naïvely, that at least the serious, reviewing newspapers would devote some attention to the book, if only to discover what all the fuss had been about. Hopefully, some senior figure might find a good word or two to say for it, might ask why it had been so badly treated by Oxford, and it might start to shift.

Self-publication, however, also poses various problems. First, of course, it means doing without an editor. Given the history, it may be wondered why I cite this as minus, but in losing an editor, an author loses, or should lose, far more than a mere spellchecker or house-stylist, they lose the vital encouragement of an ally morally supportive enough to tell them which bits of their work are too this, too that or too the other. I was once more thrown back onto solitary self-reliance. Sheer laziness and fatigue doubtless played their parts here, but fortunately, whatever I thought of the text's 1986 draft, there were now also some sound historical and legal reasons for leaving it unretouched. (In fact I still did not think too badly of much of it — the general structure, the twists of argument, some of the writing. The play, of course, remained still a rough sketch, unfinished, as I guess it always will be; but generally speaking I felt that, unlike Ryan's infamous 1986 rejection-scrawl, my second draft would *do*.) In the meantime though, the Berlin Wall had fallen and the Cold War background to Cause and Effect's conversation had thawed, so some minor contemporising changes were necessary in Chapters Six and Nine. Apart from these, I decided to leave the book almost exactly as it had been when submitted to OUP in February 1986, adding a prefatory Author's Note to this effect. My final choice on the vexed subtitle issue was, naturally, *An Idea of Philosophy.*

I had already had some experience of typesetting and layout, and during the latter stages of the dispute had had plenty of time to get *Making Names* word-processed and computer-set. After all the Oxford objections to the book's unmanageable length, it in fact worked out at a perfectly average 425 well-spaced A5 pages. I christened my imprint AKME Publications (the book's two protagonists' initials spelt 'ACME', but there already existed several 'ACME' publishers, and 'AKME' is truer to the Greek). I commissioned a Brighton artist to paint the central motif for the dustjacket-design I had suggested — a human hand penning the title on an open book's blank first page — and made no direct reference on it to the book's difficult birth; I wanted *Making Names* to be judged on its merits and not to be known as 'the book of the lawsuit'. (Hardy later opined that this was a mistake.) I thought it would be fitting to re-enact Oxford's original plan and to order first a short run in hardback, complete with sewn binding, head and tail bands and gold-blocked spine. I obtained various printers' estimates, and in February 1992, assuming the litigation would soon end, ordered a first production-run, which to my eye turned out excellently. The book's frontispiece gives no publication date, for at the time I did not know when that would be. In the event it was August 1992.

So far, so good, but as Mustill and Nourse LJJ had observed, the role of a publisher extends far beyond that of mere book-production, being more importantly that of *making work public,* that is of distributing, advertising, promoting and in the countless well-trodden ways of such organisations, disseminating and selling it as widely as possible. In this respect, my assumption of the book's automatic media attention had indeed been naïve. All the newspapers were sent copies, some even two or three, with press releases, cuttings about the case, and follow-up phonecalls from AKME's specially-hired PR-person. Not a single review or article appeared and not a single journalist picked up the story (sadly, Laurence Marks had by then been taken ill; he died in 1996). Not that there was *no* interest, for there was in fact a good deal, expressed by all sorts of people who said they liked the book and were appalled by its history: reviews and articles were genuinely promised, radio and TV mentions were enthusiastically mooted. But every time they began, communications would shortly go mysteriously dead. Of course, this is routine in the media, this is the nature of the game in which legions of hopefuls are constantly scrabbling for their fifteen minutes of attention. But, even allowing for my being an out-of-the-swim provincial and for the kiss-of-death word 'philosophy', why did this happen so repeatedly to a book that had been the focus of such an interesting and important media tale?

I have always found this silence surprising. Even allowing for the traditional British uninterest in philosophy and general scepticism of any claimed innovation, surely my six years' hard labour in Chancery and my historic legal victory should have earned the book, whatever its contents, a glance, or at least a glancing blow? There was also the extraordinary status conferred upon it by the 1992 settlement, a circumstance which, I believe, makes it unique in the entire history of writing and publishing. Here, I suppose, lies a clue, for by the same token it had become a book which the authorities at Oxford had an extra, legal motive — besides straightforward spite and self-vindication — for wanting, as Ryan so generously suggested, to sink without trace. Over the years since its launch, I have heard a number of whispered indications as to why *Making Names* may have been so deafeningly ignored, and a few clear, well-documented incidents. Of the latter I will cite just two, the first of which occurred soon after the hardback's release, the second more recently.

28

DIM Innuendo

IN AUGUST 1992 I was telephoned by a Bill Noble, who I think had been given my number by Mark Le Fanu. Noble was a Canadian, London-based author of educational textbooks who in the late 1970s had formally been contracted by OUP to write an ELT series for the then-booming Middle-Eastern market. In circumstances not dissimilar to mine, after he had written three of the books, the oil price fell and Oxford broke his contract, publishing only the first of the series, and leaving him well out-of-pocket on both his wasted work and his lost royalties. In his case, there was no dispute that there was a contract or that OUP had reneged on it, yet for years he had had to nag for restitution. Having been repeatedly fobbed off, he had initiated a legal action, had successfully won an Arbitration Order with costs, and was presently negotiating with Justine Winternitz, an in-house solicitor appointed by OUP in the wake of my victory. It seemed that, unbeknownst to each other (but both beknownst to Le Fanu), Noble and I had for some years been fighting parallel fights. About a week after my case finally settled, Noble appeared unannounced at OUP's Walton Street headquarters and demanded to see Sir Otiose in order personally to serve him with a five-figure bill. Noble was told that Otiose was overseas, but did not believe this and refused to budge until he got satisfaction. He was promptly escorted from the visitors' area to a private office, and on the way an editor whom he knew greeted him, only to find herself being manhandled off down the corridor by security guards. After the scuffle, Noble was shut in a room from which the phones were removed. Eventually, a fuming Sir Otiose appeared, together with OUP's International Branch Director Roger Boning, to acknowledge the service of Noble's bill. When in the ensuing conversation Noble mentioned the name 'Malcolm' and quoted certain lines from my case, I gather the mighty publisher turned "incandescent".

Noble bought a copy of *Making Names* and said he found it entertaining and thought-provoking. Under the headline *Cause célèbre*, he wrote an enthusiastic review of the book which through his own personal contacts was published in *The Times Educational Supplement* of Friday 25th September 1992:

"Making Names is an original *tour de force*... As its title forewarns us,
it deals with some modish issues of semiotics, but the overall contents
are more comparable to some of Bertrand Russell's later writing,
effectively communicating the essentials of philosophy and scientific
theorising to students and general readers. With its entertaining
dialogues and its realistic, direct arguments, *Making Names* should
prove a widely popular introductory text."

On the following Monday, Sir Otiose abandoned Winternitz's negotiation
and in her stead instructed Clifford Chance to act against Noble. I later
spoke to the lady at the *TES* who had authorised the appearance of
Noble's review; she explained to me nervously that "she had got into
serious trouble for letting it through."

The rules of evidence that apply to arbitration hearings are looser than
those in High Court cases, permitting the admission of material detailing a
defendant's previous similar misdemeanours, so Noble asked me for various
items from my case that would help him with his. I gradually fed him what
material I legitimately could and explained it step-by-step. Noble's interest
in the saga grew, particularly with respect to Sir Otiose's sworn statement
that OUP kept no records of its General Book approvals, and in all the
evidence which appeared to contradict this unlikely assertion. Noble
explored the American media and was asked to write a 'background piece'
on my case for *The New York Times*. He was then invited by an American
publisher to expand this into a book, and inquired if I would mind him
doing so. I said no, whereupon he embarked on some detailed research,
talking to several of Oxford's participants in the affair. In one of the many
weird and telling lies he elicited from them, Alan Ryan told him that "I had
borrowed on the equity in my mother's property to finance the lawsuit." My
mother is still waiting to hear from the visionary communitarian what
property of hers he was referring to, while I am wondering why on earth
my bank-balance should ever have been on his, er, mind. On 9th
November, Noble placed an advertisement in *The Oxford Times*:

OUP

I am an OUP author. I wish to get in touch with the OUP
staff members who, during my sojourn in your foyer on 9
July 1992, offered to help in respect of my 3 book
contracts. Regarding also my main precedent "Malcolm
versus OUP" — Can anyone provide missing documentation
such as lists of General Books titles at the Delegates' meeting
in July 1985? Please write to Bill Noble... (address)
Confidentiality will be preserved as you request

This advertisement stung Oxford Chance into injunction-mode and got the story into *Private Eye*, which in January 1993, without any prompting from me, ran a long piece on the two stories (mine and Noble's), leaked Chancers' £400,000 costs figure, referred to Sir Roger Rabbit's "increasingly hazardous reputation", and broke the lawyers' ultimate taboo by featuring that other unmentionable p-word, "perjury". On 23rd March Sir Rabbit sued *Private Eye* and its editor Ian Hislop for libel. The *Eye's* lawyers consulted me on the defensibility of the article, which, unfortunately, had not been relayed to me beforehand and was slightly carelessly worded. I thought a defence feasible but risky, and Hislop was understandably reluctant to contest it in front of the dusty-wig brigade. In September 1993 the *Eye* paid Sir Rabbit undisclosed, but I gather modest, out-of-court damages.

Noble, meanwhile, had successfully concluded his own litigation, but was now himself bound by confidentiality undertakings. Hardy and Oxford had learned of his planned *New York Times* article about my case and he was obliged to abandon it, along with the book. Our correspondence gradually dried up, but when I talked to him a year or so later he told me that during the settlement phase of his action, two large suited gentlemen from Chancers had one night visited his Hampstead house unappointed and told him, *inter alia*, "If you ever want to earn money from ELT books again, you had better drop the Malcolm story." Being in the process of putting three daughters through their schooling, and well-versed in the artful machinations of academe, Noble had reluctantly decided not to risk any further research. This ugly revelation recalled, not for the first time, another of the darker exchanges in *Making Names*, at page 156:

> **Cause:** I am reminded of another, rather strange way in which our notion of criminality is under threat, from the development of modern policing techniques.
> **Effect:** What, the spectre of everyone eaves-dropped, phone-tapped, radio-monitored, that old bogey?
> **Cause:** It's no bogey Malcolm, for some people it's already everyday life; tagging is being tried, boardroom bugging is routine, and just you wait till your research comes up with something...

I had thought that I had perhaps 'come up with something' in my original 'intellectual voyage of discovery', but as Jeremy Mynott had predicted, this was proving to be of no interest whatever to anyone, and as dead-born as Hume's *Treatise*. By contrast though, it now seemed possible that in my subsequent real-life voyage, *Malcolm v. Oxford*, I really had unearthed some interesting new truth, for the Thought Police had finally broken cover. But what, I wondered, could my awkward discovery have been?

Noble reported something else interesting too: he had never told me of any responses to his *Oxford Times* advertisement, so I had assumed that he had had none, but when I asked him casually if this was the case, he said cagily that in fact he had received some remarkable replies but could not disclose them. He added that he had copied certain of these papers to Mark Le Fanu, who had insisted that on no account should they be passed on to me; presumably they provided grounds for further menacing, and Le Fanu, no doubt wisely, adjudged this unwelcome. He reminded Noble that OUP was one of the last great independent, international British publishers competing in an increasingly cut-throat global marketplace, that it published a large number of books written by his Society's members, and that British authors' interests generally were not best served by plunging such an institution into even deeper trouble. All true, no doubt, but rich in paradoxes that readers, especially authors, may wish to ponder. That defending Oxford against Malcolm's machinations had now become a patriotic duty again chimed with a traditional ethical question aired in *Making Names*: can there be moral obligations higher than those one owes one's country? Whatever one's view, it remains a remarkable fact that the Society of Authors' quarterly magazine, which had carried two-page analyses of both the comparatively trivial *Barrow* and *Joseph* cases of 1951 and 1959, has so far featured precisely zero analysis of mine.

In 1997 there was another odd manifestation of the Society of Authors' role, which in its new *Quick Guide to contracts* asserted (7a):

> "it is usual for the form of publication (hardback, trade paperback, mass market paperback) and the approximate published price to be specified — and preferably the anticipated size of the first printing as well."

Had Mark Le Fanu therefore perjured himself on my behalf in his 1990 affidavit? Had the trade's practice, perhaps as a result of *Malcolm v. The Chancellor, Masters and Scholars of the University of Oxford*, entirely changed between 1990 and 1997? I do not believe so, and Hugh Jones' 1996 analysis confirms that a book's format, print-run and price are matters still "normally reserved for the publisher's sole discretion and control." Oxford's 'sole control' clause has not changed (though in OUP's ever-expanding *Memorandum* it has moved from 5 to 7.3), and the P.A.'s Code, revised in 1997, retains its 1982 wording verbatim: "Under the contract, final responsibility for decisions on the design, promotion and marketing of a book is normally vested in the publisher." I know of no-one in the publishing world who believes Le Fanu's new *Quick Guide* statement to be true, so why then is it so publicly, misleadingly there? Perhaps this disturbing question should inaugurate a novel branch of Oxford study, Political Psychology; most post-modern.

Another clue emerged more recently. Early in 1997 I submitted two suggestions to *The Guinness Book of Records*, which, I had learnt, was undergoing a major revamp and seeking fresh material. I suggested for its publishing spread two new categories (in capitals) and entries, the first of which was the fruit of years of exhaustive research and was absolutely certain, the second of which was my pure guess:

RECORD DAMAGES AWARDED TO AN AUTHOR
In December 1990 the UK Court of Appeal found a breach of contract by Oxford University (Press) to publish Andrew Malcolm's philosophy text *Making Names*, and after an assessment in July 1991 the author was awarded £17,445.

RECORD UNRETURNED ADVANCE
In February 1996 the New York State Supreme Court ruled that the actress Joan Collins could retain a $1.2 million advance for her unpublished novel *A Ruling Passion*. The publisher Random House had found Ms Collins' first draft unsatisfactory and sued her unsuccessfully for the return of the money.

At a meeting on 10th April 1997 of the *GBR* committee, both of these new categories were approved for the 1998 edition and both claimed records were at once accepted as authentic. By early July they were included on the *GBR's* final film sent to the book's Spanish printer, but on the 25th, on the eve of the presses' scheduled run of 600,000 copies, Guinness Publishing Director Ian Castello-Cortes personally flew out to Barcelona, held up the plant for twelve hours, and carefully expunged from the plates a single entry, mine. He hastily filled the resulting gap in the spread with an unapproved, unauthenticated translations record claimed by US novelist Sydney Sheldon.

29

The AKME Empire

B UT ALL THIS is mere tittle-tattle. Surely it is inconceivable that after so much litigation Oxford would have dared to breach any of its confidential settlement undertakings? On the subject of confidentiality, in 1992 I got another surprise glimpse behind enemy lines. Bill Noble revealed that, like me, he had been assisted by several 'moles' at OUP, and had learned that witch-hunts were being conducted to identify the leakers (he had even, unbeknownst to me, obtained a full transcript of my trial cross-examinations of the Oxford Six). I, or rather AKME, then became the beneficiary of yet another such lapse of discipline. By this time, Lilian Lewin's former home had become a filthy building site, with foundations being dug, walls being removed and RSJs being installed. The roof leaked rain, the dust lay inches thick on every surface, and bags of cement and plaster spilled their contents on all sides. However, as it was secure, had a telephone and electricity, and provided a different address from my own, I decided to locate AKME's head office there. For £10 I purchased a fine, stout old oak sideboard with tight-fitting dustproof doors, and I wired phone and power sockets into it. For some months, this rubble-strewn sideboard, with its fax and answering-machine inhabitants, became the hub of the AKME empire. I had reported AKME's important news to relevant journals like *The Bookseller*, which in turn had published AKME's address. In September this bore a most unexpected fruit: some mischievous OUP staffer mailed me the prospective contract of employment of one Sarah Brown, who had applied for the job of OUP Production Assistant (Arts and Reference), starting in November. The point of interest, I assumed, was the hilarious post-Malcolm, per-Winternitz, pre-Amis Clause 11, headed CONFIDENTIAL INFORMATION:

> While you are employed by either the Press or by Oxford University (or by any part thereof) the following terms will apply:-
>
> (a) In respect of any invention, discovery, patent process, know-how, trade secret or other confidential information (from now on referred to as "Information") which relates either to the Press or to its clients or to its suppliers and which you learn because you are employed by the Press or as a result of having been employed by the Press you agree to the following restrictions:-
>
> i You will not make known such Information to any other person, firm or corporation.
>
> ii You shall use your best endeavours to prevent anyone else disclosing or publishing such Information without authority.

iii You will only use such Information when required to do so as part of your job.

iv When your employment finishes (for whatever reason) you will immediately hand over to the Press the originals and any copies of all correspondence, documents, specifications, papers and any other items in your possession which are the property of the Press and which relate to either the Information or to your employment generally.

(b) While you are employed by the Press you must not, without your Divisional Head's written permission, which will not unreasonably be withheld, carry out work for any other person, firm or corporation which either competes with or carries on similar business to that of the Press whether or not you are an employee or a consultant and whether you are paid or not. In no circumstances will you be permitted to do such work on Press premises, using Press equipment or within your normal working hours.

(c) Unless the Delegates of the Press, through the Secretary, give their approval in writing beforehand, you must not enter into any agreement or other commitment on behalf of the Press beyond the limits of your usual authority in such matters or be concerned directly or indirectly in any transaction connected with the Information.

(d) Each clause and sub-clause of this Clause 11 shall be read separately and in the event that the whole or any part of these clauses and sub-clauses shall be found to be void but the clause or sub-clause would be valid if part or all of the sub-clause were deleted then such modifications shall apply as may be necessary to make the clause or sub-clause valid and effective.

Returning to AKME's own staff-recruitment programme, I appointed myself Sales Manager, had some stationery and cards printed under the alias Denis "one 'n' please" Dugdale (those being Charkin-n-Hardy's middle names), bought myself another Help-the-Aged suit (grey this time, with complementing blue polyester shirt and grey silk tie), invested in a fine grey attaché case, and hit the grey road, in particular the Charing Cross Road. Over the next few weeks, Denis scored some notable successes. For a brief while Blackwell's shop in central Oxford devoted an entire window-display to *Making Names*. The manager of the philosophy department in the Charing Cross Waterstone's read and liked it, proposed it as a 'Book of the Month' in their catalogue, and again promised a window display. (On the strength of this I lashed out on some glossy A1 posters, but then neither the puff nor the display materialised.) W. H. Smith's buyers read the book and were impressed — a huge coup, this — but decided to wait for a cheaper paperback edition (the hardback was retailing at £24.90). Generally though, Denis's experiences were greyly depressing; selling the odd few copies here and there did not really compensate for having to wait in grimy backrooms for one's turn in the rep-queue to sweet-talk some apathetic buyer. On most occasions, the words 'philosophy', 'AKME', and 'Malcolm case' might as well have been Chinese. "Is it anything to do with Princess Di?" was asked more than once. Without broadsheet newspaper attention, Denis was sinking, and I was once again being cast out into the wilderness role of railing crank, only this time one with a shedful of books to shift and a bank-loan to repay.

The psychological strain self-publication imposes by its alienation from the mainstream was by now the accepted, normal condition of my every action. What were less expected were some of the tensions such a venture can generate closer to home. For a start, one's immediate friends at once divide into two camps: those who even though broke, uninterested in the book and without any intention of reading it, nevertheless unhesitatingly buy a copy, sometimes even refusing an offered discount; and the freeloaders who grunt "so where's mine then?" Then there are the not-so-immediate acquaintances who request copies *as if* they are going to pay for them, but who, as one gradually realises over the ensuing weeks, are not. This is the routine stuff, of course, of everyday life, and people divide themselves into such camps all the time, but when the object is the fruit of a ten-year creative effort (never mind a six-year legal battle), the lessons can be telling. Another familiar, well-intentioned toe-curler goes: "Come on, Andrew, you've given *Making Names* your best shot, why don't you try writing something else now, not philosophy, something funny?" (Well, at last I have, so...?) And of course there are the oh-so-English mutual embarrassments with the few of one's acquaintances who *are* in the media; one doesn't like to ask if they don't volunteer, while they, I guess like my ancient school-chum at Routledge, don't want to have their objectivity compromised by a personal association. I knew, for example, the producer of a BBC TV book series who without apparent irony asked me if I had heard of any good publishing stories which she could use in her programmes. I had to tell her that I could think of none at all.

As must by now be patent, if I do have any talents or skills, public relations is certainly not amongst them; indeed, I seem to have been blessed with, or acquired, a knack for the very opposite, however that might be phrased. Way back in July 1985, when Henry Hardy had made his well-meaning polytechnic-posters suggestion, he had added "There is nobody who has more commitment to book-promotion than the author and his committed friends." At the time I said nothing to this, but did find it a troubling remark coming from an editor who worked for an international publishing house. I had always assumed that it was the author's part to *write* things and others' to take care of the rest. Surely this was the whole point of getting a thesis down on paper, so that one *didn't* then have to traipse up and down the country personally trying to explain it to people. More and more, it seems, writers, even writers of science and philosophy, are nowadays required to be 'personalities', to perform well on podia or TV chat-shows, to sound lucid on radio, and to look good in photographs — all ambitions of which I am temperamentally suspicious and in practice probably incapable. Years later, with *Making Names* at last in print and briefly displayed in a few bookshops, Hardy re-entered our rift-turned-chasm of mutual misunderstanding with a letter that I found literally breathtaking. It was dated October 1992 and bore the address of his Wolfson College sinecure:

> Dear Andrew,
>
> I hope this finds you. I just wanted to say that I was delighted to discover (only yesterday) that *Making Names* was finally in print. You may have wondered, but I have never deviated from my view that it ought to be published, and I am very pleased that it now has been. It looks as if AKME has been set up for the purpose, which means, presumably, that you're not getting the full representation and distribution you'd get from an established publisher, but I've no doubt that you're championing the book effectively nonetheless. The production job seems to me very good. Maybe you'll sell paperback rights? I gather you've had a good review in the *THES* [in fact the *TES*], but I haven't yet seen this. I should be fascinated to know how the book is selling.
>
> It's a bit odd to quote from publishers on the back without explaining the history of the book inside (except for the Author's Note, which would be entirely cryptic to anyone who doesn't know the story). But no doubt you had your reasons.
>
> No need to reply: I simply wanted to congratulate you on publication.
>
> Yours,
>
> Henry Hardy

As Hardy anticipated, at first my instinct was not to reply to this amazing turn — a death-bed repentance, as Laurence Marks described it. However, my settlement with Oxford had obliged Clifford Chance to notify the University's employees and some ex-employees of certain of its clauses, and I wanted to learn how diligent they had been in this regard. I therefore did write back, asking if Chancers had ever written to him. He sent me a copy of a letter he had received from Karen Anderson in July 1992 in which she thanked him for all his assistance and properly apprised him of his obligations. The letter's heading, however, featured the case's most glorious and telling Freudian and legal slip to date: instead of the usual "Malcolm v. Oxford University" or similar, it read: "The Chancellor, Masters and Scholars of the University of Oxford University ("the Press") re: Andrew Malcolm". Now there's a giveaway, if you like, or perhaps just an attempted Footlights joke. Evidently Chancers were keen that Hardy should not understand the implications of what had been agreed. Out of some perverse fascination, I engaged the memory-man in correspondence, trying him with many further interesting questions. The resulting exchanges read like a psychological case-history as bizarre as any by Dostoevsky. Of all his latter-day remarks, my favourite is: "I don't think you had a legally enforceable contract, sadly."

With the saga rumbling on in *Private Eye*, in January 1993 AKME took an advertisement in the magazine, editing puffs from Edgley, Noble and Hardy, and quoting Charkin's cheerful "load of rubbish" jibe. *The Bookseller's* gossip columnist William Boot "joyfully" repeated this tribute, speculating that Charkin's Minerva imprint would therefore not be signing up the paperback of *Making Names*. Boot would have been even more joyful to learn that two years earlier, Charkin's Heinemann had offered to do that very thing. Charkin then at last decided that he had better actually take a look at *Making Names* himself and sent me a slip worded (in full): "As you're using my name to help sell your book, the least you could do is send me a copy, isn't it?" I sent him a complimentary by return, but never got the benefit of his views on it. Another nice irony crystallised too. As a publisher of evidently controversial work, AKME found its Post Office box taking delivery of various other authors' stifled masterpieces, including a play about the IRA. Regretfully, Denis Dugdale was unable to find space for any of this material in AKME's current list.

A rather more gratifying surprise came in April 1993 with a telephone call from Sir Karl Popper. The call was unexpected, but not quite out-of-the-blue. I had for years regarded Popper as the last great philosopher alive, a beacon of eloquence and reason who on many matters had bravely out-faced the tides of fashion and unpopularity; I imagine that future history may well judge him to have been *the* greatest, soundest thinker of his era. When I first approached him, in 1991, I therefore did so with enormous trepidation. To my surprise he was wonderfully approachable and at once invited me to send him *Making Names*. Not wishing to burden him with superfluous introductory material, I sent him just the typescript's opening pages, a summary, and the final *Electra* chapter. This elicited from him no comment, and I did not press him for one. However, he had apparently been following my litigation in the newspapers, for some months after my appeal victory, he telephoned to congratulate me. We fell into conversation, and I was surprised to learn that he too had been dogged all his life by unscrupulous publishers. He was at that time involved in a court action in Germany to uphold his right to make amendments to his works when they came up for re-edition, and he wanted to read the judgment in my case to extract from it any points that might be of relevance to his. He said he hated his American and British publishers (as already recounted, I was later to have the pleasure of cross-examining Routledge's David Croom) and had found only one in the world whom he wholly trusted, a small firm in

Tübingen. I sent Popper the judgment and, in April 1992, the printed book, but again he evinced no opinion on it... until a whole year later. Popper invited me to tape-record his comments and to use and quote them as I wished. I here present some in the spirit in which they will doubtless be received, one of dazed scepticism.

> "I will start from the end, because, as you yourself say, that is the best part. Now, about *Electra* I want to make clear to you that I am deeply interested not only, as you know, in Greek philosophy, but also in Greek tragedy; it is really in a sense a hobby for me, one of my main interests, although I have so far talked to quite a few people about it, but have never written a word on the subject. So I must say that this part of your book seems to me in a sense quite independent of the rest, and extremely interesting. Somehow, perhaps, it is unfinished, somehow distorted because of the very artificial relation between it and the rest of the book — you no doubt know what I mean. But I was deeply impressed by your *Electra*. In spite of let us say its sketchiness, I think it is excellent. It speaks not only for your mind in general, but it shows your dramatic and poetic heart or soul or whatever... I think very highly of your gifts. I must say I read it, how shall I say, as if it were written by Sophocles. I really felt that you have caught the spirit of Greek tragedy, and I felt that you are a poet. I was deeply moved."

Once again the roller-coaster had thrown up one of those rare, dangerous moments of apparent vindication and trick-euphoria. Just as I was beginning to reconcile myself to the conclusion that perhaps, after all, *Making Names* was just another bunch of gimp trex, here came one of century's great sages tempting me with second thoughts: Andrew Malcolm Sophocles, oh sure!

Popper went on to express reservations about certain aspects of my introductory chapters, which he felt suffered from a moral relativism he judged impermissible, especially in a potential teaching book, and he invited me to visit him at his home in Kenley for a discussion of the problem. (This charge, incidentally, was one I have never quite understood; it is my fear, especially now, that the book errs too much the other way.) As luck would have it, I was at that time recovering from an eye operation and had to decline his invitation (perhaps too I was reluctant to risk any kind of a disappointment), so he outlined his worries about the book on the telephone and subsequently we engaged in a sporadic correspondence on various subjects, sadly brought to an end by his final illness. One unexpected result of our encounter was my introduction to him of a German translator for various of his hitherto unpublished works (he was unhappy with previous attempts); at last I had made a serious contribution to international philosophy. At last too, my own personal endeavour in that department had come full-circle. With his acute, intuitive dissection of *Making Names'* history, and in exact contradiction of the various Oxford views, Popper had found my 'footnote' chapters unsatisfactory but my *Electra* valuable. Following Edgley, I had finally succeeded in conveying my Brighton beach vision to another human being, and of all the billions in the world it had turned out to be Popper. Suddenly, somehow, it no longer seemed to matter much whether or not the book sold.

Another boost came in April with the publication in *The Spectator*, after a long delay, of a review of *Making Names* by Terence Kealey. Kealey was a delightful free spirit I had met some years earlier who worked as a research biochemist in Cambridge, who wrote occasional articles on scientific subjects, and who had liked both my book and my battle. (His own particular anti-Oxford bone was its refusal to grant Margaret Thatcher an honorary degree.) Under the headline "Plato meets Kylie Minogue", his piece described *Making Names* as "a valuable, comprehensive, professional textbook in an original, fun, dialogue format." Of my Chapter Eight he wrote:

> "It is too easy for schoolchildren to go through an education believing that concepts like physics and metaphysics are absolute definitions. It is important to understand that they are the constructs of very fallible human beings, and that the great scientific laws were the products of individuals wrestling with phenomena. Science is not a temple of absolutism, it is the product of individuals' creativity... In this book, by concentrating on people, the nature of science as it is practised is well portrayed, it forces people to re-examine the complacent doctrines of their school years. In summary, the book runs counter to most conventional assumptions that are generally, and falsely, held... It may well attain a certain cult status."

Hardy's prescient "no fair hearing here now" warning was evidently starting to cut both ways, for Kealey then launched into a general attack on the University:

> "I distrust OUP if only because it publishes the *Oxford Magazine*, the dons' house journal. Otiose, self-pitying and greedy on easy money, the *Magazine* is the very image of the modern don. During the 1980s, it inflamed Oxford's campaign against Margaret Thatcher by comparing her treatment of the universities with Adolf Hitler's."

30

The Perspex Ceiling

KEALEY'S PIECE concluded with a plea to his readers to go out and buy *Making Names*. Few did, but nevertheless, and despite the lack of mainstream attention, the hardback just about managed to cover its costs, so AKME's Denis Dugdale, as Production Manager this time, plunged on with the paperback. His plan, following Hardy's suggestion, was to hype the legal history, add an index, make small improvements to *Electra*, order a longer run, and retail at £9.95. The book's back-cover now set Popper's and Edgley's puffs against a collage of newspaper cuttings, while new ten-page forewords outlined the lawsuit, quoted two of the most scandalous passages from the cross-examinations of Elliott and Charkin, reproduced OUP's public statement verbatim, and distilled the various favourable judgments that had by now been passed both on the book and in the case, including extracts of Edgley's testimony at the damages hearing:

> "It seems to me that there are also two actual original contributions to philosophical problems in this book. One of the most striking of these is the account of Wittgenstein and his theory of universals, his theory of family resemblances. This criticism is quite striking and would be of great interest to professional philosophers. Another contribution is in the field of ethics, where Malcolm takes a famous argument of Hume's about "ought" and "is" and points out that Hume himself perpetrates this kind of inference which, explicitly, he is disallowing. This was certainly new to me and, again I think would be of considerable interest to professional philosophers... Malcolm does not opt for either of the standard monisms, that is either materialism or idealism. He produces a theory which is a peculiar combination of materialism and idealism, and again this seems to me to be well worth the attention of professional philosophers... Finally, there is his striking account of the language of modern particle physics which connects it with theology. I find this a very daring proposal. The specific form of his argument is, I think, unique, and again would be a contribution that could be of great interest to professional philosophers... Malcolm has done something in this book which is unique. I should be very sad if it were not published. It ought to see the light of day and it would create quite a stir if it did."

The printers of the hardback, who also did work for OUP, had by this time learned of *Making Names'* troubled history, and politely declined the new assignment (they have asked me not to divulge their identity), but it

was not difficult to find an alternative firm willing to take the risk. In
September 1993 I signed up with a Southampton company who did an
equally excellent job. With W. H. Smith and also an independent
wholesaler now distributing the paperback nationally, and with the honour
of Popper's eulogy on its back-cover, surely one of the broadsheet newspapers
would now give it a mention? Again, despite a sustained assault on the
book-review departments, AKME's championing proved utterly ineffective;
there was not a peep. The story of an article long-promised by James
Wood, the then books editor of *The Guardian*, itself turned into a uncanny
re-run of Walton Street's original antics: *Making Names* had gone out, I
was told, to no less than *three* identified readers, none of whom in fact
ever received it; a fourth who did eventually get a copy and who, I gather,
wrote a favourable review, then found that for no stated reason his piece
got spiked. I corresponded with Peter Preston about all of this, but, as
usual, his explanations made no sense whatever.

In August 1993 an intriguing letter appeared in *The Bookseller*.

> Sir, Clare Baker's article (30th July) on the Oxford and Cambridge
> University Presses reads rather like special pleading. Are they different from
> commercial publishers because their objective is the advancement of learning?
> Are they able to contemplate major long-term investment projects which a
> commercial publisher would not consider? Not to the untutored eye.
>   The fact is that apart from their ownership the two university presses
> are nowadays indistinguishable from other academic and educational
> publishers such as Macmillan, Longman or Routledge. To mention a
> single example, Macmillan will soon publish the *Dictionary of Art*, the
> fruit of fifteen years' work, tens of millions of pounds of investment, and,
> perhaps, of more man years of research than the *OED*. The dictionary is a
> scholarly collaboration of 7,000 authors from over 100 countries.
>   Does the ownership by the universities lead to a greater distinction in
> their academic and educational publishing? I doubt it. Are the two
> organisations any less hard-nosed in their commercial attitudes? Certainly not.
>   It must be increasingly questionable whether there is any justification
> for the special competitive advantage gained by the two presses through
> their tax-free status.
> Yours faithfully,
> Adrian Soar,
> Managing Director, The Macmillan Press

Having developed an interest of my own in OUP's tax-exempt status, in
November I sent Soar a copy of a recent report on OUP's "pretax profits",
suggesting that this over-protested phrase might merit his further
comment. This led to a meeting at which Soar asked me to write a book
for Macmillan about my case, but at that time I could not face a first-

person rehearsal of the profoundly depressing history, so we shelved the project. In January 1997, however, I recontacted him and at his request sent a draft of *Pariah*. He pronounced the script 'publishable', suggesting that I had at last discovered that elusive magic formula. By this time, however, Soar had lost power within the Macmillan structure and had to get *Pariah* approved by the head of the Picador and Papermac imprints, who had become, wait for it, Jon Riley, the ex-Penguin who had appeared for Oxford at my damages hearing. Sure enough, Riley could imagine no market for a book which he himself found "absolutely riveting, fascinating and very instructive." What an odd set of people, I decided, publishing folk are. Even after all this time I still do not understand a single word they say. Shortly afterwards, Richard Charkin became Macmillan's chief executive (see Epilogues, page 222).

In November 1993, completely by chance, I learnt that a lengthy analysis of my case up to the 1990 appeal, something akin to a law report, had, after all, appeared in a legal journal, the Autumn 1991 issue of *The Entertainment Law Review*, published by Sweet & Maxwell. The fact that it took over two years for me accidentally to learn of this article's existence and that its author Bernard Nyman had written it without any reference to me is a good incidental illustration of the mysterious ways in which the law, like the book trade, can move. Nyman, who presumably had as his source-material only the Court of Appeal judgment, and therefore only a fraction of a fraction of the case's eventual evidence, nevertheless made a sound job of his analysis, cleverly picking as his 'headnotes' my pivotal 'commitment' paragraph of 24th March 1985 (see page 17) and Lord Justice Leggatt's "in my judgment when Mr Hardy used the expressions 'commitment' and 'a fair royalty' he did in fact mean what he said..." passage (see page 143). In conclusion, however, Nyman again concentrated on the contract's telephoned (oral v. written) aspect, which I take to be the case's least interesting, warned editors therefore to be careful what they say to authors over lunch (fat chance: I, remember, never even met Hardy), and incorrectly suggested that the judges had found specific performance impracticable because *Making Names* would have required editing (the judges never gave a reason for this finding and Hardy expressly denied the editing point). Nyman's article concluded with a jarring observation which once more set the subterranean doors a-clanging:

> "The case emphasises what are, at the end of the day, the inadequacies of the law. Nothing will really compensate Malcolm for the non-appearance of his book on the bookshelves and that is something the law cannot achieve. He may be further from that goal now than before the commencement of the action."

Reading this gloomy coda two years after it had been published, two years during which *Making Names* had failed to generate a single column-millimetre in any national newspaper, it came as a chilling public declaration of the hard, unpalatable truth: that book-wise the whole struggle had been a perfect, lunatic waste of time. No, even better than that, it had enacted a perfect theorem of *counter*-publication, a *real* Greek tragedy; I had brought upon myself a *no*-hearing-here-now situation. Neither could I console myself with the thought that at least I had improved things for other authors, for not even the case's legal implications were being properly published. Catch-44.

Before recounting the last incident in this long, miserable adventure, I think now may be the time to conclude an earlier digression. As you may remember, at his futile meeting with me at Brown's in January 1991, Ivon Asquith had offered a few general observations about author-publisher contracts. These were revealing, firstly for their strange ethical blindness, and secondly for their illustration of the ultimate irreconcilability of authoring and publishing. "What would happen," he asked, "if publishers got litigious like you and started suing authors, for example for their frequently late delivery of scripts?" What an extraordinary point to put, I mused, or even to think. "But the publisher does not lose any money by this," I replied, "a court would never award them anything." If an author promises to deliver a script by a date and delivers it late or not at all, then there may be a late book or no book, and the publisher may be disappointed at losing their chance of a possible profit, but the publisher hasn't actually lost any money or done any work, except perhaps some scheduling. I suppose in a few exceptional situations with rushed, highly topical books, a publisher may spend advertising revenue before taking receipt of the script, but these are rare and their risks are obvious. The common case of an author who fails to deliver a contracted book is hardly balanced by that of an author who does a year's (or ten years') contracted work on one that is then shafted. "But we offer authors unrecoverable advances which we may write off," persisted Asquith. "Where was mine?" I asked, "or when did you offer compensation for my nine months' work at your behest?" Silence. "Do you work for OUP just on the *off-chance* that you'll get paid at the end of the year?" Silence. The extraordinary thing, it dawned on me, about Asquith's, and presumably all Oxford's, analysis of what had happened, is that even after the repeated incantation of my 'commitment' exchanges with Hardy, even after the Courts' emphatic castigation of their conduct, even after Lord Justice Leggatt's dangerous reference to fraud, they still did not feel that anyone at Oxford had done anything morally wrong, either in their original treatment of me or in their handling of the litigation. Even now they saw the affair just as a lapse of internal procedure, not as an exposure of corporate trickery.

In 1995 I met another author who thought he had fallen foul of similar Oxford trickery, the historian John Vincent. He talked not of being led up the garden path by OUP, but of being escorted up the aisle by them, only to find himself, after a long engagement, jilted at their Walton Street altar. In 1992 Vincent had been invited to write a students' introduction to historiography, a study of the ways in which history has in the past been written and interpreted. He had spent considerable time on it, under enthusiastic editorial guidance, only to find his finished script rejected at the last moment by an anonymous axe-person on the grounds of its "political incorrectness". The story reached the newspapers, provoking a *Sunday Times* piece by Mark Lawson headlined "Fugitives from the book police" and an outraged leader article in *The Times* of 30th January accusing Oxford of toadying to the fads of the American market. (By the way, a new American OUP translation of the Bible has "God the Father-Mother" and "the human one" for the Son of Man, and so on.) Vincent asked me to read his file of OUP correspondence and to lay-advise him on whether or not he had a contract. It was quickly clear that he did not, but it was equally clear that his editors (two, tellingly) had been ever-so-carefully avoiding one ("encouraging him," as Charkin would probably say, "keeping his position less than black-and-white"), whilst nevertheless inveigling him through to the book's completion. One of OUP's early letters pointedly began "I'm glad that I've persuaded you to write..." and there were frequent "subject to the Delegates' approval..." caveats: Giles Gordon's Ruritanian condition has evidently arrived. Reading the correspondence, one could almost hear Ms Winternitz putting OUP editors through a post-Malcolm crash-course in script-teasing contract-avoidance: work in pairs, positive and less positive; keep the goalposts ever on the move; play up any uncertainties which the author himself raises; always ensure some little issues remain unresolved — the contents of the last chapter, the book's exact length, and so forth. If this is another result of my case, it is hardly a desirable one. Again, *caveat auctor.*

In Vincent's story, it was the political correctness rather than the breached contract aspect that made the headlines, but keen-eared observers may have heard whispers of a political correctness theme in the *Making Names* saga too. Although during my detailed negotiation of Oxford's revision requirements with Hardy, no suggestion was ever made that the book was in any way sexist, Galen Strawson did say he found it problematic that its dialogue was between two men, and a year later Bion and Ryan alluded to unspecified "sexist aspects" of the revised script (in fact, I had deliberately reslanted the whole thing the feminists' way, making Electra, rather than Orestes, the book's final dramatic hero). The international writers' group P.E.N. maintains a watch on writers' censorship and oppression, and keeps files on notable political correctness cases. Their 1994 report featured an amusing example of a children's writer who had been asked to rewrite a story about a family that lived in a house with a lawn; the publisher felt the story would be offensive to readers who did not have lawns. *The Evening Standard* has also run articles about such instances and reported the case of an OUP children's author whose stories were set on an English farm and who was obliged to remove from them all references to pigs, in order supposedly to placate Oxford's Muslim readers and markets. In his eventual affidavit, arch anti-racist Ryan described *Making Names'* protagonists as "boorish", and there is indeed a brutish scene in Chapter Seven where the two men tuck into roast pork at High Table in Effect's college. If *Malcolm v. Oxford* was, after all, just a camouflaged wrangle over political correctness, then surely it has to go down as the longest, silliest and costliest to date. The fact that it happened, however, and that all its farmyard animals behaved as they did, may not, I fancy, prove so easy to keep forever airbrushed out.

31

Authors and Publishers

REVISITING ASQUITH has raised the matter of authors' advances. For obvious reasons, this is not exactly my specialist subject, but I gather that for some time the trend has in fact been towards the legal *returnability* of such payments. The PA's 1982/97 Code of Practice states:

> "7. If an author fails to deliver a completed manuscript according to the contract or within the contracted period, the publisher may be entitled (*inter alia*) to a refund of moneys advanced on account... If the work has not been produced in good faith and with proper care, or the work does not conform to what has been commissioned, the publisher may be able to reclaim the advance."

As confirmed by the 1998 *Guinness Book of Records*, this aspect of author-publisher law, at least in the U.S., was examined in the unsuccessful claim of Random House against Joan Collins, another celebrated victory for authors' rights. Long before I intruded upon it, the formerly freewheeling world of gentleman's agreements and honourable dealing had turned down the road of carefully-defined legal obligations and minimum terms. The calculated trickeries exposed by my case and by Vincent's jilting demonstrate that fundamentally, the author-publisher relationship has become irreparably soured. Not that there are not many examples which still work happily, but that at its legal heart it has now ingested too much poison, too much suspicion. So who needs it? Why bother with it? In his Court of Appeal judgment in my case, Lord Justice Nourse wrote:

> "The functions of an author and his publisher are quite distinct, a state of affairs which has been humorously expressed by the saying that each regards the other as a necessary evil. The function of the author is to produce the raw material of a script. The function of the publisher is to present and promote that material in such a way that it will be as widely acquired by the reading public as is practicable."

Is this necessarily true? Do authors need publishers? Do publishers need authors? Do all authors automatically want their works to be as widely acquired as possible? Could it not be that the price paid for such mass-marketing may be their works' undesirable cheapening (in all senses), and that in any case this does not necessarily increase authors' incomes?

Presumably, if evils can be avoided they should be. It is worth remembering that publishers and publishing as we know them have developed only comparatively recently: two hundred years ago, most books were financed by booksellers and printed in the backrooms of small shops (remember brave, or perhaps just drunk John Noon?) Nowadays, the streamlined systems of distribution and the powerful, monopolistic media empires can seem to render all but a few chosen authors with proven product-lines impotent and helpless, but simultaneously the means of book-production, by ever cheaper and better computing, are moving back to the domestic scale (see Appendix 4, page 243). Also, quite apart from the growth of purely electronic reading-matter, more and more actual book-*buying* is now being done via the Internet. OUP itself is at it: it recently launched a system offering net-users a book's contents page and first chapter free of charge, in the hope that it can then download them the rest for a fee. After the demolition of Reed (now dismantled and asset-stripped and sold and re-sold — business, as usual), Richard Charkin himself for a while left the world of printed books and went, electronically, back to medical bulletins. In the Winter 1996 issue of *The Author* (yes, *The Author*), he even wrote an article extolling the virtues for writers of putting their work on the World Wide Web, although he sounds like a modem salesman and his piece is a convincing argument for good old-fashioned paper. (I am having second thoughts about *Pariah*.)

Obviously, in such a brave new bookselling world, an author's number of copies sold might at first be much reduced, but their earnings-per-copy might also be correspondingly increased. Who is to say that most authors, impoverished as they generally are anyway, would not become rather richer distributing their work by this exciting, direct, middlemen-free means? Also, perhaps most precious of all, authors would not be assigning their rights to teams of spivs. AKME is impotent, but at least it is mine. The fact, incidentally, that I have not assigned the rights to (in? over?) *Making Names* raises some interesting legal conundra. Try this: suppose I shred my remaining stocks of the book (one cannot lug one's grand pianos and dead mules forever), and bequeath the rights in it to no-one, or even expressly prohibit its reproduction (surely I would not wish my heirs to fall under its self-evident curse?), what happens if after my death someone in the publishing trade happens upon an old copy and finds in it some merit? Suppose, just suppose, that they come to share Hardy's view of its first eight chapters, or Popper's of its ninth, and want to exploit, or even for no gain just to broadcast the book's thesis. Presumably, under copyright law, for seventy years — the current European Union period — they would not be allowed to do so. Like its sad, embattled heroine, the imagery in my *Electra*, which I believe to be perfectly plagiary-proof (yes, still so naïve after all these years), could remain imprisoned for some while yet. Where it best belongs, her DIM-squad jailors would doubtless argue, but still, the fantasy is intriguing.

On the other side, freed from writers, and spared all their tiresome royalty-wrangling and the endless fussing over their rotten scripts, the publishers and their retailing friends would at last be able to pursue untrammelled their profitable management of the book trade. For a start, like Oxford, they could keep flogging ever-greater quantities of ever-cheaper editions of out-of-copyright classics. Mustill LJ objected to my reworking of Warby's calendar case which cast OUP as little more than printers, but in such circumstances this characterisation comes roughly true: the publisher's chief remaining role lies in cover-design and warehouse-operation. Reed's primary business, remember, was paper-milling. Another way, of course, is for publishers to assemble ('package', as they say) their books themselves, especially, again like OUP, in the fields of education, reference and non-fiction. They can identify niches in markets and employ – or better still, sub-contract – armies of editors, researchers and contributors on salaries, hourly rates or fixed fees to exploit them. Their received beliefs and theories, just like their paper, can be repeatedly recycled and recycled. It is happening already!

What a lot of aggravation would be alleviated if this natural divorce were now to be driven through to its logical absolution. Both parties would at last be free to pursue their own true interests, and could finally abandon the irksome pretence of 'shared goals' and 'mutual benefits'. Publishers could in clear conscience conduct their real business of value-added paper-shifting, while authors could indulge unfettered their whimsical passions for intellectual and literary exploration; fools like me who once thought they had stumbled on some or other helpful insight could scribble away to themselves without bothering, or being bothered by, the great public world; and with a bit of luck, everyone could still make the odd crust and neither side need ever again trouble the other. I understand that, in response to Charles Clark's preface, these precise issues are currently being hotly debated in international writers' circles, where it has even been mooted that author-publisher contracts should be made altogether *illegal*, so as to ensure writers 'a level playing-field'. I personally would not wish to see things taken this far, but I would like to note that, as so often happens, what started out looking like an ethical or a legal problem has ended up finding its probable solution in technology, with philosophy playing no part in the case whatever.

Ah well, it's only an idea.

Glossary and Epilogues

Tergiversate (Latin *tergum*=back, *versate*=turned). To shuffle, to evade responsibility, to espouse or even initiate a cause and then faithlessly desert it. To get the ball rolling, to encourage, to gallop ahead, then vanish from sight, sink without trace, flee. See also back-slide, turncoat, *sb.*

On returnng to Oxford after my case, Alan Ryan, the 'professor of political theory' who, perhaps more than anyone else was responsible for its epic scale, was appointed Chairman of, you've guessed, the University's Equal Opportunities Committee, succeeded Harvey McGregor Q.C. as Warden of New College (declared assets £60 million) and is now Chairman of the Conference of Oxford colleges, a body whose chief purpose is to maximise the University's sources of funding. In *The Guardian* of 19th November 1997 he contributed an article eloquently headlined "Give us the money" urging the new Labour Government not to withdraw Oxbridge's preferential State grant of £35 million (£1,800 extra per student per year) supposedly needed to sustain the universities' dubious tutorial/ supervision systems. He justified his plea by claiming that "Oxbridge students write better and think more exactly than their peers... the Manchester United of the educational system... a good education is like Everest... *et cetera.*" Goal! Needless to say, within a week, Tony Blair had caved in to the "exact thinkers" and coughed up. "Is it really worth the candle?" was the Government quote. No, of course it isn't. Port-cannon ahoy!

In Walton Street, Sir Roger Elliott was replaced in 1993 by James Arnold-Baker, a man from BBC Enterprises who had merchandised Mr Blobby, and in January 1998 Arnold-Baker unexpectedly decided not to renew his contract. The favoured 'internal candidate' for his replacement was said to be Ivon 'calculating to mislead' Asquith, but in May *The Bookseller* announced that 'dark horse outsider' Henry Reece had got the hot seat instead. OUP's recorded sales for 1996/7 topped £278 million, in 1998 it came 49th out 58 in a *Bookseller* productivity survey, and its website now carries, in true scholastical grammar, the following Ruritanian caveat:

> "Please note that Oxford University Press is obliged by its charter to have all books published by us to be ratified by the University. We don't as a rule publish works of fiction, unless it forms part of an educational course or examination."

In 1996 OUP's "separate Delaware corporation" published a biography of Black Panthers' founder Malcolm X, wittily entitled *Making Malcolm*.

In 1998 Sir Michael Atiyah retired and was succeeded by Tony Blair's appointee, Third World poverty guru Amartya Sen (see pages 80-82) as Master of Trinity College, Cambridge (declared assets £150 million).

In yet another inexplicable lapse of Oxford memory, the current (November 1997) edition of *McMouse on Damages* (Sweet & Maxwell, £195) omits any mention of *Malcolm v. Oxford*, even on the subject of damages for an author's loss of reputation (see Appendix 2, following).

In 1997, the increasingly expectant Richard Charkin became Chairman of the Whitechapel Art Gallery, notable for its fondness for Freudian figures (Lucian's, that is), and in January 1998, after unsuccessful spells at Reed and BioMedNet he rejoined mainstream publishing as chief executive of Macmillan. In *The Bookseller*, he described his management style as "inclusive". By delicious irony, in 1998 he had to pay out substantial damages and costs, probably over £100,000, in the *Malcolm*-based case of *Myers v. Macmillan* (see Appendix 3, following). Having bungled Macmillan's attempted takeover of Cassell (which merged instead with Orion), in November 1998 Charkin announced Macmillan's launch of "Print-on-Demand" publishing, an interesting new sharp practice in which OUP is aalso implicated (see Appendix 4, following). Shortly before Charkin's arrival at Macmillan, and amidst much acrimony, Jon Riley left and was appointed Chief Editor at Faber & Faber, while in June 1998, Stuart Proffitt was appointed Publishing Director of Penguin.

In 1998, reportedly related to Oxford's fears for the future of its preferential government funding, pressure from the Vice-Chancellor on OUP to maximise its income resulted in its axing of its "insufficiently profitable" music and modern poetry lists, a public relations disaster the fallout from which included a cavalcade of Oxford Eng. Lit. dons queuing up to disown their own imprint. On 3rd February 1999, Arts Minister Alan Howarth delivered a powerful speech in Oxford warning of "the public interest" in OUP, while *The Times Higher (Education Supplement)* of 12th February, delivered a colourful attack by Valentine Cunningham headlined *Mammon's Imprint*, and *The Times Literary Supplement* published a 'justification' by Sir Keith Thomas entitled *The Purpose and the Cost* (5th February) and two articles by me entitled *The War for Jericho* (2nd April) and *An Ultra Short Run* (18th June, see Appendix 4, following).

Just a few months after the poetry fiasco, it was revealed (in *The Times* business section, 17th July) that in addition to its declared donation to the University of about £10 million per year, OUP has over the past fifteen years amassed an additional £130 million 'surplus' in a hitherto undisclosed 'Property and Reserve Fund' (see Appendix 5, following). It is rumoured within the trade that Rupert Murdoch wants to acquire a financial interest in OUP, and both are presently hotly eyeing the enormous educational and ELT market emerging in China. In August 1999 OUP launched its CD-ROM encyclopaedia in a joint promotion with *The Sun* (yes, *The Sun*) newspaper, for just £1.99.

In June 1999, Roy Edgley died, after a long battle against illness. In the words of his friend and obituarist Joseph McCarney:

> "In all circumstances of his life, Roy was true to the individual spirit within, the distinctive impulse that drove his thought and action. Integrity is too weak and moralistic a term for that achievement. It approaches much nearer to what should be called, in a phrase of one of his favourite poets, 'unity of being'. Those of whom anything like this might be said are exceptional human beings, and the world seems shoddier and more commonplace for Roy's passing. His memory will help us not just to endure its condition but to strive for the kinds of improvement to which he devoted his life."

And in November 1997, I finally got around to fly-posting Oxford – with blurbs for *The Remedy*, which I was then producing in computer-printout form. As I negotiated various amusing Porters' Lodge incidents and staple-gunned the common room noticeboards, it seemed as though my whole career was coming full-circle: years ago as a varsity undergraduate, this was how I had distributed my scurrilous magazine.

As for AKME, paperbacks of **Making Names** (ISBN 1-874222-01-0, A5, 425pp), following Oxford's inflation-model, are available at £15, hard-backs (ISBN 1-874222-00-2) at £25 and further copies of *The Remedy* at £15 (U.S.$19.95), all inclusive of postage and packing, from: **AKME Publications, 7 Southover Street, Brighton BN2 2UA, U.K.** Please make cheques payable to AKME Publications and allow up to 3 weeks for delivery. The paperback of **Making Names** is also available retail at £14.95 from the Philosophy Bookshop, 16 Golden Square, London W1R 3AG, tel. 0171-434-3337/8, has secured US distribution at $19.95 by philosophy specialists **Hackett Publishing Co., Inc.** P.O.Box 44937 Indianapolis, IN 46244-0937 and is listed on **www.amazon.com** and **www.amazon.co.uk**.

AKME's website **www.btinternet.com/~akme**, carries information and reviewers' comments on *Making Names* and *The Remedy*; annotated versions of *The War for Jericho* and *An Ultra Short Run*; a **Cuttings Library** of published articles about Oxford's poetry fiasco, the university's finances and other scandals; a News Items file featuring more brewing trouble; and a free, dedicated online **Law Library** for authors contemplating litigation against publishers. In addition to the complete court judgments in *Malcolm v. Oxford*, this provides the numerous other important author-publisher cases and related materials indexed overleaf.

The AKME on-line Literary Law Library

Planchè v. Colburn 1831 Binghams Common Pleas, Volume 8, p. 13 *Author contracted to write volume for a periodical series - Publisher abandons series - Author entitled to remuneration without delivering work - Quantum meruit basis*
Sweet v. Cater 1841 11 Sim 572. *Piracy - Copyright - Agreement - Construction*
Stevens v. Benning, 1854 1 K. & J. 168; 6 De G. M. & G. 223 *Author and Publisher - Copyright - Injunction*
Reade v. Bentley 1857 3 K.&J . 271; 1858 4 K. & J. 656 *Copyright - Agreement - Author and Publisher - Partnership - "Edition" - Stereotype - "Thousands"*
Warne v. Routledge 1874 Equity cases L.R. Vol. XVIII 497 *Oral agreement with publisher - Exclusivity not implied - Copyright - Suit to Restrain publication of second edition by licensee fails*
Griffith v. Tower Publishing Co. Ltd. [1897] 1 Ch. 21 *Contract - Author and Publisher - Agreement by Company to Publish - Copyright - Debenture-holder's Action against Company - Assignability of Agreement*
Abrahams & another v. Reiach 1921 1 K.B. 477 *Author-publisher contract - Articles published in magazine, therefore no uncertainty as to text - Discretion of Publisher - Measure of Damages - Reasonable publication*
Tolnay v. Criterion Films 1936 All E. R., Vol 2 1625 *Author of screen play - Breach of contract - Screen credit promised - Loss of publicity for authors as well as actors - Damages*
Ackland v. World Screenplays, 1950 *The Times*, Feb. 23, 1950 *Screen credit - Size of Lettering - Damages*
Barrow v. Chappell 1951 [1976] R.P.C. 355 *Oral contract for publication of musical scores in journal - Author's right to be published unedited and with expedition - Breach of contract - Damages inadequate - Specific performance (publication) ordered and damages awarded for delay*
Joseph v. National Magazine Co. Ltd. 1956 [1959] 1 Ch. 14 *Contract to publish article in magazine - Article under author's name - Refusal of author to allow stylistic and factual alterations by editor - Whether contract repudiated by author - Whether author entitled to specific performance (publication) - Damages for loss of opportunity to enhance reputation*
Steans v. West 1997 West London County Court (*Guardian* report) *Vanity ('subsidy') publishing contract - Poor quality of books' bindings, covers - Books unsaleable - Damages.*
Pilling v. Reed Consumer Books 1997 Whitehaven County Court *Author (poet)-publisher contract - Sparse correspondence - Formal document unexecuted - Editor as witness - Damages - Loss of reputation*
Myers v. Macmillan Press Ltd. 1998 Queen's Bench Division (see Appendix 3, following) *Author-publisher contract - Correspondence and oral commitment sufficient - Agreement with other publisher not repudiation - Oral notification sufficient - Damages calculated by either lost royalties or work done - Estimate of lost royalties more realistic - Lost sales projected into future.*
Kent and others v. Valeforce Associates 1999 Wandsworth County Court *Vanity publishing contract - Poor quality of books - Failure of publisher to market books - Publisher's bad faith - Misrepresentation.*
The Publishers Association Code of Practice 1982, 1997 *Guidelines for Publishers in dealings with Authors*
A series of articles by literary lawyer Nicola Solomon from *The Author*

Other materials are in preparation and invited.

Appendix 1: The Court of Appeal Judgment

NOURSE LJ:

The only question of substance for the decision of this court is whether, during their telephone conversation on 20th May 1985, Mr Hardy and the appellant entered into a contract for the publication by the respondents of the appellant's book. Like many questions of its kind, it is both short and difficult.

The three material extracts from the conversation are fully reproduced in the judgment of Lord Justice Mustill (see *The Remedy*, pages 20-23). The first of them comes right at the beginning. Mr Hardy, having acknowledged that the appellant wanted a commitment sufficient to take him through the last stage of revision, offered him such a commitment conditional on the revision's not, in the opinion of the Press, making the script worse. As to that condition, the judge [Lightman] said:

> "But whilst this condition gave the university wide scope for rejection of the revised draft, the power on the part of the university of rejection had to be exercised bona fide, and indeed there is no dispute that this condition has in fact been satisfied. I am therefore quite satisfied that a clear commitment was made by the university."

The second extract comes about half way through the conversation, after a long discussion about cutting, subtitling and style. At that point Mr Hardy said that he would like to have the script accurately cast off, which would not take more than a week or so. Then he could do costings and could talk to the appellant again about length. The Press would have some costing done on the basis of the actual length and he and the appellant would talk more precisely then about what kind of saving might yield what kind of price-reduction; that again would depend on whether the Press did it in hardback only or in hardback and paperback. Mr Hardy was still wavering on that one.

The third and crucial extract, which comes at the very end of the conversation, must be quoted again in full (see page 22). What then was the effect of this conversation in law? Although the judge was referred to *Abrahams v. Herbert Reiach Ltd.* (1922) 1 KB 477, I cannot think that the real significance of that decision was brought to his attention. Its significance resides in an assumption, first made in argument by Mr William Jowitt and evidently shared by a division of this court consisting of Bankes,

Scrutton and Atkin L.JJ., that an agreement between a publisher and an author for the publication of a book for a stated consideration and no more is a complete and enforceable contract. A common assumption made by judges as eminent as these is as valuable as any decision of this court. Having sought to give the matter an independent consideration, I am confident that we ought to apply the assumption by way of decision.

The functions of an author and his publisher are quite distinct, a state of affairs which has been humorously expressed by the saying that each regards the other as a necessary evil. The function of the author is to produce the raw material of a script. The function of the publisher is to present and promote that material in such a way that it will be as widely acquired by the reading public as is practicable. And so a contract in the form which has been postulated, however unusual or imprudent it may be, is not one which the law regards as incomplete. It simply requires the publisher to perform his distinct function, leaving to him the decision of all questions of presentation and promotion, subject only to a requirement that he must act in good faith towards the author and not so as to detract from the purpose of the contract.

Accordingly, there was not, as the judge thought, any need for agreement on questions of print run, hardback versus paperback, sale price and so forth. On the other hand, there could not be a contract without agreement as to the consideration which the appellant was to receive from the respondents. Can it be said, on an objective view of the words in which the parties expressed themselves, that there was that agreement here?

If the last part of the conversation had stood alone, I would have said that it could not. It would have appeared that everything was to remain fluid until the cast off and the costing had been done, when there would be talk "about some sort of contract", it being highly probable that at that stage there would be an agreement for the payment of a royalty at a specified but fair rate without any advance.

How then is this view of the last part of the conversation affected by the judge's finding, based primarily on the beginning of it, that "a clear commitment was made by the university"? Mr Hardy offered the appellant the commitment he wanted, a commitment to publish the book on the faith of which the appellant could have the confidence to undertake the last stage of revision. The solemnity of such a commitment is obvious enough in itself. But that was not all. There was attached to it a condition which can only have been intended to protect the respondents. This is consistent only with the commitment's having been intended to have contractual effect.

It is within the aura of this contractual commitment to publish the book that the last part of the conversation must be reconsidered. The two expressions on the part of Mr Hardy which are most against the appellant are:

> "...and then we can er talk about some sort of contract."
> "...I mean what I think we should agree is that you have a fair royalty..."

The first is suggestive of there being no agreement at all; the second of there being no agreement as to the consideration. The first, if taken literally, is contradictory of the contractual commitment to publish the book. But immediately afterwards Mr Hardy said:

> "It seems to me that because it's such a risky venture I'm not going to be terribly generous financially, ermm... I mean etc..."

That shows that when Mr Hardy referred to "some sort of contract" he actually meant the consideration which the appellant would receive.

The second of Mr Hardy's expressions is more problematical and has caused my mind to fluctuate from time to time. The consideration which the parties clearly intended that the appellant should receive could have taken one of three forms: an advance, a royalty or a combination of the two. Any thought of an advance was rejected by Mr Hardy with the assent of the appellant. That left only a royalty. On the whole I think that what the parties intended was that the appellant should receive a fair royalty, at a rate which would be agreed when the cast off and costing had been done. Having got to that stage, mindful as ever of the contractual commitment to publish the book, I see no real alternative to positing an agreement that the appellant should receive a royalty at a rate to be agreed and in default of agreement at a fair rate. That is an agreement to which the law will give effect.

I am therefore of the opinion that, during their telephone conversation on 20th May 1985, Mr Hardy and the appellant entered into a conditional contract for the publication by the respondents of the appellant's book; the appellant to receive a royalty at a rate to be agreed, in default of agreement at a fair rate. The condition having since been satisfied, the contract is enforceable at the suit of the appellant. I would emphasise my belief that this opinion has been formed on an objective view of the words in which the parties expressed themselves and without the implication of any term or terms.

LEGGATT LJ:

It is common ground that Mr Hardy gave Mr Malcolm an assurance that he would be paid "a fair royalty." The question is whether this was said with contractual intent. The respondents' alternative argument that the parties intended the amount of royalty to be determined by subsequent agreement depends on the same considerations: did they intend that there should be no legally binding agreement until the amount of the royalty had been agreed between them?

The respondents say that Mr Hardy's reference at the beginning of his telephone conversation with Mr Malcolm to the fact that he was "not offering a totally unconditional commitment" made plain that he was not entering into an enforceable agreement. Mr Malcolm retorts that the sense in which the commitment was not totally unconditional was explained immediately thereafter when Mr Hardy said of his unwillingness to offer such a commitment that it was "because obviously if what you do seems to us to make it worse then we would write and say so." This was the basis of the Deputy Judge's finding that what Mr Malcolm was given was an absolute commitment subject only to the condition upon which Mr Warby himself relied at trial that the revised draft should not be worse than the first. About that the Deputy Judge held that "there was no dispute that this condition has in fact been satisfied" (see transcript page 10D). Indeed he had earlier held (at p.4F) that "[i] It is common ground between the parties... that the revised script was, in the opinion of the University, better than the original." Against that finding there is no appeal.

It is difficult to know what the Deputy Judge meant by a "firm commitment" other than an intention to create legal relations. Nothing short of that would have had any value whatever for Mr Malcolm. He had made it clear that without a commitment he was not prepared to undertake the work of revision expected of him. To suggest that Mr Hardy intended to induce Mr Malcolm to revise the book by giving him a valueless assurance would be tantamount to an imputation of fraud. So Mr Warby has preferred to explain the notion of "commitment" as being no more than a valueless expression of a revocable intention. I do not believe that that is what Mr Hardy thought he was giving. It must be borne in mind that not only did he say at the beginning of the telephone conversation that he knew Mr Malcolm wanted a commitment, and that the Press felt confident enough to tell Mr Malcolm to go ahead and revise the book (subject only to the condition which was in fact fulfilled), but on the following day he wrote to Mr Malcolm to say, "I am pleased that we are going to do your book." I find it hard to construe that expression as anything less than an acknowledgement that the Press was contractually bound to do so. To this Mr Malcolm replied that he too was pleased that the Press was going to do his book, and that he had waited for over ten years for this moment to arrive.

When Mr Hardy was reproached by Mr Charkin for failing to observe the internal requirements of the Press he replied, "The reason why I spoke in terms of a contract, rather than willingness to consider a revised transcript, was that the author estimated that the revision we sought would take six months' solid work." He also remarked that "this is not a case of offering a contract out of the blue for a book that happened to take my unconsidered fancy." The question therefore is whether, despite Mr Hardy's belief that in these circumstances he had committed the Press contractually, he had not in fact succeeded in doing so.

It is in that context that the latter part of the relevant telephone conversation must be viewed. Mr Hardy first mentioned that when he had done the costs and the cast-off he could talk about "some form of contract". That to me is equivocal: although it might refer to the making of a contract in the first place, Mr Hardy then went on to speak in terms of consideration alone, saying, "I mean what I think we should agree is that you have a fair royalty so that if the book is a success you will do well out of it", adding, "but I don't want to pay you in advance money that's been very riskily invested." The conversation concluded with Mr Hardy saying, "Well let's hope it does well." In my judgment the proper inference in the circumstances from the use of these expressions is that Mr Hardy was inviting Mr Malcolm to agree, which he did, that he should be remunerated by a fair royalty without an advance. I would therefore hold, contrary to the Deputy Judge's finding, that the respondents did expressly contract to pay Mr Malcolm "a fair royalty". It follows that in my judgment when Mr Hardy used the expressions 'commitment' and 'a fair royalty' he did in fact mean what he said; and I venture to think that it would take a lawyer to arrive at any other conclusion. There was therefore an enforceable contract for the publication of Mr Malcolm's book.

Appendix 2: Authors' Entitlements to Damages

The fact that the current (1997) edition of *McMouse on Damages* (Sweet & Maxwell, £195) omits any mention whatever of *Malcolm v. the Chancellor, Masters and Scholars of the University of Oxford* [C.A. 1990] begs further examination of the case's implications for damages law, implications which can perhaps best be regarded as an appendix to my earlier implication 5 (see page 147). Without contention I was held to be eligible for damages under two heads, the loss of opportunity to enhance my reputation (publicity) (1), and my loss of income from *Making Names'* royalties (2). I will examine these in reverse order.

Lost Royalties

The starting point is our old friend *Abrahams and another v. Herbert Reiach Ltd.* 1921 1 K.B. 477. Here the publisher, remember, had already published Abrahams' and Liddell's athletics training articles, as contracted, in a magazine on fixed terms, but had then failed to publish them, as contracted, together as a book which was to have yielded the authors an agreed royalty of 4d per copy sold. The authors successfully sued for breach of contract and in a lower court before Sankey J they were awarded damages of £500 calculated on an imagined sale of 30,000 copies. The publisher appealed that this award was excessive. No reason is stated in the report why the publisher reneged on the agreement, and the easy assumption that it resulted from the publisher's reduced estimation of the book's likely sales may not be correct.

In the Court of Appeal Mr Jowitt, counsel for the publisher, invoked the well-established principle that in the case of a contract which affords the breaching party alternative obligations, a court cannot award damages greater than the least onerous, and argued that within the contract's terms the publisher was not obliged to publish more than one edition [copy] of the book. The court did not accept this, but sought instead to determine what in all the circumstances would have constituted "a reasonable publication", making no apparent distinction between the number of copies that would probably initially have been printed and the number that would probably have been sold. No reasoned estimate was made of the publisher's likely first print-run or of the book's likely eventual sales. It is mentioned, however, that the publication was to have coincided with the 1920 Olympic Games in Antwerp, suggesting that it was perhaps regarded by both parties as a one-off venture, with only a single "reasonable" printing being envisaged. Also, Bankes LJ invokes the principle in *Reade v. Bentley* (1857) 3 K&J 271 that a publisher who has agreed to publish a work must publish it, but is not bound to continue publishing it.

In *Malcolm*, by contrast, things are moved on quite a way. Here *Reade v. Bentley* is eschewed and it is accepted that a reasoned estimation was to be made of how many copies of the book would actually have been sold in different editions over a period of time. I sought the period of five years because (a) books usually sell best during their first few years, and (b) this was roughly the time that had elapsed between the original planned publication date and the damages assessment; I assumed, perhaps wrongly, that if I were to seek a longer period, McGregor would successfully be able to argue that I had by then become free to take the book elsewhere. In any event McGregor agreed without argument to my five-year suggestion, the principle of which has subsequently been extended in *Myers v. Macmillan* 1998 (see Appendix 4, following).

It was agreed too on all hands – by myself, by the Court in the person of Chancery Master Barratt and generally speaking by Oxford – that the only way to arrive at such an estimation was to relate *Making Names'* imagined prospects to the actual sales of arguably comparable books. I say "generally speaking" because although Oxford in its pleadings did present various books' sales figures, from time to time McGregor also reverted to Mr Jowitt's initial line in *Abrahams*, that *Making Names* would nevertheless have sold zero copies, thereby perversely assessing his own clients' book evaluators and sales personnel as totally incompetent and their much-coveted imprimatur as worthless (all arguable, I suppose).

McGregor further muddied the waters by repeatedly insisting (see page 189) that the more appropriate precedent was *Chaplin v. Hicks* 1911 2 K.B. 786, an important case on the subject of damages that can be awarded for the loss of a chance. Ms Chaplin, an actress, had entered a national beauty competition organized by a theatrical manager for a London newspaper which offered substantial financial rewards to the winners. She had succeeded in reaching the final fifty selected from a national entry of about 6,000, and numerically she stood a one-in-four chance of winning a prize in the final round, but was then denied the opportunity of competing in it by the organizer's inadequate notification. She sued successfully for breach of contract and a jury awarded her damages of £100, against which the organizer appealed on the grounds that the damages were too remote and were inassessible. Their lordships embarked on some learned analyses of remoteness and inassessibility, but unanimously concluded that both the lower court's judgment on the organizer's liability and the jury's assessment of £100 should stand.

I suggested to Master Barratt, successfully I think, that McGregor's introduction of *Chaplin* was inappropriate, for he thereby seemed to be suggesting that books' sales were a matter of pure luck, and nothing whatever to do with their content – another strange position for a guardian of OUP's reputation to be adopting. If there was any analogy, I added, Oxford's nine months of refereeing *Making Names* by its three expert judges *was* my beauty contest, with their agreement to publish it being my first prize. Surely Oxford, I asked, do not choose which of four scripts to publish by tossing them in the air and seeing, say, which one lands the most prettily? If OUP had published my book, there was no chance, whatever McGregor said, of it selling *zero* copies, and Hardy's PPF had predicted that OUP's short initial print-run of 2,000 hardbacks would sell out.

For a court to predict with any certainty what would have happened beyond that was, as Master Barratt wrote in his findings, very difficult:

> "Assessing damages for loss of royalties resulting from the non-publication of a book is a highly speculative exercise. By comparison with other books of similar type, it is not too difficult to ascertain the likely range of publication price for hardback and paperback copies during specific years. Even the royalty percentage that could have been expected by the author must fall within certain clear limits. Evidence given at the hearing by experts in publishing and others enables some accuracy to be achieved on both these elements of the calculation. But what is bound to remain a guess, however carefully considered, is the number of copies that would have been sold, whether in hardback or paperback... Although publishers are experts in their own field, they, like all experts, are not necessarily infallible. Stephen Hawking's *A Brief History of Time* had a similar record of rejection before eventual publication as a best-seller, running into many editions, with sales of millions of copies throughout the world. The Plaintiff, in his letters to some of the publishers to whom he submitted the idea or the typescript of *Making Names* referred to it as "an unusual and risky project" and in one letter he even accepted "the book's apparent unmarketability" and said "It certainly does not fall into any of the presently established publishing categories" It just might have been a gamble that was destined to succeed, like Stephen Hawking's book, but the weight of expert opinion from people whose job it is to assess the marketability of books, would make an assessment of damages on such an assumption totally unrealistic."

But although Barratt talks of the book's publication being "a gamble" and his estimate of its sales as "a guess", the figures he then proposes are not the products of pure luck but are reasoned and justified. Barratt himself asked to hear not only from experts who could testify as to royalty rates and suchlike, but also from authorities *who had read the book*. While there are doubtless many cases in the annals in which courts have given reasoned determinations of uncertain damages, I cannot imagine that there has ever previously been such a detailed attempt to assess a work of art or literature's likely financial earnings. If so, *Malcolm* set an important precedent, if only by demonstrating that such an enterprise is practicable (see again *Myers v. Macmillan*, following), and it may well have provided a useful model upon which future similar claims can be based. Or it may, on the other hand, have better demonstrated that specific performance would have been a more practicable remedy.

It has long been established in law that the fact that the wronged party's losses in a breach of contract may be indeterminate does not render them inassessible. This ground is well covered in *Chaplin*, and in 1911 there was already a wealth of precedent on the principles held to be relevant. One such principle that is universally recognized is that any damages should reflect, if possible, the potential rewards that were in the contemplation of the parties at the time the contract was formed. This may not always be very easy for a court to gauge, but fortunately, I was blessed with much evidence of Oxford's high expectations in 1985 for *Making Names*. Not only did I have Alan Ryan's (two) and Galen Strawson's favourable reports of 11th February and 18th and 14th July, with the former's mentions of the bestsellers *The Outsider* by Colin Wilson and *Gödel, Escher, Bach* by Douglas Hofstadter, I also had all the enthusiastic written and recorded remarks of Henry Hardy, the OUP editor who was going to be responsible for the book's publication. He had written that he hoped it would be "a terrific success", confided that he had planned to launch it simultaneously in hardback and paperback – a most unusual vote of confidence – and had even spoken of its potential for adaptation as a 'tele-script'.

Here, I was less successful with Master Barratt, who in his findings quoted not a single line from Oxford's original evaluations, but preferred to rely instead upon Alan Ryan's, five-copyless-but-dispassionate-years-later view that "*Making Names* would have sunk without trace". Barratt even quoted the views of Kim Pickin, Giles Clarke and Colin Mitchell, despite the fact that none had ever opened the book. Besides Barratt's purely mathematical mistakes — his low royalty rates and so forth, his failure to place any weight upon Oxford's original contemplations would have been a major line of argument for me at the aborted damages appeal. I, of course, would never have gone ahead and spent nine months revising a book for a publisher who believed that it was destined to sink without trace.

Loss of Reputation or Publicity

In the new edition of his great textbook, McGregor writes at paragraph 55(b) [I reproduce his ellipses and footnotes in his numbering]:

Loss of future reputation, of publicity, of credit.

Loss of reputation generally makes for a non-pecuniary loss but it may also involve a pecuniary one for which damages may be awarded in contract. As Hallett J. said in *Foaminol Laboratories v. British Artid Plastics* [1941] 2 All E.R. 393 at 399-400,

> "A claim for mere loss of reputation is the proper subject of an action for defamation, and cannot ordinarily be sustained by means of any other form of action... [but] if pecuniary loss can be established, the mere fact that the pecuniary loss is brought about by the loss of reputation caused by a breach of contract is not sufficient to preclude the plaintiffs from recovering in respect of that pecuniary loss."

It is thus established that a plaintiff can recover for such a pecuniary loss in three particular types of case: (1) where the wrongful dismissal of an actor[75] causes him loss of future publicity[76]; (2) where there has been a failure or a mismanagement of the advertising of the plaintiff's business; and (3) where the defendant fails to honour the plaintiff's drafts thereby causing him loss of credit, or otherwise fails in breach of contract to sustain the plaintiff's financial credit. This head of damage may also be recoverable in other types of case,[80] but that these are likely to be few is suggested by the fact that in the three established types of case the loss was particularly contemplated by the parties to the contract.

The type of case of interest here is clearly (1), and McGregor explores this later at paragraph 1243:

> There is, however, one clear exceptional case in which damages for loss of reputation, or, as is more often put, loss of publicity, is recoverable by the plaintiff; this is where the enhancement of the plaintiff's reputation by publicity was particularly contemplated by the contract, so that it might be regarded here as a head of damage contemplated by the parties themselves when entering into the contract. This was first established with regard to actors in *Marbé v. George Edwardes*, which case was tested and confirmed by the House of Lords in *Clayton v. Oliver*. The main point decided in these two cases was that such a contract imposed on the defendant an obligation to allow the plaintiff to appear before the public as an actor, and not a great deal was said about damages, except that Lord Buckmaster in *Clayton v. Oliver* said that he thought that "loss of reputation" was not the exact expression

but "loss of publicity" should be used. More assistance is given in the later case of *Withers v. General Theatre Corporation* [1933] 2 K.B. 536, C.A. where, the anterior point of liability being by then settled, concentration fell on the question of the basis of the assessment of the damages. The position was put most clearly by Greer L.J.

> "When a proprietor of a music-hall or theatre engages an artiste to perform, he is promising two things: he is giving a consideration which consists of two different elements: first, a salary which he promises the artiste for his services, and secondly, the opportunity to play in public some part which will attract attention. ... For the loss of the opportunity... and so enhancing or maintaining his reputation, he is also entitled to recover damages".

It was, however, held by the Court of Appeal that no damages were recoverable where the plaintiff's only loss was injury to his already existing reputation as an actor. Yet it is submitted that this limitation should be discarded if there eventually prevailed what is thought to be the proper interpretation of *Addis v. Gramophone Co.*[21]

This head of damage for loss of publicity was extended from actors to authors, or at least to an author of a screenplay entitled to a screen credit, in *Tolnay and another v. Criterion Films*[22]. Goddard J. pointed out that "all persons who have to make a living by attracting the public to their works, be they... painters or... literary men... or... pianists and musicians, must live by getting known to the public". He thought that the loss of publicity to an actor, whose worth the public can only estimate by seeing him perform, is more serious than in the case of the author... The approach of the Court of Appeal suggests that damages for loss of publicity are germane only to theatrical or closely analogous contracts; Greer L.J. thought that very special considerations apply to theatrical contracts since the consideration to the artist, certainly to the artist in the early stages of his career, is as much, if not more, the opportunity to appear as it is the mere wages.

Here, of course, one may wish to protest, on behalf of authors of written works, that publicity or reputation is as important to them, and as important a part of their contracts whether specified or not, as it is for actors like Marbé, Oliver and Withers, especially when they are unknown. Writers' contracts, after all, are entered into with *publishers*, and with a solo literary work, unlike a complex joint venture like a film, there is no question as to who is to be identified as its creator. In *Tolnay*, it should be mentioned, two screenplay writers were contracted to adapt a novel by another writer, and their agreement expressly stated that they were to be credited on screen as the film's joint authors; they were awarded substantial damages assessed as £100 each for their loss of publicity. Amongst Goddard J.'s concluding remarks edited out by McGregor are these:

"An unknown author, we all know, has a great struggle in the same way as an unknown musician or actor has a great struggle... One way in which they can expect remuneration and expect employment is by getting their name before the public."

Strangely, McGregor does not mention in his book another case which further extended the scope of this type of recoverable damages and which he himself invoked in court in my assessment hearing, *Joseph v. National Magazine Co. Ltd.* [1959] 1 Ch. 14. In summary, Joseph, an expert on jade carvings, was in 1956 contracted to write an illustrated article for *The Connoisseur* antiques magazine, but found his work so heavily rewritten by the magazine that he disowned the piece it intended to print and sued for the publication of his own version. In lieu of specific performance, Harman J. awarded him £200 for the loss of his opportunity to enhance his reputation as an expert on jade.

In my own case, Gavin Lightman makes this powerful statement in his Chancery Court judgment:

"I cannot think that any order for specific performance [OUP's enforced publication of *Making Names*] in this case would be practicable. I would, however, have been minded to indicate that a substantial award of damages was called for to recompense Mr Malcolm for loss of the opportunity for him to enhance his reputation by securing the imprimatur of the Oxford University Press on his work."

While, in his findings, upon which I will refrain from comment, Master Barratt writes:

2. Loss of opportunity to benefit reputation

The other head of damages which can be awarded in this action is for loss of opportunity for the Plaintiff to establish or enhance his reputation. *Making Names* would have been the Plaintiff's first published book. If it had borne the imprimatur of O.U.P. it would have been launched under the most favourable circumstances possible for a work of philosophy intended for both academic and general readers. The benefit to be derived from the O.U.P.'s imprimatur could have been counteracted by adverse reviews and it is clear that O.U.P. has chosen to incur considerable expense and trouble to withhold its imprimatur from *Making Names* and to avoid any responsibility for the book. The conclusion to be drawn from the reluctance of so many publishers to accept this book is that they did not consider it to be of outstanding quality.

Even if *Making Names* had been published by O.U.P. and had achieved sales comparable to those of Colin Wilson's *The Outsider*, it could well have brought the Plaintiff no greater future benefits than had been achieved for Colin Wilson. However, if the Plaintiff's first book had been published by O.U.P. and had achieved even modest success, the text of his second book would have been considered more favourably than is now likely. Even the prospect of academic employment might have been improved for him. Such benefits, dependent as they would be on a favourable reception for his book, would be spread over many years and would only arise if the Plaintiff's subsequent endeavours provided suitable circumstances.

Guidance from reported cases as to the scale of compensation appropriate to such loss of opportunity to enhance an author's reputation is rare. The amounts awarded in the *Tolnay case in 1936* and the *Joseph case in 1958* are both equivalent to only about £2,000 in present money. Any figure selected can be no more than a guess. However, on the basis of two other assumptions, namely that 15,000 copies of the book would have been sold and that its reception would have been reasonably favourable, the damages for loss of beneficial publicity are assessed at £6,000.

It therefore at the very least seems clear that *Malcolm v. Oxford* has extended the scope of such 'lost publicity' awards markedly further, firstly by now including a purely literary work, a text, and to boot a philosophical text, and secondly with respect to the £6,000 awarded, three times the inflation-adjusted equivalents of the *Tolnay* and *Joseph* awards of £100 and £200 sought at my hearing by McGregor.

Why then does McGregor not mention *Malcolm* (or even *Joseph*) in the new edition of his great textbook? Authors and lawyers advising authors could easily get the impression from it that damages for loss of publicity are rarely if ever recoverable in law and that at best they can only be modest, when in fact it now seems perfectly certain that they are recoverable in reasonable measure, especially by first-timers. Even the comparatively slim textbook *Treitel* now mentions *Malcolm* and paints a different, rather more straight-forward picture:

> "An actor *or author* can recover damages for 'loss of publicity', that is for loss of the chance to enhance his reputation." (my italics)

McGregor might, I suppose, try to claim that neither the *Joseph* nor the *Malcolm* award was argued at sufficiently senior level (he says, remember, that "the approach *of the Court of Appeal* suggests that damages for loss of publicity are germane only to theatrical or closely analogous contracts"), but he himself never disputed my entitlement to recover damages under this head, and Oxford's pleadings, which he drafted, expressly concede the point.

In an interview for *The Times* (20th January 1998), after a cabaret rendering of Noel Coward's frightfully witty song *A Bar on the Piccola Marina*, McGregor assured his interlocutor of "his logical mind and very good memory", and certainly it cannot be that he has allowed his distasteful experiences of 10th and 11th July 1991 to cloud his judgment and thereby mislead his £195-a-go clientele. He, like Treitel, notes that damages are not yet held to be recoverable for injury to an (actor's or author's) *existing* reputation, so where, I wonder, does this mysterious omission leave his own?

McGregor's footnotes

21 [1909] A.C. 488. The submission in the text is, since its completion, now justified by the House of Lords' overruling of *Withers* in *Malik v. BCCI* [1997] 3 All E.R. 1, H.L.

22 [1936] 2 All E.R. 1625. Similarly in *Ackland v. World Screenplays, The Times* February 23, 1950.

75 And similar persons, such as the author of a screenplay: *Tolnay v. Criterion Films* [1936] 2 All E.R. 1625. So too a dismissed apprentice can recover for his loss of training: *Dunk v. George Waller & Son* [1970] 2 Q.B. 163, C.A.

76 *Marbé v. George Edwardes* [1928] 1 K.B. 269, C.A.; approved and applied in *Clayton v. Oliver* [1930] A.C. 209.

80 See, e.g. *Anglo-Continental Holidays v. Typaldos* [1967] 2 Lloyd's Rep. 61, C.A., where travel agents were awarded damages for loss of goodwill when the shipowners with whom they had arranged a cruise substituted a smaller and less attractive ship with a less attractive timetable of stopovers at ports en route; and *Barrow v Chappell & Co.* [1976] R.P.C. 355, where the award in respect of the defendant's delay in publishing a musical work composed by the plaintiff may be attributable to this head of damage...

Appendix 3: Myers v. Macmillan

The Summer 1998 edition of *The Author,* besides featuring an advertisement for the first printout form of *The Remedy,* coincidentally mentioned the successful conclusion of another author's hitherto unreported breach-of-contract action. This turns out to be the clearest demonstration so far of the effectiveness for authors and costliness for publishers of the judgment in *Malcolm v. Oxford* (specifically implications 2 and 5, see page 146), which by delightful irony rebounded on our earlier hero Richard Charkin, in his new capacity as chief executive of Macmillan. It may also have had something to do with that publisher's curious about-face over *Pariah* (see page 214). *The Author's* 16-line report, remarkable for both its brevity and its odd observations (the one in brackets, for example), goes:

Myers v. Macmillan Press
The facts of the case were complicated... One particularly interesting part of the judgement concerned damages. As well as looking at what Mr Myers would have earned by way of advance and royalties (the usual way of attempting to assess damages), the judge also considered what would have been a reasonable sum for the work done... On that basis he would have awarded Mr Myers damages of £24,000 plus interest since 1989. However, the lost royalty claim was larger and Mr Myers was instead awarded more than £45,000 plus interest.

The judgment in the case is, as *The Author* says, complicated, but only by Macmillan's extraordinary final, disreputable defence against the claim. Their breach of contract was in fact again starkly simple, and even in its turns of phrase provides ugly echoes of both *Malcolm* and *Noble v. Oxford.*

In October 1986, Geoffrey Myers, an English language teacher living and working in Switzerland, who had already had a secretarial ELT course and other books formally contracted and published by Macmillan, had a meeting with the company's international publishing director Terence Creed to discuss a new project, a two-part, six-book Business English course to be called *Can I Help You?* At Creed's invitation, Myers wrote a specimen unit for the course, and upon its consideration was told by him in February 1987 to "go ahead with" the project. In June 1987 they agreed that Myers would receive an advance of £500 on receipt to the completed units for Part I (three books), and be paid net-receipts royalties of "10 percent of the first 30,000 copies sold and 12 percent thereafter". By August 1987 Myers had completed Part I of the course and was paid the £500 advance, and by December 1988 he had completed and submitted all three further books for Part II. In March 1989 Myers returned Macmillan's corrected proofs of both Parts incorporating various amendments requested by Creed. Then... nothing happened. For a long time, despite Myers' gentle badgering, there was no sign that the course was actually going to be published. In June 1989, Terence Creed had been replaced by a Ms Susan Holden, and in June 1991 Myers wrote to her asking:

> "What about *Can I Help You?*, the book commissioned by Mr Creed in 1986, delivered in 1988, and then put on the shelf in an alcohol-free version (for the Middle East)?"

A year later, in June 1992, Holden replied:

> "Once we are clear exactly what market we are aiming at, and how best to adapt the material to fit it, I would be happy to go ahead, with a target publication date of 1994."

Myers remained resolutely polite and co-operative for a further year, but then received this beauty:

> "I appreciate that you worked on this material at the request of Terence Creed in 1986, but I'm afraid that it has never been included in my own publishing programme. I am responsible for the whole of Macmillan's ELT publishing programme, and although I try very hard to enter into any agreements entered into by my predecessor, I have to temper this with an appreciation of current marketing requirements... There is absolutely no point in publishing material that cannot be sold."

The judgment does not, of course, report the negotiations that may have followed this rejection, but obviously they were unsuccessful, for in 1994 Myers went to law. Nor does the judgment recount the details of the early litigation, but it is clear that, like Oxford in my case, Macmillan and their lawyers resisted the claim tooth-and-nail, invoking every sort of defence they could muster. They argued that the suit was invalid on procedural grounds, being barred by some obscure statute. They stated that they had lost all of their files on the proposal (Creed, of course, had no clear recollections at all). And when Myers produced his copies of their correspondence, they argued that it did not amount to a contract.

On the eve of the trial, after three years' of litigation, *Malcolm v. Oxford* was invoked, and Macmillan was obliged to abandon its 'no contract' defence, offering Myers £30,000 in a confidential out-of-court settlement. Myers however, being by then advised to expect a higher award from the court, opted for trial, and Macmillan then launched a technical counter-claim, arguing that Myers' use, with their permission, of 13 percent of the course-material from *Can I Help You?* in a different German-language course book published by — you've guessed — OUP(-Cornelsen) and aimed exclusively at the Swiss market in which Macmillan does not operate, by implication constituted Myers' repudiation and therefore annulment of their agreement. By the time the case came before the judge (Neuberger J, in the Queen's Bench Division), this unlikely arcanum had thus become the chief issue left to be resolved, and hence generated the spurious complexity of the judgment (3rd March 1998), in which Neuberger carefully rubbishes almost every aspect of the publisher's disgraceful last-ditch defence.

Liability settled, Myers offered two bases for the calculation of his damages: lost royalties on the estimated sales of the books; and *quantum meruit* remuneration (remember *Planchè v. Colburn*?) for his work done, which he claimed to have been 2,346 hours (59 40-hour weeks) at £20 per hour. The judge assessed his damages on both bases, weighing up both sides' submissions, and arriving respectively at the figures quoted in *The Author*: over £45,000 plus interest spread over a number of years and £24,000 (1,600 hours at £15 per hour) plus interest since 1989. He offered Myers the choice, assuming that he would opt for the former, for although it yielded less interest, which he left the lawyers to negotiate, it would undoubtedly produce a higher total. However, he also observed:

> "While both bases have their difficulties so far as assessment is concerned, I agree with counsel that, in light of the evidence, the second [work done] basis is less satisfactory because it involves carrying out an exercise which does not reflect what happens in practice... assessing the damages on this second basis is unrealistic: so far as all the witnesses are aware, such a basis of remuneration has never been agreed with an author of a book such as *Can I Help You?*"

True to Oxford form, Macmillan then argued that Myers' earnings from his other, under 10-percent-overlapping, German-translated, OUP Swiss course books should be deducted from the damages total. Mercifully, in this final meanness too, the publisher was unsuccessful.

Several parallels with *Malcolm v. Oxford* should be noted. Myers, like me, had no formal *Memorandum of Agreement* (or equivalent) for Macmillan's publication of *Can I Help You?* He had had their formal memoranda for his earlier publications — indeed it was only because these existed that Macmillan was able to attempt its "Swiss work" defence — but for *Can I Help You?* his complete contract resided entirely in oral exchanges and correspondence. By the time the case reached Neuberger J, this was no longer an issue. Incidentally, in the detail of Macmillan's "Swiss work" defence is to be found a technicality — an apparent clash between the small-print clauses of the companies' two standard forms

(OUP-Cornelsen's and Macmillan's) — which the judge dismissed as purely theoretical, demonstrating how the routine signing-up to unread printed memoranda can sometimes be more confusing and less contractual than a straightforward negotiation. Myers, like me, also suffered from a change of personnel, with the incomer expressly reneging on the commitments of her predecessor. And Myers, like me, after a year's hard work was fobbed off with the good old "change in the market" routine.

In the damages argument there was more familiar detail too. Myers' net-receipts royalty rates were in writing and so not in issue, and the books' retail prices and their rises were agreed, but Macmillan's average discount was not specified. Myers argued that it would have been 40 percent, Macmillan claimed 65, and the judge compromised at 50. Myers suggested that total sales of Part I would have been 80,000 and of Part II 45,000, and expert witnesses for both sides agreed that these would have been regarded as "only satisfactory" by market leaders in the ELT field. The judge, however, accepted Macmillan's self-deprecating submission that it was not a market leader and that the market generally had contracted, and he reduced Myers' figures to 48,000 and 33,000 respectively. One interesting departure from my own assessment, however, came with Myers' claim that the calculation should cover the whole 'shelf-life' of the course, which he set at 14 years. The judge broadly accepted this, projecting the books' sales 13 years forward to the year 2002, although tailing off his later figures more sharply than Myers'. All-in-all, it seems that Neuberger's assessment was a far more genuine compromise between the two sides' divergent figures than Barratt's was in my case, but then the sales of ELT course-books are doubtless far more predictable, and susceptible to reasoned expert opinion, than those of one-off philosophy texts. Neuberger's calculation certainly provides an important and encouraging new model for future similar claims.

The *Myers* judgment, however, also raises many questions and mysteries, not the least of which concerns The Society of Authors. Why, yet again, does *The Author* make only a very measly mention of what is obviously an important victory for authors generally? Could it be that for the Society successful author-litigants, the awkward-squad actually advancing the frontlines, are an embarrassment? Pending further research, this appendix should be taken as only a first draft, still awaiting the formal approval of AKME's Delegates.

Appendix 4: Print-on-demand Publishing

Published by *The Times Literary Supplement*, **18th June 1999 as** *A Very Short Run*.

Two controversies generated by electronic technologies currently preoccupy students of publishing law: first the apparent nonsense made of publishers' territorial rights by the growth of bookselling via the Internet; second the arrival of "Print on Demand", whereby very short runs and even single copies of out-of-print books can be computer-printed to an individual purchaser's order. I believe this latter development may logically invite a radical reappraisal of the whole author-publisher-reader relationship.

The Bookseller of 6th November 1998 reported that Macmillan, following Wiley UK, has launched such a scheme to include up to 1,000 out-of-print titles in 1999: "The service will enable Macmillan to supply single copies without holding books in stock or reprinting huge amounts... It is Macmillan's mission to keep works of academic value in print on a permanent basis." This announcement prompted an interesting exchange of letters between Mark Le Fanu (27/11/98 pp. The Society of Authors), Richard Charkin (11/12/98 pp. Macmillan) and Maureen Duffy (1/1/99 pp. The European Writers' Congress). In America, Simon and Schuster already has over 9,000 books similarly available, and Oxford and Cambridge University Presses have both licensed an American company to produce substantial numbers of their out-of-print titles on demand. CUP has owned up to the practice, but OUP's overworked Public Affairs Department has repeatedly and categorically denied any involvement in it, despite the appearance in some recent OUP authors' contracts of the phrase "single copy reprint", and the fact that OUP's licensed website is there for all to visit.

What has facilitated print-on-demand? Laser printing has developed in-line machine systems (the IBM Infoprint and Xerox Docutech, for example) which either from computer disk or from scanned originals can automatically, and in literally a minute or two, produce the collated sheets, printed on both sides, of small-format books. This bundle of sheets can then be trimmed and perfect-bound (glued) into a choice of covers – rudimentary for cheapness, colour-laser-printed for verisimilitude – to produce what would probably, under usual dictionary definitions, qualify as 'a book'. The details of the cover, binding and trimming may of course vary, and the finish of such facsimiles is certain to be of lower quality than their lithographed originals, but the margins, both technical and financial, between the old print processes and the new are rapidly closing; the days of short-run, plain text, lithographed books are numbered.

Wiley and Macmillan produce their 'on-demand' books in glued bindings with undesigned board covers printed in black with just the book's title, author and publisher's colophon. CUP (like OUP) uses an American licensee which specializes in facsimile work and reproduces the books' original 4-colour covers. Oddly, neither Wiley nor Macmillan could provide a list of which of their titles are now being printed on demand; when an order comes in, they simply fulfil it this way if they find the original lithographed 'hard copy' to be out of stock. CUP, on the other hand, has seventy on-demand titles listed on its licensed website (alongside OUP's forty-five), though these may represent only fractions of their totals. When a purchaser orders from Wiley, they are not told that they may be getting a PoD copy, which is unreturnable, while Macmillan pre-confirms with its purchasers that PoD will be acceptable, and CUP maintains that its PoD product is indistinguishable from the original so no such problem arises. Wiley's, CUP's and OUP's PoD copies sell at their original prices, while Macmillan's are always more expensive. Neither Wiley nor Macmillan could confirm that they inform their authors of their books' PoD production, and CUP asserted that they are under no contractual obligation to do so.

My guess is that very few authors whose books are now being printed on demand are being informed of the fact. All the publishers who have so far embarked on PoD expressly claim that by keeping these titles "permanently in print", they are ensuring that the copyright in them need not revert to their authors under their contracts' traditional 'reversion' clauses, and incidentally absolving them, they hope, of any contractual obligation to report any change in production. (Their claim and hope aside, it does not, however, absolve them under the the Publishers' Association Code of Conduct, 1982P97, which states that "the publisher should keep the author informed of important design, promotion and marketing decisions... The fullest reasonable consultation with the author on such matters is generally desirable, both as a courtesy and in the interests of the success of the book itself. In particular the author should, if interested and available, be consulted about the proposed jacket and jacket copy...")

Contracts have always varied, of course, from publisher to publisher, agent to agent, author to author, and book to book, but many terms have been standardised. For example, the 'Reversion' or 'Cancellation' clause from OUP's printed *Memorandum of Agreement* dating from way back and applicable through the 1980s goes:

> "If after the Work is out of print and is not available in any edition
> issued by the Publisher or authorized by him the Author shall call upon
> the Publisher to reprint the Work and if the Publisher shall not within
> eight weeks after he shall have received a written request to that effect
> agree thereto the Author may require the Publisher to resign all rights
> in the work and the Publisher shall thereupon at the Author's request
> and expense assign the same to the Author absolutely without prejudice
> to any claims the Author may have under this Agreement and to rights
> in the Work already granted to third parties under this Agreement."

In other words, subject to written request, if a book goes out of print for
more than eight weeks, the copyright in the text reverts to the author, who
is then free to try to get it republished elsewhere or to do with it what they
will. Suppose, for whatever reasons, the author of a book which was now
being printed by their publisher on demand sought the reversion of their
copyright. Could the publisher sustain at law a counter-argument that
under such a clause they were thereby keeping the book 'in print' and so
retaining their rights in it?

In practice, this question will be answered only when someone brings a
test case, a development which may not be far off. A cardinal principle any
court has to apply in deciding the implications of any contentious contract
or clause (for example the meaning in the above of the word 'reprint') is to
try to establish what was contemplated by the parties when the contract
was agreed. By this test, with respect to all older contracts, the publisher's
claim at once would certainly fail. The print-on-demand process is new,
while what was contemplated by the parties when they signed up was a
substantial print-run (or reprint) of properly lithographed and bound and
jacketed copies. Indeed, the very inclusion of such a clause demonstrates
that the possibility of push-button, single-copy production was not at the
time contemplated by either party. Then there is the literal point that
"stored as a computer file" cannot possibly mean the same as "in print" or
"available in an edition". Publishers who think that they can perhaps
circumvent this by always keeping in their office at least one saleable laser-
printed 'hard copy' of every book (and a CUP spokesman advised me that
"it would be more helpful to think of a single on-demand copy as just an
ultra-short print-run") should be reminded that there is now a fair amount
of law in the archive as to what constitutes "a reasonable publication,"
law which a court would probably extend by implication to "a reasonable
reprint". It was contended, for example, in *Abrahams v. Reiach* (1921)
that a publisher's obligation to publish under the contract would have
been fulfilled by their production of just one copy, but this was immediately
rejected by both courts (the case went to appeal), who instead assessed "a
reasonable publication" (of an athletics training book) as respectively

30,000 and 6,000 copies. In my own 1991 assessment hearing, Harvey McGregor Q.C. for Oxford, briefly argued the same line, but quickly abandoned it, and in the end I was awarded damages based on an assumed sale of my philosophy text *Making Names* of 15,000 copies. Last year (1998), in a case founded on mine, Geoffrey Myers was awarded similar damages against Macmillan on an imagined 12-year sale of over 80,000 copies of a business-English course book.

Are there any grounds for asserting that the inferior quality of PoD fails in any case to constitute a book's proper publication? Suppose, to save costs, (for example, in an attempt to 'fulfil' contracts about which they had changed their minds, like those of the twelve poets dropped by Reed in 1995) publishers were to start using this technology for their short first print-runs as well as their reprints, would authors have grounds for claiming that such production breached their agreements?

As was established in the *Abrahams* case and my own, matters concerning a book's production and marketing (most notably its format, print-run and price) are nowadays normally at the publisher's discretion. Perversely, although clause 5 in OUP's *Memorandum* expressly stated that "the Publisher shall print and publish the Work in such edition(s) as he considers appropriate... and shall have sole control of all details of production advertising, price, sale, and terms of sale of the Work," and despite the facts that their editor had actually arrived at a consensus with me on these points and that he had then demonstrated his 'sole control' of them by issuing internal instructions without further reference to me, Oxford argued on appeal in 1990 that our contract was incomplete on the grounds that these figures had not contractually been agreed. This obliged me to present evidence that formats, (minimum) print-runs and prices were rarely specified in contracts, and I had to recruit expert witnesses, including Mark Le Fanu, to testify on the point. Oxford opposed the introduction of this evidence, but when it was admitted, conceded its truth, and thus I won the case. Curiously, in the Society of Authors 1997 *Quick Guide*, Le Fanu contradicts his testimony with the statement: "It is usual (in a contract) for the form of publication and the approximate published price to be specified - and preferably the anticipated size of the first printing." Is this wishful thinking, or has the practice, perhaps as a result of *Malcolm v. The Chancellor Masters and Scholars of the University of Oxford*, changed over the intervening years? I do not believe that it has, and I have met no-one in the trade who believes that it has. OUP's clause 5, renumbered, has not changed, nor has the P.A.'s code, which states, now as then, that "the final responsibility for decisions on the design, promotion and marketing of a book is normally vested in the publisher," and Hugh Jones'

1996 text *Publishing Law* (Routledge) expressly confirms that these matters are still normally at the publisher's sole discretion. Publishers may therefore think that under most contracts they have the legal right to laser-print a book if they so choose.

However, whatever may or may not be the case with respect to what is and is not normally specified in such contracts, it does not follow that a publisher has, shall we say, *carte blanche* in the fulfilment of them; however much discretion the publisher is expressly or implicitly allowed, failure to achieve certain minimum standards could certainly constitute a breach. This was demonstrated in the case of *Steans v. West* (West London County Court, 24th June 1996), in which a an authoress successfully sued a crooked vanity publisher on the grounds that the books he produced from her script were defective in respect of their typesetting, their printing and, most notably, their cover and binding. There seems to be absolutely no reason in law why similar defects should not constitute similar breaches in respect of ordinary commercial publishing, especially given that here an author's reputation is an added consideration (and an established head of recoverable damages). An author who discovered that his or her book was being laser-printed and plain-bound might, *inter alia*, argue that their reputation was thereby being harmed. Also, there would be an overwhelming amount of evidence available on past (lithographic) custom and practice, which is certainly being changed with the introduction of these new techniques.

As far as I know, no-one has so far brought a case which specifically hinges on the laser-printing point, but if anyone were to do so, and if the court, suitably apprised of the publishing-law minefield presented by the new single-copy technology, were persuaded of the need to 'draw a line in the sand,' for example as to the meaning of the words 'print' and 'reprint', then the laser-printed (or computer-printed) versus lithographed distinction might well provide it with the clearest, most easily demarcatable ground on which to do so.

But why would an author being printed-on-demand want their rights to revert? Surely they, along with their readers, should be grateful (this, of course, is the line of Macmillan's Richard Charkin), that their work is still being kept available? Surely it would be crazy to suggest, now that this wonderful new single-copy technology is here, that publishers should not use it, or should waste masses of paper and money on print-runs of books only very few of which they will ever sell? No doubt many PoD authors don't care how, or even whether, their books are printed, or about their meagre earnings from them, and indeed many may be past caring altogether, that is, dead. But some might think differently. They might feel that being printed on-demand was not what they had in mind when they signed up. If all the publisher does is laser the text from a computer disk or a scanner, add a cheap cover and charge £75, then perhaps the author could do this at home (or down at the nearest Docutech shop), probably better, and for a fraction of the cost.

Günter Grass famously described modern publishing houses as mere filing cabinets full of contracts, to which might now be added safes full of computer disks and drawers full of mailing lists. In a world where most authors write on computer, sometimes even in typesetting programmes, and readers' telephoned, single-copy orders are printed one at a time, the publisher seems to have become little more than a handler, a disk-agent marrying readers with scripts. On the face of it, such a service might be thought worth a commission of, say, 15 percent, yet under existing contracts, publishers may be entitled to an astonishing 90+ percent of any profit (in my damages assessment, Oxford argued that less than five percent was a fair paperback royalty), which in a 'net-receipts' deal they would calculate after the deduction of their own huge administrative costs. It is hard to believe that this simple, entirely risk-free 'service' represents good value for either the author or the reader.

The notion of risk is legally all-important. Over the years, most of the rights ascribed in law to publishers have rightly been based on the premise that in the publication of most works, it is the publisher who takes all the financial risk. Traditionally, it has been the publisher who pays for the typesetting, cover-art, blockmaking, printing, advertising, distributing and sundry other expenses involved, including any advances paid to the author. For making all this risky investment, the publisher is recognized as being entitled to a fair share of any profits earned from the book, and when the author sees their effort nicely printed, glossily bound, displayed in bookshops up and down the land, and perhaps even reviewed here and there, they may think their ten percent royalty a reasonable stake in the whole complex operation. But when none of this applies, and the 'publisher' has become instead just a 'to order' button-presser, the author, and the law, is likely to take a very different view of what constitutes 'a fair split.' Incidentally, all this also argues for authors' increased proficiency with computer DTP programmes so that, perhaps to a publisher's requested page-layout, they can provide their texts already typeset, thereby retaining these rights too (the CUP spokesman actually claimed that out-of-print authors would not be allowed to get their books scanned themselves because the publisher held the rights in their *design*).

Non-technophobic authors may conclude from all this that self-publication is now the way to go, and will perhaps discover that in the Internet Age this need not be as difficult or distasteful as it sounds. Who needs a disk-agent, when the WorldWideWeb is a mass of free public archives, search-engines and mailing lists? Surely burrowing readers and specialist authors can find one another personally, and make their own arrangements, especially in the worlds of scientific, technical and academic research, most of whose institutions are permanently on-line. And if authors or their heirs don't want to deal with their readers directly or hate the hassles of laser-printing, they may prefer a better 'disk-agent' deal than their present one, a deal which offered, say, 85 percent. Before publishers snort in derision at such margins, they should be reminded by a glance through the law library (e.g. *Reade v. Bentley* in 1857, *Griffith v. Tower Publishing* in 1896), that not so long ago a 50/50 profit split between author and a *risking* publisher was common. In his *Bookseller* letter, Mark Le Fanu raises the further possibility of out-of-print Macmillan authors securing proper, and perhaps better re-publication deals with other presses. In short, there are several powerful reasons why authors with existing contracts might wish to enforce the reversion of their copyrights in their out-of-print (printed on demand) works, and there is waiting to be set an important legal precedent which would at once allow them all to do so.

What of future contracts? Obviously, clarity is the chief requirement. A publisher and an author can contract whatever they want, provided their terms are unambiguous, and, as far as possible, any problems are foreseen. Over recent years, contracts have thus steadily lengthened as publishers have incorporated into them more and more detail about envisaged electronic media, CD-ROMs and suchlike. The appearance of Oxford's "single copy reprint" clause now demonstrates the urgent need for a complete rethinking and public clarification of the whole rights-reversion principle. Le Fanu does not mention older contracts, but suggests that in future reversion should be related to books' annual sales, suggesting a threshold of 100 copies, and I gather that some agents' contracts already apply such a formula. OUP, however, has informed some of its academic authors that their books cannot now be viably reprinted (lithographed) unless annual sales of at least 1,500 are anticipated – hardly a bridgeable gap. To me therefore, it seems more important than ever that authors (and their agents) should extract from publishers minimum undertakings as to the format, print-run and price not only of a book's first printing, but also of its print- and reprint-and-binding methods or models too. Some authors might wish, for example, expressly to prohibit the laser-printing of their scripts, if only on the grounds that they can do that themselves. Again, before publishers go into impractical snort-mode, a glance at *Sweet v.*

Cater (1841), a case, appropriately, concerning the publication of a law book, will remind them that it is perfectly easy to formulate, in about thirty words, a complete agreement on all of these matters: "2500 copies of the work" were to be printed, to be "sold to the public in boards for £3" and "to correspond in type and page" to a previous book. The model specified was *The Treatise of Powers*. Enough said.

PoD Postscripts (which did not appear in the *TLS*)

If I am right (a) that the days of the short-run, lithographed, plain-text book are numbered and (b) that in the near future an author with an existing, older contract will be successful in establishing the general legal right of such authors to recover their rights in their printed-on-demand (i.e. out-of-print) works, one may envisage an interesting new scenario and ask some interesting new questions.

What happens, for a start, to the (stock-market) value of the big commercial publishing houses (or OUP) with their extensive, prestigious backlists? If computer-printing becomes the rule for short-run books (first editions and otherwise, academic and otherwise), and computer-printing becomes the legal 'line in the sand' for reversion under authors' older contracts, everyone would then theoretically be (re)starting from scratch. Although nobody, presumably, is yet making much significant money out of printing-on-demand, this explains why all the established publishers are so keen to jump on the 'single-copy-reprint,' 'ultra-short-run' bandwagon. If their 'permanently-in-print' claim were to fail at law, they would at once all notionally be asset-stripped. Another recent correspondence in *The Bookseller* suggests that the proportion of the big publishers' profits derived from their backlists is surprisingly high, between 60 and 80 percent.

OUP's and CUP's American on-demand licensee is Lightning Print Inc., at www.lightningprint.com, a subsidiary of US book wholesalers Ingram Corporation. AKME's website www.btinternet.com/~akme includes an on-line, annotated version of the above article, together with links to Lightning Print, collated lists of OUP's and CUP's PoD authors and other participating publishers, and the *Bookseller* correspondence.

This paperback version of *The Remedy* was itself printed on a Docutech, so at this moment you literally have the future of publishing in your hands.

Appendix 5: OUP's Tax-exemption

In shorter form, this was written as a newspaper article, was invited in August 1999 by two of the Sunday broadsheets, but then went unpublished.

In *The Times Higher (Education Supplement)* of 12th February, in the wake of OUP's shameful axing of its modern poetry list, Oxford English literature don Valentine Cunningham contributed a brave and colourful article entitled *Mammon's Imprint*. Under a strapline which began "OUP enjoys charitable trust status", the *THES* launched an online 'soapbox' debate on whether the university presses in general still justify their tax-exemption, while Cunningham argued that by its naked commercialism OUP in particular, the Leviathan of the species, has surely now abrogated that precious privilege.

This debate was further fuelled by the revelation (*The Times* business section, 17th July) that, besides their annual donation of about £10 million to their parent University, OUP's Delegates had over the past fifteen years quietly amassed additional profits estimated at about £130 million (and rising) in a 'Property and Reserve Fund', from which over the next three years £60 million is to be spent on restoration work at the Bodleian Library and on the building of a new chemistry faculty. Now I hate to spoil a good party, but didn't I hear somewhere that tax-exemption is conditional upon non-profitability? As someone against whom during that period this 'Learned Press' abortively defended a six-year, half-million-pound breach-of-contract action, if not simply as a taxpayer, I declare an interest.

In all the celebration of OUP's worldwide trading success, the Press's troubling tax dispensation is rarely mentioned. The word 'charity' appeared nowhere in the *Times* report, until Cunningham's piece it had largely escaped mention during the poetry fiasco, and in the long 'justification' of OUP's ruthlessness that appeared in *The Times Literary Supplement* (*The Purpose and the Cost*, 5th February), both it and its sentiment were scrupulously eschewed by its Finance Committee chairman Keith Thomas. A sign, however, that all is not as it should be, and that Thomas knows it, is the recent appearance of the following strange new petition on OUP's notepaper and on their books' imprint pages:

> "Oxford University Press is a department of the University of Oxford.
> It furthers the University's objective of excellence in research, scholarship,
> and education by publishing worldwide"

These are AKME's aims too, of course, so here goes. It is generally assumed, or glossed, that the university presses enjoy charitable status by virtue of being owned by their universities, which themselves automatically qualify for charitable status as educational institutions as defined by the Charities Acts. Not so. This in fact turns out to be an argument rather than an axiom. As far as the charity lawyers, and therefore the Inland Revenue Special Commissioners are concerned, the universities and their presses are financially distinct entities. In law the charitable purposes of the university presses' operations stand in independent legal requirement of their own intrinsic definition and validation, and until surprisingly recently none was tax-exempt.

So it was that in 1940 Cambridge University Press applied to the Inland Revenue (but not to the Charity Commission) for tax-exemption and was refused, on the eminently reasonable grounds that, because it did not confine itself to book distribution within the university but traded alongside commercial publishers in the open market, its business went beyond the charitable, educational purposes strictly defined for the University itself. It was held that conferring such a privilege on CUP would have given it an unfair advantage over its tax-paying competitors. This is a consideration often invoked in such charity-law disputes, and it was a view that was then widely held even within CUP, many of whose managers did not want to be seen to be receiving any special, unbusinesslike privilege, and correctly supected that if they were granted one, they would become generally resented by the rest of the trade. It was also feared darkly that seeking tax exemption for the Press might somehow jeopardise the government's funding of the University itself. When it failed, the application was therefore not pursued.

In 1975, however, CUP's chief executive Geoffrey Cass tried again, and several features of his determined reattempt should at once be noted. First, as in 1940, it was not a conventional application to the Charity Commission, which would have required a public 'governing document' of aims and limitations (such as the memorandum and articles of a limited liability company), but a private request for tax-exemption made to the local Inland Revenue department. It was thought that to risk legal proceedings, whatever their outcome, would be to invite the bad publicity the Press so dreaded, so this more 'discreet' method was favoured. (It has been suggested that the strikingly unpatriotic timing of CUP's previous application was chosen to keep, as it successfully did, reports of it out of the wartime newspapers). Even Cass's new, quiet, backdoor approach never achieved the status of a full submission, but consisted only of a 'preliminary letter', albeit a sixty-page one, threatening the tax officials with a deluge:

"This letter is not our formal submission: but there seems to me no reason nevertheless why it could not provide a basis for an Inland Revenue decision to exempt the Press, at this stage. Our formal submission, when completed in the Spring [of 1976 – it was never completed], is likely to be several hundred times bigger than this letter. Yet the complete dossier of evidence and historical documents will, in the main, merely reinforce each of the key points of this letter a hundred times over. I have extracted for this letter the crucial items which would determine the case."

One result of this unusual tactic was that there was never, as is customary, a formal hearing to decide the question, a question whose implications if applied to other university presses would arguably make it one of the most important decisions in charity law this century. When the Inland Revenue privately decided in 1976 in CUP's favour, there was thus no reasoned judgment to dissect, no law report to ponder, no solemn written conditions or undertakings, and not a single mention of the momentous ruling in any newspaper. Perhaps, therefore, it is now high time to re-examine Cass's 'crucial items' of 1975 to see how they have fared over the years, and to decide, for example, how they relate to OUP's current ethos and latest grand munificence.

Cass's first argument was that from the constitutional and legal point of view CUP had no separate corporate status apart from 'the Chancellor, Masters, and Scholars of the University of Cambridge', itself an educational charity. Apart from being merely a repetition of the mistaken 'no distinct identity' assumption mentioned above, this is perfectly illogical. If the issue was that simple, why was any application necessary? Why Cass's 60 'preliminary' pages, let alone his planned 6,000? And why had CUP's 1940 attempt been rejected? Why had the university presses hitherto been liable for corporation tax? Had no-one noticed that they were owned by their universities? There is the technicality too that, strictly speaking, it is not the *universities* of Oxford and Cambridge which enjoy educational charity status, but their individual colleges, each of which is obliged to file separate accounts; this apparently puts CUP and OUP in an even less certain situation than that of their non-collegiate counterparts.

Then there is the point that if university presses' tax-exemption were reliant solely on their parent charity's status, they would be free to publish whatever they liked, or whatever made them the most money; they could sell tax-free pornography. By the same argument, suppose, to alleviate its poverty, Oxford University were to open a wholly-owned chain of fast food shops in the city (DIM burgers, DIM nuggets, DIM cola, Big DIM and fries to go, so forth), would it expect or be entitled to tax-exemption simply on the grounds that its profits were to go to a seat of learning?

Charities, it is true, are sometimes allowed to run non-charitable trading subsidiaries – the Guide Dogs for the Blind Association Xmas gift catalogue, for example – which can covenant all their profits untaxed back to their parent charity. But firstly the parent body's registration and 'governing document' render all such operations open to public scrutiny, accountability, limitation and constraint. Secondly, the covenanting rules are strict and absolute: there can be no question of amassing surpluses in undisclosed funds, or of using them to fund construction projects (surely, in any case, there must be a hundred better ways to restore Bodley or to buy a new lab?), or even to expand indefinitely in the publising trade. Thirdly, again and as always, it depends upon what the subsidiary actually does. And fourthly, both the particular cases and the general rules are subject to constant revision. I understand, for example, that the charitable National Trust's operation of a chain of untaxed high street gift shops in competition with tax-paying rivals is currently under reconsideration. Perhaps, if properly constituted, OUP's profits could all formally be covenanted in some such way, but one immediate result would presumably be a mass resignation of Walton's Street's salaried staff, who see themselves (and are employed) as publishing professionals, not as charity workers. Their morale must already be at an all-time low.

Certain aspects of charity law, however, are absolutely clear: while 'education' may be a recognized charitable aim or purpose, the distribution of books *per se* – whether for profit or not, and whatever they contain – is not. Even if, implausibly, OUP were able to persuade the Commisioners that teaching the Chinese to speak English is a legitimate charitable aim within the remit of the University of Oxford (in which case it would be a legitimate charitable aim for anyone else), nothing could be inferred from this about the shifting, or flogging, of pallets of paper. The only exception might be where a book directly furthered a specified charitable aim: The Foundation for the Study of Infant Deaths, which is a registered charity, might, for example, want to distribute a book warning parents about cot death. This distinction between education and book-trading becomes especially clear in our new Internet Age: if the University's and its Press's aims are purely charitable and educational, why don't they simply download all of their teaching materials onto a free Chinese website? In fact, OUP's electronic ventures so far have been confined to advertising: tempting readers with a book's first chapter in the hope of persuading them to fork out a fee for the rest. By contrast, a perfect example of a truly charitable, educational operation is AKME's own non-profitmaking online Law Library.

Whatever the niceties of the charity law that Cass preferred not to invoke, his 'no separate corporate identity' assertion is in any event now certainly untrue of OUP. In 1987 during my legal action, I discovered that the Press had registered no fewer than thirty-five limited companies, most of which appeared to be non-trading 'dummies'. It seems that around 1984 some rival entrepreneurs had started a publishing business in the city also exploiting the 'Oxford' name, and that OUP had hurriedly bought them out, and registered other similarly tempting titles, in order to protect the 'brand exclusivity' of its own. 'Cattle crossing", I suppose, just doesn't have the same ring to it. Incidentally, an odd, vacuous rigmarole presently appearing on the frontispieces OUP books goes: "Oxford is a trade mark of Oxford University Press". Again, if OUP has no corporate identity other than *The Chancellor... et cetera,* what on earth is it doing buying up other commercial publishers right and left, taking over dodgy South American outfits, tying up with shady French wholesalers, and crossing swords with tricky Lebanese middlemen? In my lawsuit, Oxford's city lawyers at one stage described OUP (USA) as "a separate Delaware corporation" whose papers the University was unable to obtain. And could Roy Jenkins even *list* his thirty other overseas subsidiaries?

Next, Cass's letter claimed that every CUP publication had to be individually approved by the Press's governing committee of 'Syndics' (or OUP's 'Delegates'). This, it was said, was no mere formality; all appraisals were academically rigorous, and the Press's salaried staff had no power to accept books themselves. Again, this is certainly untrue of OUP, whose huge General Books Division operates largely free from Delegatorial control. This was another point demonstrated by my court-case, in which the Senior General Books Editor Henry Hardy and the Chief Executive Sir Roger Elliott both testified to the Division's autonomy, the latter referring to the Delegates as merely "retroactive scrutineers". In his American affidavit of 1991 (see page 171), senior Delegate Alan Ryan (now Warden of New College) was especially clear on the point:

> "General [as opposed to Academic] books were submitted to the editorial committee for approval, and if approved, then reported on to the Delegates. The Delegates did not have the same role in their approval, because the intellectual name of the Press was not at risk: such books were aimed at the general reader rather than the scholar, and do not carry the academic imprint of the Press."

In fact, many of OUP's moneyspinners now have little to do with Walton Street, which increasingly "outsources" its projects to independent book packagers. It closed down its own encyclopaedia department, for instance, and now has its 'Oxford' books assembled by a firm in Aylesbury, with controversial results. Amongst the post-poetry chorus of public complaint about OUP's falling editorial standards, the former managing editor of the *Oxford Illustrated Encyclopedia* observed that in its subsequently culled paperback version, Czech literature now gets greater coverage than English. Conversely, Oxford's newly-launched *Atlas of the World's Religions* was produced by a London packager whose work was excellent but had nothing to do with OUP; Walton Street's only contribution to the book was its hilariously bungled dustjacket displaying a third-century Gandharan Buddhist sculpture of Princess Diana.

Every CUP publication, Cass further insisted, was approved solely on the grounds of its contribution to the advancement of knowledge, education or religion, purposes recognised as charitable under the Acts. Whatever their truth, these were interesting claims, for they implicitly conceded that the validity of the Press's sought tax-exemption would depend directly upon the quality and content of the books that it published. While many of OUP's publications undoubtedly do still fulfill these criteria, increasing numbers certainly do not, and in his *TLS* creed Keith Thomas himself laments the dwindling of the scholarly monograph market. One wonders, for example, how his own *Oxford Book of Work [nice if you can get it]* or *Oxford's scratch 'n' sniff Smelly Old Histories: Medieval Muck* would today convince the Inland Revenue's Special Commissioners, now cast as they are by their *ad hoc* decision into the unlikely role of educational-book-quality monitors.

It was argued too that CUP's Syndics (and OUP's Delegates), unlike the directors of a company, were appointed by a nominating committee, were unpaid, and had no personal financial interest in their Press. Strictly speaking this may be true, but given that all are paid, and some handsomely so, by the charitable University in which they hold office, the point has a certain disreputable circularity. Another assertion made by Cass was that because of its peculiar constitutional status, CUP could never be bought, sold or taken over, but in OUP's case this too was given the lie in 1987 when a group of Oxford dons proposed selling a 49 percent stake in their then-failing Press to Robert Maxwell.

The keystone, however, of Cass's application, the assurance that kept all the others in place, was that any 'surpluses' made by the Press (charities are not allowed to make 'profits') would be ploughed back into further scholarly, educational and religious publishing and be set aside only as necessary to ensure the Press's continuing viability. It was expressly stated that 'profit' as such was not to be considered or required by the Syndicate of any publication, and that the Press had always recognised as its prime function the publication of works which commercial firms would not undertake, a point that will not be lost on Oxford's exiled poets, sacked music department, or the eminent academic whose promised OUP reprinting was recently refused because it was unlikely to achieve its 1,500 annual sales target. It is ironic that the university which so self-righteously snubbed Margaret Thatcher should finally have admitted what its ears find most truly musical and poetic.

By corollary, CUP's application continued, the University would make no call upon any cash reserves which its Press might accrue, and Cass expressly disowned as "errant" its last signficant benefaction, the endowment of the Pitt Professorship back in 1944. By modern contrast, the word 'profit' is now happily and openly bandied – flaunted even, and Keith Thomas feels free explicitly to disavow such an idealistic ethos, declaring instead that "OUP has to make a reasonable financial return to its owner." Oxford's Delegates are *proud* of their £140 million nest-egg, which seems to have been announced almost as a *challenge*.

Lawyers may at this point be interested to learn that the chief legal authority hypothetically relied upon by Cass was an appeal for charitable status successfully made four years earlier by a team of (less than twenty) law reporters, and without going too deeply into the minutiae of charity law, a glance at the other similar claims therein cited – the City of Glasgow Police Athletic Association, for instance – leads at least this lay-lawyer to doubt the relevance of such a case to the business operations of an international general publisher which has over 1,200 staff on its payroll and whose annual turnover is presently hitting £300 million.

This prompts some entertaining speculation as to what might happen were the issue ever to be properly examined and resolved, by a court, say, or by the Charity or Inland Revenue Commissioners. As in my case, where non-Oxford judiciary had to be specially recruited, only senior, non-partisan adjudicators would be eligible for the job, with alumni from Oxford or Cambridge being automatically barred, and doubtless the field of candidates being thereby greatly narrowed. The corollary, of course, may help to explain why the present anomaly persists.

Two final points should also be noted. Firstly CUP did not, apparently, have very high hopes of its application succeeding, for during the years it was in preparation and under consideration, the Syndics set aside a fund of the notional tax they would be obliged to pay if it failed; it was the sudden release of this money that financed their construction from 1977 of the

Press's massive new Edinburgh building and Shaftesbury Road complex, completed in 1981. Secondly, throughout his submission, Cass repeatedly contrasted CUP's scale, lists, circumstances and policies with those of OUP, which he publicly disparaged as being "not purely a university press". He actually went out of his way to stress that the uniqueness of CUP's history and ethos meant that a decision in its favour would create no precedent with respect to any other university press. Notwithstanding Cass's view, OUP's similar application, again by backdoor letter, again in virtual secrecy, and now based on the precedent of CUP's conditional exemption, was granted on the nod a year later in 1978, a fact which goes oddly unrecorded in any of OUP's own self-histories.

The result of all this is that, *THES* strapline notwithstanding, the university presses in general, and OUP in particular, do not, strictly speaking, enjoy the status of charitable trusts after all, having never applied for such status, but are merely in possession, or proxy-possession, of kind but vulnerable letters from their nearby taxmen. (Most university presses, remember, both here and in America, are by contrast *subsidised by* their universities.) If OUP had true charitable status, its notepaper would have to display not some measly mission-statement, but its registration number. And the answer to the *THES's* general question is that if any university press were to apply to the Charity Commissioners in the normal way, its case might – and only might – have a chance of overcoming the basic 'trading in the open market' objection if it fufilled the sort of conditions lengthily listed by Cass, especially his keystone requirement of ploughing any 'surplus' it makes back into non-commercial publishing like poetry. Whatever else, OUP's £20 million-a-year cash-cowing would certainly disqualify it.

In an archaic whine reminiscent of Sir Roger Elliott's fine 'public apology' in my own Court of Appeal hearing (see page 138), Geoffrey Cass concluded his 1975 'preliminary letter' with a quotation from a 1614 order of the Lords of the Privy Council:

> "Forasmuch as learning hath antiently had this spetiall favour and priviledge, that upon any occasion of grievance, or complaint offered unto the Two Universities of this Realme, whensoever they have made their immediate recourse to the King or his Councell for speedie redresse and for avoyding length and charges of suit in an ordinary legal proceeding of Justice, they have never beene refused, but allwayes gratiously accepted."

Ye case resteth.

Epi-epilogues

Prior to the launch of this paperback edition, AKME decided to advertise it with a targeted leaflet drop in Oxford using the service operated by *The Oxford Star* newspaper (now American-owned by the Gannett Corporation). AKME had 25,000 leaflets designed and printed, and contracted with *The Star* for their distribution. The University learned of the plan and on the day before the leaflets' distribution, with 24,000 already delivered in batches around the county, *The Star's* editor Pat Fleming received a phonecall warning that if the distribution went ahead he could expect to receive a DIM-squad writ (type unspecified). He duly complied and all 24,000 were re-collected. *The Star's* sister *The Oxford Times* then made it a front-page story instead.

AKME's website **Law Library** at **www.btinternet.com/~akme** (see page 223) now includes the following further cases relating to loss of reputation or publicity and to charitable tax-exemption:

> Chaplin v. Hicks 1911 C.A. 2 K. B. 786 *Beauty contestant denied chance to compete - Breach of contract - Damages - Remoteness - Inassessability*
> Marbé v. George Edwardes (Daly's Theatre) Ltd. & anr. 1927 C.A. 1 K. B. 269 *Contract - Engagement of actress - Damages - Loss of publicity - Libel Qualified privilege - Malice - Judge's discretion - Defendant to call evidence*
> Withers v. General Theatre Corporation Ltd. 1933 C.A. 2 K. B. 536 *Contract - Theatrical engagement - Construction - Breach - Damages - Loss of publicity - Option as to theatrical hall - Misdirection of jury*
> Clayton & Waller v. Oliver 1930 A.C. 209 *Theatrical engagement Construction - Obligation to find actor a part - Damages - Loss of publicity*
> Tolnay v. Criterion Films 1936 All E. R., Vol 2 1625 *Authors of screenplay Breach of contract - Screen credit promised - Loss of publicity - Damages*
> Ackland v. World Screenplays, 1950 *The Times*, Feb. 23, 1950 *Breach of contract over screen credit - Size of lettering - Claim for damages*
> Tennent Plays Ltd. v. Com'rs of Inland Revenue 1948 C.A. *Income tax exemption - Charitable purposes - Finance Acts 1921, 1927*
> Associated Artists Ltd. v. Com'rs of Inland Revenue 1956 1 W.L.R. 752 *Income Tax - Exemption - Charitable purposes - Income Tax Act, 1952*
> The Incorporated Council of Law Reporting for England and Wales v. Attorney-General and anr. 1971 C.A. *Development and administration of judge-made law - Publication of accurate reports of benefit to legal profession Charges made for reports - Whether reports beneficial to community*

The last of these was the case hypothetically relied upon by CUP (and OUP) in its 1975 application for tax-exemption.